HOWARD BLOOM

HOW I ACCIDENTALLY STARTED

THE SIXTIES

HOWARD BLOOM

HOW I ACCIDENTALLY STARTED

THE SIXTIES

Vireo • Rare Bird • Dragonfly Books & Media
Los Angeles, Calif.
2017

This is a Genuine Vireo Book

published in association with Dragonfly Books & Media

Vireo | Rare Bird
453 South Spring Street, Suite 302
Los Angeles, CA 90013
rarebirdbooks.com

FIRST TRADE PAPERBACK ORIGINAL EDITION

Set in Dante
Printed in the United States

Cover Photograph by Jason Schneider, 1965

10 9 8 7 6 5 4 3 2 1

Publisher's Cataloging-in-Publication data
Names: Bloom, howard, author.
Title: How i accidentally started the sixties / Howard Bloom.
Description: First Trade Paperback Original Edition. | A Genuine Vireo Book | New York, NY; Los Angeles, CA: Rare Bird Books, 2017.
Identifiers: ISBN 9781945572913

Also available in e-book

This stuff really happened. Several names have been changed to protect me from my attorney. However, any lack of resemblance to actual people, living or dead, is solely due to the incompetence of the author.

CONTENTS

PROLOGUE—LIFTING TIMOTHY LEARY

Before we begin, let me tell you a story, the tale of how Timothy Leary's praise of *How I Accidentally Started The Sixties* came to be. It was 1995. I had come down with an illness seven years earlier, in 1988, that had left me in solitary confinement in a bedroom in Park Slope, Brooklyn, too weak to talk for five years and too weak have another person in the room with me. My wife had tried to keep me company by laying on our king-sized mattress next to me reading. But the sound of a newspaper page-turning tore through me like a cannonball. And eventually, thanks to the illness, she would leave me.

For three years, the doctors didn't have a clue to what I had. Turned out to be Chronic Fatigue Syndrome, also known as myalgic encephalomyelitis. And it's far more wicked than you might think.

Staying alive was rough. I needed entertainment with zero stress that would somehow keep my brain busy. And I needed social contact. I needed friends.

For problem number one, stuff to keep my brain busy, I discovered humor. Humor and two of its masters: Dave Barry and P. G. Wodehouse (the creator of Jeeves the Butler). Their books were hilarious. And hilarity has a peculiar property—it can lift you out of your miseries and put you, no matter how briefly, into an alternative universe, a virtual reality. It can lift you out of a body that is failing and awaken your capacity for joy.

Problem number two was social connection. Without connection, we die. Our immune system goes into a nosedive and our thinking capacity whiffles into the dead zone. I was in solitary confinement and could not utter a single syllable. What's worse, one of my scientific colleagues, evolutionary biologist Valerius Geist, says all communication boils down to two things—attraction cues and repulsion cues. When you're sick, you give off repulsion cues. People flee from you. Even those who formerly seemed to be your best friends.

How can you get people to interact with you? You need to give off attraction cues. And what's one of the greatest attraction cues of all? Humor.

So I wrote a series of letters to my friends, letters telling tales that I'd told for years out loud when my tongue and larynx had still been functional. Tales that my tiny audiences had found mind-boggling. Why? They were tales of my adventures accidentally helping start The Sixties. Tales of hitchhiking on the West Coast, riding the rails, seeking the Zen Buddhist form of enlightenment, *satori*, experimenting with peculiar new drugs, and discovering sexuality. Tales of inadvertently cofounding a human tidal wave the press would later call "the hippie movement."

The internet was still so new in 1990 that only techie friends like Peter Gabriel were on it. So I wrote my letters horizontal in the bed using a keyboard across my lap, a keyboard connected to the two computers an arm's length to my left. Then I had my assistant/caretaker send the epistles out on paper via snail mail. And to the best of my ability I wrote these episodes in the style I'd learned from Dave Barry and P. G. Wodehouse. But I wrote in a Wodehouse and Barry style transformed and transmogrified by a very strange mind, mine.

It worked. I found two friends who would stick with me. Then over the course of five years this process produced the first draft of a book: *How I Accidentally Started The Sixties*.

Keep in mind, I began to write How I Accidentally Started The Sixties in 1990. I put it together in book form in 1995. And I wanted to get it published, whether I was imprisoned in bed or not. So I aimed to get some quotes on the book from people famous for their centrality in The Sixties.

The first folks I thought of were the Jefferson Airplane. Why them? Well, their song proclaiming that *One pill makes you larger, and one pill makes you small, and the ones that mother gives you don't do anything at all* was a Sixties anthem. I'd listened to it in 1967—the Summer of Love— in a Manhattan apartment in the East Village laying in the bed of a girl I was madly in love with. I had removed her two small stereo speakers from their normal position on a shelf and relocated them around my head just an inch or two from my ears. That was during the Summer of the Great Polygamy Experiment, whose undulations you can read in *How I Accidentally Started The Sixties*.

But there was one more reason to zero in on Grace Slick and her merry band. I had a friend, rock manager Eric Gardner, who had started his music career as a roadie for the Jefferson Airplane.

So I snail mailed a letter to Eric asking if he could get *How I Accidentally Started The Sixties* to the Jefferson Airplane. He snail mailed me back saying that he had someone far better in mind, another client of his, Timothy Leary. So my assistant printed out a massive pile of paper, a copy of the *How I Accidentally Started The Sixties* manuscript, and shipped it to Eric.

Eric allegedly got the manuscript to Leary. And a month later I received this in the mail:

"This is a monumental, epic, glorious literary achievement. Every page, every paragraph, every sentence sparkles with captivating metaphors, delightful verbal concoctions, alchemical insights, philosophic whimsy, absurd illogicals, scientific comedy routines, relentless, non-stop waves of hilarity. The comparisons to James Joyce are inevitable and undeniable. Finnegans Wake wanders through the rock 'n roll sixties. Wow! Whew! Wild! Wonderful!"

—Timothy Leary

Frankly, I didn't believe that Leary had actually written this. I thought Eric had done it, as a favor.

Then, in roughly 2000, Douglas Rushkoff, the author of books like *Media Virus*, *Coercion*, and *Cyberia*, came to my bedroom to see me. By then, I could talk again, and I could have others in my room. Doug brought with him a San Francisco visual artist, a male with long blond hair, a haircut that smacked of Haight-Ashbury. In our conversation, something became obvious. Doug and his artist friend had known Leary. More than that. They had spent Leary's last six months of life watching over him in his bedroom and keeping him cheered and occupied.

Now, remember, I didn't believe that Leary had written the quote that Eric Gardner had sent. But I had a printer in the bedroom. So I printed out two copies of the alleged Leary quote and handed one to Doug and one to his friend. They sat in chairs at the foot of my bed, read the quote, and lapsed into a frightening, tomb-like silence. I knew exactly what was going through their minds. They could see that the quote wasn't from Tim, and they were trying to figure out how to tell me without hurting my feelings.

Finally, Doug spoke. But in a very strange tone, a sepulchral tone. "This is Tim," he said. And you knew why he was sepulchral. The quote had brought Timothy Leary alive for a moment to Doug and his friend. In a Brooklyn bedroom. It had brought Tim alive with all the pains of his illness. And with the terrible loss when he died.

As you recall, I had written this book in a style designed to lift even those of us undergoing disaster out of our woes. I'd written it to take readers to the alternative reality of humor. What Doug and his friend explained to me is that Timothy Leary had read *How I Accidentally Started The Sixties* when he was terminally ill with prostate cancer. He'd read the book six months before he died.

I'd tried to write in a style that could lift people dehumanized by illness out of their body and up to another plane. And that's what *How I Accidentally Started The Sixties* had apparently done for Leary. When he was in bed dying. One extremely sick person had reached out to lift another. And it had worked! That's apparently why Leary had written such a powerful quote. *How I Accidentally Started The Sixties* had worked the magic it aspired to.

But why had Leary compared *How I Accidentally Started The Sixties* to a work by James Joyce? After Rushkoff's visit, I went online and found Leary's obituary in *The New York Times*. Joyce, said the obituary, was Leary's favorite author on planet earth.

Let's hope that Timothy Leary was right about *How I Accidentally Started The Sixties*. If he was, you may be in for the ride of your life.

HOW I GOT INTO THIS MESS
TO BEGIN WITH

It was a rainy August day in 1969 on Max Yasgur's farm just outside of Woodstock, New York. Good for the crops. You could tell. There were over 400,000 of them. Kids. Lots with long hair (including some of the girls). Some naked from the waist up (including some of the boys). Others cross-pollinating in nature's ultimate fertility cream—mud. Yeah, there was mud by the acre. This wasn't an event for industrial pollutants like Astroturf.

No, the chemical additives were mostly in the kids. Cannabis, peyote, LSD, amphetamine, and a lot of elephant tranquilizer.

Then there was the greenery. Half the kids who'd swallowed pills were green. So was most of the cash. That was being handled by a friend of mine, Michael Lang, who was having it carted by the hay load to his bank back in New York. He'd decided to throw this little harvest. Musicians, hallucinations, and declarations of political rights for plants in bloom ("flower power"). I'm Bloom. But I wasn't there. Didn't need to be. I'd sown the seeds seven years earlier. Long hair. Lysergic acid. Entering the vaginal canal of any willing girl in sight. But I hadn't done it on purpose. Honest. The whole thing was an accident.

◆

IF YOU ARE LIKE most of us, you think The Sixties began in 1964 when Ken Kesey, the author of a wildly successful novel—*One Flew Over the Cuckoo's Nest*—came up with a strange idea for publicity. And an even stranger idea for inspiration. Instead of begging the nine muses to blow on the smoldering coals of his imagination, he saturated the six layers of his cerebral cortex with lysergic acid—LSD. Then, to draw attention to the novel that limped and crawled from this process, *Sometimes a Great Notion*, this enterprising scribbler packed fourteen friends from the fringe of lunacy into a wildly graffitied ancient bus at his ranch in La Honda, California. All fourteen were dedicated to an overarching mission: scrambling their brains like Scrabble tiles. Kesey called his improvised tribe the Merry Pranksters, and set off toward the 1964 World's Fair in New York City, thus carrying a first hint of the drug culture and of its goal, mind expansion, from the sunset golden beaches of the West to the sunrise silver beaches of the East.

In 1965, when the acid-saturated busload of Pranking passengers returned to the Kesey ranch, they invented The Electric Kool Aid Acid Test, a trial-by-liquid in which they made you drink a cup of punch richly riddled with LSD, forced you to listen to the music of a band that would later call itself the Grateful Dead, and challenged you to keep your sanity from shattering in a "freak out" like a teacup dropped from a Boeing 727.

Yes, if you have all your marbles still in their original package complete with instructions, you are probably under the impression that The Sixties began in 1964, which was also the year in which Timothy Leary, Richard Alpert, and Ralph Metzner—after experimenting with the hallucination-inducing formulation called psilocybin at Harvard—wrote their book *The Psychedelic Experience*, and gave their age a name—the psychedelic era. What's more, if your pre-frontal lobe has not petitioned your brainstem for removal to someone else's skull, you almost certainly know that The Sixties climbed toward its peak in 1967 when the Jefferson Airplane sang that one pill makes you larger, the other makes you small, and the ones that mother gives you don't do anything at all. In addition, if you know that your ears are up and your ankles are down, you realize that The Sixties soared even higher four months later when Janis Joplin and Jimi Hendrix burst out of nowhere at the Monterey Pop Festival.

Surely those were The Sixties, weren't they? Yes, like a rampaging rhododendron bursting with blossoms, those were the overground explosions that grabbed attention. But could it be that the real story is not in the blossoms but in the roots? Not above the ground but beneath it?

Two years before the Merry Pranksters and Timothy Leary, five years before Grace Slick's "White Rabbit," and half a decade before the Monterey

Pop Festival, the members of a tiny tribe with no name at all were marinating their brains in strange substances, twist-tying their axons and their dendrites, using bizarre molecules to confuse innocent neuroreceptors, and polluting hapless potassium-sodium-ion channels with peculiar chemicals. That nameless tribe was also pioneering the copulatory freedoms that would rocket to fame in 1967's Summer of Love and The Sixties Sexual Revolution.

In other words, when that tiny, anonymous gaggle was surfing the waves of emotional mystery, The Sixties that you and I know and love had not yet begun. But to understand where the Age of Aquarius and the Era of the Hippy came from, what box it sprang from like a goggle-eyed toy, you have to look back to 1962, when most calendrically-challenged Americans still thought it was the Fifties. You have to peer into a tide pool of hidden escapades, secret adventures in the chemical maddening of the brain, slapstick sloshings in the inner terra incognita that would become the roots of more deliberate insanities yet to arrive on the scene.

And if you are lucky, you may catch a glimpse of the embryonic pulse and twist of delirium that would later splotch the world with tie-dyed T-shirts, bell bottom trousers, and psychedelic concert posters. If you are even luckier, you may be able to see the motives behind the madness: a bloodhound sniff-fest, a determined hunt, a pursuit of higher truths. And a quest for truths that are far, far lower.

Why? Because sometimes the lower truths are the most important truths of all.

FROM THE MOUTHS OF MURDERERS

I t feels a little funny to drag these stories from the depths of memory now that us baby boomers are all supposed to be picking out the patterns for our tombstones, counting our wrinkles, and trying to replicate the secret of Ronald Reagan's perpetually dark hair.

But speaking as a voice from the crypt, let me see if I can impart some mangled semblance of wisdom to this seriously brain-damaged world. To follow this tale of moral profundity, you'll have to travel with me back to the dim and distant days of a long-forgotten era, before Roomba robots, apps that identify bird calls, gaming consoles you can communicate with by twerking, garden hoses that miraculously avoid tying their own creative variations of Boy Scout knots, and drones with which you can watch your wife doing things with some other guy that she's always refused to do with you. Yes, we are fumbling through the swirling mists of the past to those years of astonishing antiquity when even Donald Trump, David Letterman, and Jay Leno were still in their teens and when Lady Gaga, Taylor Swift, and Miley Cyrus had not yet been born, THE *EARLY* SIXTIES!!!

More specifically, it was 1962. I had just left college without finishing my freshman year, a high crime. Escape from an institution of higher learning before your sentence expired was so unheard of for a middle-class Jewish kid that there wasn't even a name for the crime—just a mushroom cloud of incoherent curses that erupted when your parents discovered your abominable act. The word "dropout" wouldn't go mainstream in the American vocabulary for years to come.

I'd camped out in the basement of a Seattle anthropologist with a remarkably hospitable nature—so hospitable, in fact, that the basement's opposite end was occupied by a charming drag queen who could have given Josephine Baker lessons in *haute couture*. Somehow, this master of the plumed gown and feathered boa had no influence on our host. But apparently, I did. In fact, I accidentally became our host's spiritual master. My hunt for satori—for Zen Buddhist enlightenment—was so intense that it gave the impression that I knew something. In reality, I knew nothing. All I had were questions. But when you are certain that your questions point to truths that are gut-deep, you apparently develop a misleading charisma.

Our anthropologist host was just about to finish his PhD thesis. The topic? Ornamental penis cones in the South Pacific. He showed us pictures. His South Pacific subjects were nudists. They wore not a stitch of clothing. But stitches exist in fabric. And fabric was not what these macho warriors preferred as apparel. Instead they had wooden cylinders the size of the sausages Italians feed you with onions and peppers, sausages with deep hollows drilled in their centers. And they slipped their penises into these things, then paraded about, proudly thrusting their pelvic appurtenances into the viewfinder of any passing anthropologist's camera and wearing these penis cones all day long.

Why bother? Because the penis cones were a language. A pecking order language. A language of hierarchy, of who is on top and who is not. Penis cones, like $4,000 suits, displayed status. Thus, a lesson was inserted into my brain about the central role of status in the lives of men, a lesson that would eventually shape my theories and my books. But that's in the very distant future. Let's get back to 1962.

Despite the fact that he had almost finished his thesis, the anthropological type decided to abandon his mortgage, forget about his teaching job, leave his shot at a PhD, stop paying for his girlfriend's orthodontia, grab that girlfriend, and follow me and two of my friends to California.

Our arrangements for departure were all set. We would head for the nearest freight yard and catch a box-car headed south. Unfortunately, I got a cold, and my followers left me to catch up with them when I could get better. Not a nice thing to do to your spiritual leader.

But they weren't heartless about it. They found me a room in one of those environmentally-conscious University of Seattle off-campus hovels where no student has washed the dishes for six months and every platter and fork is turning mossy in the ecosystem of the sink. I had a mattress of my own on a nice, organic, hardwood floor. The boards were biodegradable.

You could tell—they were rotting. And my acolytes had provided for my recovery with a leaking pitcher of orange juice, a pile of sandwiches, and the company of a remarkably sympathetic horde of cockroaches.

Four days later, thanks to the healing powers of this nature-rich habitat, I finally got my health back. I went to the local supermarket, gently laid a quart of milk and a loaf of bread in my shopping cart, then stuffed my athletic supporter with provisions—cream cheese, smoked oysters, and a variety of other delicacies. I paid for the milk and the bread, accepted the more expensive items as a donation, and headed back for the moss-covered kitchen, where I cleared a space between the fungi, spread out my twenty-four slices of bread, made twelve sandwiches, packed them in the plastic bag provided as a bonus by Wonder Bread, made a gallon of Kool-Aid in a Clorox jug, rolled the food into my sleeping bag, headed for the open road, and stuck out my thumb. Jack Kerouac, one of my idols at the time, would have been proud.

My apostles, the ones who had left me on the floor of a Seattle cockroach dance hall, had ridden the rails. I had decided to travel by road. Unfortunately, hitchhiking is an unreliable form of transportation. There are no regularly scheduled pickups. You depend on the milk of human kindness. And the cows that produce this stuff are apparently an endangered species. So, as usual when I propped myself in the gravel by a stretch of tarmac, I was stuck. In eight hours, I'd zoomed a full seventy-five miles. Now I still had 529.6 left to go before reaching my destination—the San Francisco Bay.

For four hours, I had been sampling gourmet exhaust fumes on a two-lane blacktop that ran through a collection of five buildings called Eugene, Oregon. Every twenty minutes or so, an approaching car lifted my hopes, then dropped them without a parachute as it disappeared over the horizon. I attempted to summon each vehicle's return with wistful looks. But much as Walt Disney had assured me that "when you wish upon a star your dreams come true," Walt—and innumerable drivers—seemed to be letting me down. Maybe my problem was that it was still daylight. Which meant there wasn't a star in sight.

As dusk turned the countryside gray and the first pinpricks of light appeared in the black and blue sky, my fate went through a sudden alteration. An old, hearse-black Hudson rattled in my direction, flapping the random pieces of tin from which it was made in an effort to warn any farm animals grazing on the asphalt of its approach.

My spirits, as usual, went up like a weather balloon. The car grew near, slowed down, and veered right, toward the gravel shoulder. Then the inhabitants apparently looked me over carefully, noted that I was barefoot and had a haircut of a kind unknown to Western Civilization for roughly 300 years (the Beatles hadn't arrived to make long hair acceptable yet, and even when they would, their mop-tops would not emerge from their scalps like foot-long worms curled in terminal pain). The auto's inhabitants saw that I was carrying a thoroughly disreputable sleeping bag packed with food and my one extra piece of clothing, an ultra-baggy, bargain-basement white sweater. A sweater of a brightness designed to distinguish me clearly from the empty air above the roadside gravel as I plaintively stuck out my thumb in the blackness of the night. The folks in the car were unable to spot my major virtue—I showered every morning. The inspection was apparently unsatisfactory. They picked up momentum, spat gravel, and left me in their dust.

The sun had sunk, the clouds on the horizon were red, and so were the whites of my eyes. Eugene, Oregon, was disappearing into the gloom along with my hopes, the sort of experience that makes a rejected hitchhiker feel as if his emotions have been plunged into liquid nitrogen. Then a miracle occurred. The funereal Hudson appeared on a side road about 250 feet behind me. Disney's star had worked! Maybe because I looked like Jiminy Cricket. The car's inhabitants had debated about me, changed their minds, taken a left, looped around a patch of farmland, and returned.

The dusty rear door of the ebony car opened, spilling two dozen empty beer cans into the road. A pale, white hand emerged from the dark interior and gestured. I snatched my sleeping bag and ran, hoping to catch up with this sweet chariot before it could swing across the Jordan without me. It was the beginning of one of the strangest nights of my life.

◆

To ENTER THE CAR, I had to find space for myself on a back seat whose legroom was occupied by four cases of beer. Inside, the figures were spectrally silent. A gaunt, tall man clutched the steering wheel, staring straight ahead. In the dusk, his eye sockets looked like huge black holes. The passenger seat held a smaller person with slick, dark hair who never turned his head. And ensconced on my left was the most genial of my hosts, a round-faced fellow who silently bid me make myself comfortable before he, too, riveted his eyes to the view from the front window and imitated an extra from *Night of the Living Dead*.

I asked where they were going, knowing that at best if I was in luck I'd be carried fifty or sixty miles before I was let out to unfurl my white sweater once again. A voice welled up somewhere in the car—I couldn't quite tell from whom—with the most welcome—though ghostly—syllables I'd heard in days: "San Francisco." These saviors were destined to take me my full 529.6 miles!

One of the joys of hitchhiking is conversation. It's a delight to yank life stories from the unsuspecting benefactors who haul you around. My luck in this sport had always been superb. I had pulled inner secrets out of a carnival barker, a narcotics agent, a Bible College graduate who was fleeing from a conspiracy between flying saucer people and the CIA, and even from an insurance salesman who explained with extraordinary warmth why his kids and wife were more important to him than his career.

"What do you guys do for a living?" I asked. This question was the guaranteed key with which to roll open the top of the conversational sardine can.

But not tonight. My three hosts stared straight ahead. The eye sockets of the driver grew more cadaverous. The last light disappeared from the sky beyond the windshield. No one said a word. I tried a few more questions. Silence. Except for those rare occasions on which a hollowed-out voice would ask the slightly pudgy figure in the gloaming on my left for another can of beer.

I resigned myself to looking out the side window at the blackness of the countryside. Then, after half an hour, one of my dark angels of transportation asked a brief question. "You don't mind a little heater action, do you?" It *was* getting chilly. So I answered that I didn't mind at all. But no one reached for the dashboard switch that would have pumped out some warmth. Then slowly it dawned on me—a faint recollection of Sergeant Joe Friday on the 1950s TV show Dragnet. A "heater" was a gun.

I sat in a cold sweat with mental pictures of my limp body tied to a telephone pole in the desert, slightly marred by a bullet hole in the head. After all, who else was there to shoot? The answer emerged ten minutes later when we pulled into a lonely country gas station—one of those gray, unpainted, deteriorating, wooden, all-purpose retail shacks that'll sell you everything from a spark plug and a Snickers Bar to an extension cord. The pudgy gentleman next to me and the fellow from the passenger seat disembarked and headed for the modest hut's screen door. The tall skeleton at the wheel kept the engine running and his nerves glued to the open road.

Through the plate glass window, I could see an elderly man behind a counter. I waited for a bang, spurting blood, and the spectacle of the gray-haired fellow falling over backwards with a startled look on his face, knocking a couple of cans of pork and beans off the shelf. Then I expected to see the duo in whose car I was scrunched run from the hovel with greenbacks spilling from their fingers.

Nothing of the sort occurred. When the gunmen headed back to the car, the old man was still upright. His would-be terminators were less so. In fact, their postures had been infected by a definite slump. The two slipped back into their places in the Hudson and angrily slammed the doors. We took off.

Turned out my companions had been attempting a quick-change routine. Such was their expertise that they'd gone in prepared to offer a twenty and get change for a hundred. They'd ended up with change for a ten. Oregonian country store operators are apparently a shifty lot.

The failure was humiliating. So humiliating, in fact, that the trio felt compelled to rescue their dignity. Thus they finally confessed their line of business. The driver and his partner in the front seat were specialists in armed robbery. They were particularly proud of their ability to break into fur vaults in the wee small hours and make off with skins that numerous small animals had donated to provide warmth for status-starved females of the human upper crust. Minks and ermines, for example. At the moment, the pair were out on bail pending trial for one of their more spectacular heists.

The guy in the back seat was the one who had botched the short change deal and made the whole gang look like suckers in front of a total stranger. Despite his moronic fuck-up, they allowed him to announce his claim to fame. He was a con-man. Judging from his recent performance, it was a miracle he made a living.

It would take more bragging than this to recover the pride the group had lost, and they knew it. So the driver removed the coffin-lid from his larynx and confessed the details of his hobby—murdering his fellow men. Well, in reality, his victims weren't really *men*. They were Native Americans, a species he was sure fell on the evolutionary ladder somewhere below toilet algae. But that didn't keep the sport from having its moments of excitement. Like there was the elderly red man our driver had beaten up and shoved over a cliff at a garbage dump. There was the guy he'd chained to a bed in a basement without food or water. And there were a variety of others on whom he'd demonstrated his marksmanship. So, he'd missed a few of his shots. But, he assured me, when he really concentrated he could actually hit a target.

Turns out they'd picked me up because they were heroin addicts and the supply of drugs in their home town, Vancouver, had dried up. They were hoping to score some dope in San Francisco and the sight of my outfit—long hair, no shoes, etc.—had convinced them I'd be able to provide leads on where to find injectable materials. Unfortunately, the only drug dealers I was aware of sold aspirin.

Before their poppy-starved metabolisms could freeze a Thanksgiving bird and turn them into cold turkeys, they were attempting to stave off agony with substitute chemicals. Hence their oversized supply of beer.

Eventually the tale of noble deeds—robbery, homicide and such— petered out. They put a final frosting on their image of machismo by trading lengthy epics of all the women who had given them oral sex, comparing fine points of lingual techniques too technical for me to follow as they attempted to ascertain which woman had the most acrobatic mouth in Western Canada. But finally, they ran out of peculiarly-shaped throats and other feminine orifices to compare, and were left with nothing to say. After all, it takes a long time to drive 529.6 miles.

The lack of entertainment and the deprived status of their endogenous morphine receptors were beginning to drive them crazy. Finally, in a last-ditch effort to entertain themselves, the homicidal threesome started to ask questions about what *I* did to sustain myself. I told them how I had dropped out of school to seek satori—the ultimate state of Zen Buddhist enlightenment. This did not exactly thrill them. I offered them some of my cream-cheese and smoked oyster sandwiches. When they heard that the oysters had been transported from the A&P in my jock strap, they mysteriously lost their appetites. What's worse, this revelation of my life of crime (to wit, nourishing myself and my friends at the expense of large supermarkets), threw them into a frenzy of moral disturbance. They feared for the fate of my soul. When we got to the fact that I hadn't seen my mother in over nine months, they became hysterical.

It was obvious that they had an emergency on their hands—a human about to self-destruct. Like a team of paramedics, they mobilized to affect my rescue.

First they outlined the error of my ways. I was living without real goals, they said. No human being could do that. Second, you needed a nice, steady relationship to give your life some meaning—like the ones they had with the girlfriends they cheated on back home. If they didn't save me fast, they could see I was going to tumble straight into hell, and they were desperate to catch me before I fell. What's more, I HAD to go home to see my mother!

So the visions of being tied to a telephone pole disappeared from my head, and between midnight and dawn I received caring, fatherly lectures on how to lead a moral life from folks who poked lead into other people's brains for amusement. Damon Runyon was right. There's honor, and even generosity, among thieves.

An hour after sunrise, the moral lectures stopped. Something almost too exciting to contemplate was coming up. We were about to cross the Golden Gate Bridge. This was the first chance in their lives for my traveling companions to see the Disneyland that every con man and murderer dreams about, the ultimate tourist attraction for felons: Alcatraz. As they caught a glimpse of the fabled island in the mist across the water, all three of them squealed like five year olds.

The strange thing is this. Over the next few years, I'd get a lot of advice from truck drivers, migrant fruit pickers, psychiatrists, psychologists, corporate presidents, and even rock-and-roll stars. But in the end, I'd make a simple discovery: When it came to the meaning of life, the murderers had been right. You need a woman.

ALL HAIL TO THE KING
OF SPRINGFIELD AVENUE

How'd I end up hitchhiking on a roadside in a forlorn corner of Oregon?

Rumor in my grammar school had it that I was hatched from an egg, and not even an earthling egg at that. Those in the know implied that a batch of inept Martians had misread a road map as they rushed to an obstetrical facility to help their embryo crack its way out of the shell and had landed on the wrong planet. Without competent medical guidance, they'd barely hauled me out of my calcium casing. Then they'd become so confused repacking the flying saucer that they'd forgotten to toss their new offspring into a bassinet. Thus was I abandoned in the alien landscape of Western New York State.

My parents deny this story. But it's hard to take their word for it. I know for a fact that the two of them have never had sex.

On the off chance that my dad and mom are *not* pulling a fast one, however, I've been prodding relatives to reveal all they remember of the family past, and have constructed a rough outline of my roots. This, in slightly garbled form, is the result.

My putative great grandfather lived in the section of Russia that Jews were restricted to (White Russia, a territory that was either Russian, Polish or Ukrainian, depending on which century you happened to be consulting your map). The old man, who was quite young at the time, managed to pull off the impossible. Jews were not allowed to have government jobs. But he got one. He was a courier in the service of the czar. To wit, a messenger boy. This was unheard of, totally *verboten*, and not bad for a guy who thought that Orthodox meant you wore a yarmulke, not that you made a big deal about Easter and Greek.

What's more, it meant he could do something with his kid, my grandfather that was forbidden to Jews. He could send him to a Russian government school. Again, the family seems to have gotten a little off track. You'd think, "Aha, Jewish kid, probably pretty smart, bet he's going to be a big-time scholar and invent psychotherapy and everyone will call him Dr. Freud." No such luck. The kid with the big break went off to the hot shot Russian school and was trained as—a brain surgeon? A physicist? The inventor of the nuclear samovar? No, are you ready for this? A boot maker. Ah, well, we can't all have Erasmus Darwin as a grandfather.

So my granddad learned to make heels and toes, became capable of chatting with customers in six languages, left Russia in the 1890s, and landed at Ellis Island where they couldn't spell his moniker, Wechelefsky. They looked at his rosy complexion and wrote on his passport "Bloom." He left the island trying to remember his new name and looking for work making leather encasements for feet. (The concrete foot-encasement concession was strictly Italian.)

Turned out, there was a naval base where they were fiddling with real high-tech stuff—lighter-than-air machines, blimps and dirigibles—in Lakehurst, New Jersey. The idea of being lighter than air appealed to my grandfather. I mean, us Jews like to rise in the world. What's more, a military installation had officers, and as any Russian kid knows, officers wear boots. If they didn't, their subordinates would have nothing to lick.

So my noble ancestor set himself up sheathing the legs of naval brass in the finest leather, then took his earnings and started a general store in Asbury Park, New Jersey. And somewhere along the line he got married.

I sent my father a letter asking what his parents' relationship was like. I got back…nothing. So when my dad came to visit, I hit my alleged parental sperm donor with the question again. His answer was simple. "In those days," he said, "husbands and wives didn't *have* relationships."

Meanwhile, the family patriarch with the struggling general store and the nearly-invisible wife had a whole bunch of daughters—five, to be more precise. My grandfather read to his girls every night, sometimes in Yiddish, and more often in English, which he had persuaded a teacher to pound into his tongue the instant he hit North American soil. But he was desperate for a son, some sprig of manliness sufficiently broad-shouldered to carry the family name. Despite the fact that that name, Bloom, was ridiculous for humans. Good for flowers, but not so good for *Homo sapiens*. So desperate was my grandfather that he offered a deal to God, the Almighty, Lord of the Universe, creator of the ten plagues. Yes, he made an offer to Jehovah, who, according to the scientific literature, had given up on mankind and was perfecting eight million species of beetles. The offer? If God gave him a son, his faithful servant, my grandfather, would build the first synagogue in Asbury Park, New Jersey.

Occasionally, the poor male-offspring-deprived man would stop his prayers for a few minutes, and, despite his lack of a relationship with his wife, would roll on top of her in the feather bed. Honoring the code of silence that apparently existed between the pair, he pretended it was an accident. Eventually his accidents paid off. One of his wife's semi-annual discharges was a male.

The old man rejoiced, built the promised house of worship, and was so elated that he added a bonus: in gratitude he would close his store on the Sabbath, on Saturdays, which meant that to feed his hatchlings, he was going to have to start retail hours on Sunday, a violation of the town's Blue Laws. My grandfather battled the bureaucracy for his right to adhere to the dictates of his religion. And he stomped the legal system into the ground. All in honor of his one and only son—Isidor.

Then he discovered in his newly rearranged spare time that he had a nose for real estate. In fact, if it was anything like my nose, it was a very large one. As a result of his success in sniffing out winning properties, neighbors who hoped that he would share the wealth called him the King of Springfield Avenue. It worked. He rewarded his flatterers with royal gifts whenever they tumbled into trouble.

Meanwhile, my father surreptitiously switched his name from Isidor to Irving. He was afraid of being confused with Isadora Duncan. Though I think his dancing would have given him away.

Meanwhile, the King of Springfield Avenue could be seen each morning walking the future champion of the family name—my father—to school. He would lovingly watch as his son strode into the institution's front entrance, then march off to buy up more of Asbury Park as his offspring slipped out the school's back door and headed for the train station, where he watched the locomotives and dreamed of adventures in distant lands, mythic Shangri-Las like...New York. All of this would have an impact on my later escapades.

This series of events spat out a problem. Because of God's tardiness in providing a male heir, his Yiddisha majesty, my grandfather, died when his son was a teenager. The old man's wife had already preceded him on the thorny path to heaven. Her internal organs could no longer take being accidentally squashed and poked by a man she scarcely knew.

In Anglo-Saxon society, the family possessions go straight to the eldest son, and everyone else in the brood sponges off of him for the next fifty or sixty years, living in his country pile. In Jewish families, royalty descends through the princesses. So my Aunt Beck, a boulder of strength, took over the palatial family abode, the real estate treasures, the bank account, and the responsibility for raising my father. She also handled the budding young flapper who was the family's youngest sister, and the many children of the two oldest Bloom girls, who both died of pneumonia at the tender age of thirty-nine. My aunt Beck's imprint on my psyche would later haunt my sex life. Viciously.

◆

EVENTUALLY, FOR REASONS LOST in the ashcans of history, my dad went off to make his fortune in the land of opportunity—Buffalo, New York. How he picked this god-forsaken town I'll never know. He met Buffalo Bob Smith (I kid you not), who had a great idea about a puppet, but my dad wasn't into pulling strings, and television hadn't happened yet, so he missed his big chance to wear a clown suit and become famous as the sidekick on the first really big children's television show in history—*Howdy Doody*. Yes, had fate been celebrating Practical Joke Day, my dad could have been Clarabell the Clown, a superstar of the Fifties. A man every five-year-old laughed at. Ah, the bitterness of fate.

As a result, when the Depression came my dad was poor like everyone else. He ate a can of beans a day and saved the labels for a late-night snack— but at least he was eating, which is more than some people could say.

Then he collided with my mother. One of the most unfortunate accidents that could have befallen him.

You've met my father's folks, the ones descended from a courier for the tsar in White Russia, a nation known to its intimate friends as Belarus. My grandmother on my mother's side was a tough young socialist, freethinking (e.g. atheistic) teenager from Riga, Latvia, a city suffering from a seven-hundred-year-old subcultural split. A split that would later splash its way into, of all things, the very same spot my aunt Beck would come to haunt, my sex life. But that's a tale for later.

The allegedly gorgeous young red head, my maternal grandmother, decided to make a break for it and go to the land where the streets were paved with gold and ended up married to a tailor in Buffalo and the Depression came and they were poor, too.

But my mother was extremely articulate, had a vocabulary that would have turned Noah Webster green, and possessed intellectual aspirations. Or was she possessed by them? What's more, her fingers were Olympian in their capabilities. She could play Beethoven's greatest finger-tanglers on the piano, and could type ninety-five words per minute. So she got a job as the secretary to the head of the New York State Liquor Authority. Which, she once implied, meant that she kept the whole statewide secret sauce (or is it secret souse?) authority operating while her boss went out with the boys for their daily eighteen-course, sixteen-cocktail, expense-account lunches.

My mom met my father, wasn't very impressed with him, married him, still wasn't impressed, and helped him get a liquor license using the contacts from her state job. He started, surprise, a liquor store. Then my dad was yanked into World War II. Uncle Sam wanted him. Considering the questionable taste of a man who wears a white beard, a red bow tie, and a top hat with a blue band dotted with great big white stars, it's hard to tell if that was a compliment. My pop's three-year disappearance would prove crucial. But how and why is a story for later.

When Irving Bloom returned three years later to the city that Lake Erie forgot, he discovered that his store was still a hole in the wall and that he and my mother were still as poor as they'd ever been, so he worked thirteen hours a day, seven days a week, until he built the thing into the biggest retail alcohol supply center in Western New York State. As for my mother, she *still* wasn't impressed.

But we're getting ahead of ourselves here. That's the story of the family's roots. Now let's look at the family's leaves. Or maybe that should be the leftovers. Which is where I come in.

AND UNTO THEM A CHILD WAS BORN

Dear Mr. and Mrs. Bloom,

This is Ed McMahon, and on behalf of the Publishers Clearing House Sweepstakes I'd like to congratulate you as winners of our super-duper, once- (or maybe twice at most)-in-a-lifetime Grand Prize. As you know, the lucky folks who respond to the megatons of junk mail with which we generously dole out curvature of the spine to the postal workers of America have a chance to win fabulous fortunes—millions and millions of dollars, 400-foot yachts (courtesy of Donald Trump, who failed to sell his little beauty to the Japanese in 1990 and finally let us have it if we agreed to accept his vintage collection of docking bills and parking tickets), trips to the fabulous Roach Motel in beautiful Desert Gulch, Nevada, just 150 miles outside of exciting downtown Las Vegas, and a host of other prizes too delectable to mention. And every time hell freezes over, we faithfully hand out one of these prizes to some family who will agree to drool with gratitude on television.

But you, Mr. and Mrs. Bloom, are special. You have ignored every one of our marvelous offers of fantastic magazines—like the Lint Collectors Weekly—at only twice their normal newsstand prices. So for you, we have a prize so super, so special, so unbelievable that we will have you shot by our security service if you ever reveal that it came from us. Yes, in honor of your years of faithfully ignoring every sweepstakes we've waved under your nose, we have given you what every red-blooded American man and woman fears more than anything else in the world—a completely maladjusted, pathological, baffling, prematurely eccentric infant. And here's the best part—he's all yours, complete with a personalized collection of your very own genes (which have been only slightly scrambled by our massive research and development staff, who was distracted by his janitorial duties).

So, Mr. and Mrs. Bloom, be proud that you are citizens of the USA. For only in America could you get a child with allergies, illnesses, and an entire

encyclopedia of psychological abnormalities from a mail-order scam operation.
This is Ed McMahon, wishing you luck with your spectacular bonus award. May
it bring you many years of happily gnashed teeth and joyfully rewarding tsouris.
(Hey, Frank, what's a tsouris? If it's over ninety proof, I could use one.)
    Congratulations again,
    Ed McMahon

My memory of entering this world is a little fuzzy, possibly because the Martian egg story is true, but here's the best data I can dredge up. I emerged from the womb in Buffalo, New York, at the famous Somebody-Or-Other Memorial Hospital on June 25, 1943, at either 6:00 a.m. or 6:00 p.m., but I think it was p.m. The doctors were anxious to have dinner, and were highly annoyed to discover that my mother was hemorrhaging, I was drowning in blood, they were going to have to open her up, and someone was going to have to plunge in and save me before I went down for the third time. Why they call this form of can-opening a Caesarian I'll never know, because I hadn't come, I hadn't seen, and I certainly hadn't conquered.

At any rate, they managed to get me out, much to my mother's chagrin (she had wanted a girl and I didn't turn out to be one, nor did I show much interest in even trying out the role). I imagine the spectacle spoiled the appetites of a good many medical rescuers laboring at the scene.

Those of you with an astrological bent will want to know the precise geographical coordinates of my birthplace. But Buffalo, New York, is a town which, as Rodney Dangerfield would say, don't get no respect, so I think its latitude and longitude have been revoked. Alas, not only was the location peculiar, but my timing was a tad off. You recall that my mom helped shoehorn my dad into the dusty box that the pair called a liquor store. Then a nasty little German with a Charlie Chaplin mustache and his allies—inventors of the California tuna roll, the Japanese—threatened to wipe America off the map and replace it with Argentina. Or with sushi, depending on which would cover more territory. By 1943, when my mom was pregnant with, of all the unlikely people, me, the situation was so desperate that the government began to draft men over thirty who wore eyeglasses, had pregnant wives, and who had been obsessed with methods of transportation in their childhoods.

My dad fit the description perfectly. Remember how he slipped out of the back door of his school to go to the train station?

The Navy tossed my dad into a satchel, sent him to Philadelphia, and stuffed him into Wharton for something that should have fit a railroad-obsessed man perfectly—training. At this astonishingly high class business school, my dad was taught…to type. A skill that didn't stick. Hopefully they did better at educating him in the art of filing 3x5 cards.

After six months in Philadelphia, the military cognoscenti packed him into the vehicle of his dreams, a railroad car, and schlepped him to a newly opened naval base in San Francisco, Treasure Island, the home of the machines for whose officers his father had made boots: blimps. There, the Naval brass forced him to risk his life and save America by doing highly perilous clerical work—those paper cuts could kill you. To demonstrate how crucial his job was to the war effort, they gave him a title: chief petty officer. I kid you not. You may recognize this position from its equivalent in the Army—Army Specialist First Class Of It-Really-Doesn't-Matter. Apparently, someone has to be an expert in the infinite piles of trivia that will never amount to a thing.

This means that my mom was left to run the store and to abandon the new baby (me) with, well, that was the problem. Terminology. Words matter. The phrase au pair did not exist in English. The term babysitter did. But my mom, who was normally as quick as a roomful of nuclear physicists chasing a neutrino, did something strange. To watch over me, she hired what were called in those early days of American history "cleaning women." Now look, when you hire a babysitter it means you want someone to watch over your baby. Possibly even to coo to it and to catch its eye with a shake of a rattle once or twice a day. Heck, on rare occasion a babysitter might actually get carried away and indulge in a hug and a rocking session. But when you hire a cleaning woman, you imply a radically different priority. Yes, a lot of hugging and cooing may occur. But it's all directed at a precious object that isn't your baby. It's focused on your vacuum cleaner. With a little spare attention reserved for another piece of electronica, your toaster-sized radio, which is playing the latest episode of a hot soap opera. Helen Trent was very big with the women my mother hired. The name of the sudsy radio saga I remember. But the cleaning lady's names I don't. They never introduced themselves. And they were too busy with their treasured pair of household appliances to get close enough for me to see their faces. In fact, I don't even remember whether they *had* faces.

Which means that the Second World War created a monstrous problem for many of us who were infants at the time: it got us ignored. The apartment my family lived in should have been easy to clean. We lived on the second floor of a house my father, mother, and grandmother had chipped in to buy. But, remember, they were poor. So the expansive domicile that fell within their price range was just a squoomph bigger than a Velveeta cheese box. Which means that our apartment was roughly the size of a postage stamp from Baffin Island. Not more than three particles of grit could crowd into the place at a time. If there had been a bouncer at the door, he could have had specks of grunge anxious to dance in the place lined up around the block.

Despite the lightness of the chores, it appears that none of the ladies keeping my mother's slightly-smaller-than-a-face-towel-sized carpet from accumulating unsightly particulates could stand the sight of my blond curls and handsome little face (yes, in those days I was good-looking; it wasn't until puberty that my mug began to resemble an elongated eggplant).

How do we know that the cleaning ladies regarded me as an obstacle to the Electrolux? The underworked specialists in spotless flooring put up a wooden baby gate and locked me in the narrow corridor that went from the living room in the front of the apartment to the two tiny bedrooms in the back. This was a dark, windowless hallway where the sun never shone and where there were no nice warm rugs to cover the cold hardwood floors on which my crawling palms were planted.

I sat on the frigid planks remembering what it had been like one Sunday when my mom was home and I had been allowed to sit in the bay window. For some strange reason, I could see the motes of dust that had managed to squeeze into the place drifting in the rays of the sun, rays that saturated me with warmth. I say for some strange reason because that ability to see nearly invisible threads of dust do a slow waltz in the light has utterly disappeared now that I'm an adult. Could that be because I've spent my grownup years in places so dirt-free that the dust no longer celebrates its ability to outfox the cleaning lady?

Sitting in the sun had felt wonderful. But now, locked behind the baby barrier, I saw the bay window from a distance so great that it was smaller than my fingernails. I sat in darkness longing for the light. Awful as this was, it would later squeeze forth an advantage. It would turn me into a perpetual outsider, a non-stop outcast. It would amplify my role as a visitor from outer space.

What's the bonus produced by this perpetual exile? What's the prize at the bottom of the alien Rice Krispy box? Sometimes those who are frozen out of the social circle can see more clearly than those who are locked in. Sometimes rejects can even see something that most of us miss: how flotsam and jetsam from seemingly random corners of the cosmos fit into a big picture.

◆

IN 1945, WORLD WAR II ended and the Navy returned my dad in slightly used condition. He still had all four limbs, both eyes, and another piece of essential original equipment, his nose—a large one. And he had gained a vague memory of what it had been like to type. But he had lost his hair. A devastating war injury.

I was roughly two and a half years old when my dad came back. And having him around was glorious. Briefly. One Sunday I woke up at an hour that two year olds think is party time for jumping beans, grasshoppers, frogs, and fleas who can leap to 150 times their own height. Not to mention Olympic tryout time for toddlers who want to shame all of these virtuosos-of-jump by springing from bounceable surfaces into low earth orbit. Alas, adults are under the sorry impression that 6:00 a.m. on a day off is a good time to get in an extra four hours of snoring. I opened the door to a room I'd never entered before, my parents' bedroom. The sun, which goes to work early even on the day of the weekend that carries its name, was blazing through the windows. Ahhh, release from darkness. I mountain-climbed up the bed to the plateau of the mattress, where my mom and dad were deep in snooze-land. And I did what any sensible two-and-a-half-year-old intoxicated by sunshine and seized by the leaping instinct would do—I woke them up. How do you wake people who appear to be corpses supplied with musical snorts by artificial means? You use their box springs as a trampoline. And because you've had no athletic training, you occasionally trampoline on your parents' backs, buttocks, and cheeks. What bliss. What joy. I finally had something I'd never experienced before—a family.

But remember the practice in my dad's bloodline of rolling over on your wife from time to time in the middle of the night? In my granddad's case, that nocturnal practice had produced five daughters and, at long last, my dad.

In those days just after my father's return from his duties saving the world for democracy, my mom had not yet worked out the practice of keeping him at a respectable distance. And she had not yet installed two parallel single beds with a wicked gap of three feet between them.

This negligence had consequences. One day, shortly after my exuberance at finally gaining two parents had begun, my newly reunited nurturers announced that they had a surprise for me. Oh, goodie. Toys were rare in my life, so this was the first surprise they'd ever sprung on me. Alas, it was not a battery operated tank with genuine rubber treads that could climb over bedroom slippers. It was not even a GI Joe whose jeep jerked up and down like a cat trying to cough out a poisoned canary. In fact, as unexpected revelations go, it was not a good one. I was about to have a brother. And after what seemed like only one Sunday jumping up and down on my progenitors, along he came.

Since this was the first child my parents had experienced together, they treated him as, well, their first child. They put him on a table in the living room and changed his diapers with a beaming pride that defied belief. They gave him vivid, joyful, emotional attention. Something I'd never received. And here's the capper. The table on which they changed him was, guess where? In the sunshine of the bay window. And where was I? In the darkness at the back of the living room, a few short feet from the corridor where I'd been imprisoned for the first three years of my life. This cemented it. The outsider role was here to stay.

◆

THERE WAS ONE THING that should have helped but didn't. My grandmother lived on the first floor and occasionally let me into her apartment. And, yes, bounced me on her knee, called me "boychick" and taught me that cows go "moo," dogs go "bow, wow," and donkeys go "heehaw." Essential survival skills for urban two and a half year olds who do not live on a farm.

She also spoke Yiddish a lot, and once or twice she put me into a stroller and wheeled me over to Hertel Avenue's Jewish poultry shop, a little bit of the shtetl transferred to the streets of Buffalo. All the chickens, geese and ducks sat in cages chatting. In Yiddish. You chose your bird—alive— and came back later to pick it up, considerably less talkative, headless, and denuded of its down jacket. How it stayed warm from that point on, I do not know. The oven may have helped.

The poultry shop smelled of burning feathers. Somehow, none of the fowl realized that this should be construed as a warning, and that concerted militancy in the cause of social justice might have been a good idea. I mean, there were only two humans lording it over a joint filled with 150 flight experts. If the poultry had gotten their act together, they could have clapped the butchers into the cages and changed the place to a pet food store. You know, bring in your puppy, have him pick the butcher of his choice, come back two hours later, and he's neatly packed in 300 Alpo cans. But political organization and entrepreneurship were apparently not big in the avian world at the time. All this has changed since the rise of the environmental and animal rights movements.

What sort of warmth did my grandmother inject into my life? The clue was in her baking. She made hard rolls so rigid that you could have used one in a hockey championship and, when the game was over, the roll would have remained undented. According to one of my aunts, my grandmother had the same quality. Warmth did not suit her.

What's more, when my father got back from the war and my mother returned to household duties, I was terrified of my mom and didn't exactly encourage the idea of a motherly relationship. And mothering was not on her list of urgent matters. Some women get joy from their babies and become addicted to mothering. Other women are terrified by this mass of body tissue that squalls for reasons no one can see. They flee the motherly role. My mom was in the flight category. She plunged into charitable endeavors, rapidly rising to the presidency of every organization in sight. Which meant that I was still left with cleaning ladies who loathed me. For some reason it never occurred to my mother that I might be better off in some day-care situation with the company of other kids. Maybe she was afraid of germs. Polio was fashionable at the time. Or maybe she had a premonition of another minor problem.

I was, well, how shall we put this, not exactly a social hit. At the age of four, my peers organized a group called the Hartwell Gang (named for our one-block-long street, Hartwell Road). Nominally, I was a member. But I was singled out for a uniquely privileged role. When the boys were playing games like house or doctor with the girls, I was discouraged from attending. One day, the kids erected tents made from their mothers' sheets in Sheila Eisenberg's back yard. Lord knows what game they had in mind. But they sensed a danger that could wreck their afternoon. Me. So they stationed a sentry in the driveway. When he saw me coming, he blocked me from leaving the sidewalk and heading up the drive to the back yard to see what was going on.

However, when the entertainment turned to beating someone up, I was enthusiastically invited to participate. In fact, I was indispensable. I was the beat-upee. On some days, the group got its aerobic exercise by chasing me around the block. On others, they became lazy, threw me into a basement, put a block of laundry soap on the stairs, and told me that if I attempted to climb out of my dungeon, I would slip on the soap and shatter my vertebrae. I believed them. My knowledge of physics, in those days, was less than rudimentary.

On top of everything else, as I've already hinted, I felt a need to wall myself off from my mother. I was desperate to protect my four-year-old feeling of independence. As a result of that, and the fact that my mother was the kind of person who longed for physical contact but didn't know how to go about giving or getting it (she was probably as frightened of it as I was), there was no hugging in my life. Then one Sunday morning I was out on the sidewalk with my father. A dog licked my face. I was terrified and on the verge of tears. My father explained this mystery by telling me that the dog had kissed me. Well, that was it. I was hooked. Here was a way of getting kisses without giving up any independence or descending into the nightmare world of my parents' interpersonal tensions. Animals! Animals who got a burst of joy out of your very existence. But more about the animals later. And we are not talking Eric Burden.

Dogs were not the only thing that saved me from a total interior freeze. If you don't experience warmth in your childhood, you may spend the rest of your life chilled by a coldness deep within you. You may never believe that others can actually delight in you. Why? Most adults light up when they see a child. After all, children are born with what ethologists call "supernormal stimuli," walloping, megaton triggers of cuteness. And adults are built with a corresponding biological ignition switch, one that lights them up and makes them smile, beaming like a bonfire the size of the US Capitol Building. If you as a baby kindled smiles, you are in luck. The capacity for joy and warmth is likely to flare in your heart from time to time for the rest of your life. But if all you got were frowns, woe be unto you. Your emotional core is likely to freeze over like a surplus bag of ice cubes abandoned by picnickers at the South Pole.

My mom frowned when she looked at me. The spontaneous smile of a mother never lit her face. And my dad was absent. Working. Dogs, on the other hand, danced with joy when they saw me coming. Heck, they even wagged their tails. But they were not alone. A twelve-year-old cousin traveled the 408.5 miles to Buffalo from Asbury Park, New Jersey, my father's homeland, at the end of her eighth-grade school year. I was roughly three. My father's oldest sister, my Aunt Beck, had noticed that my mom was struggling with life, motherhood, and me. "When you get out of school," she said to one of three gorgeous nieces she was raising, "I want you to go up to Buffalo and help Ann." And help my mom, my cousin Jackie did. How? When she emerged from her seven-hour bus ride, arrived at our shoebox of a house, and saw me, she thought I was the cutest thing she'd ever laid eyes on. So her smile ignited like a match factory doused with lighter fluid. Her visit only lasted a week, but it helped.

Then came something that would have repercussions way, way down the line. And in a far more psychedelic time. My mother's younger sister, Rose, invited me to the apartment she shared with her new husband a half a mile away in an almost-block-long, three-story Tudor apartment complex on Delaware Avenue. When I arrived in Aunt Rose's living room, she had the afternoon planned for me. She loved the arts. So she took me to her phonograph and played me one of her favorite pieces of music, Peter and the Wolf, a symphony that the Russian composer Sergei Prokofiev had written for Moscow's Central Children's Theatre in 1936 to introduce kids to the instruments of an orchestra. But Peter and the Wolf is not a heavy-handed, Stalinist piece of music. It is rich in melody. And it has a plot. Peter and his animal friends have to avoid the clutches, teeth, and stomach of the wolf. And one of those animal friends, the duck, lands in the wolf's belly... then is saved. Sort of. The wolf ends up in a zoo, and, "If you listen very carefully," says the script, "you'll hear the duck quacking inside the wolf's belly, because the wolf in his hurry had swallowed her alive."

But that wasn't all. Aunt Rose wanted to introduce me to literature. Sort of. Walt Disney had just made a movie and an accompanying record album out of an adventure story written by Scottish novelist Robert Louis Stevenson in 1881. The tale featured Long John Silver, a pirate with a peg leg and a parrot on his shoulder. And it had an oddball hermit, old Ben Gunn, who climbed mountain cliffs with an agility that made all the local mountain goats stop chewing, take the grass out of their mouths, poke each other in the ribs, and say an astonished "well, I'll be." Peter and the Wolf would show up one distant day down the line in my sexual enlightenment. And Treasure Island would appear in a peculiar form the first time I took LSD. But that's in the distant future.

Most important was this. Let's go back to the smile that lights you up when you see a little kid and you think he or she is adorable. The smile that makes you one of the rays of sunshine in that child's life. My mother never had that smile with me. But my cousin Jackie and my Aunt Rose did. Jackie's only lasted a week. Then she took the bus back to New Jersey. And Rose's only lasted one afternoon. Then she had kids of her own, her life got serious, and she became somber. But dogs' tongues and those two smiles installed a potential for love deep inside of me. However, the emotions they inserted would be seriously challenged before they could fully, well, ummm, bloom.

◆

WHEN I WAS EIGHT, Buffalonians were apparently drinking themselves into a stupor, because the wealth was beginning to roll in. We moved to a big Tudor house overlooking a forest of five-story-high trees in a 506-acre, Frederick Law Olmsted-designed park with a zoo a few hundred yards away, hidden by the woods. Frederick Law Olmsted, who began work on Delaware Park in 1868, was the greatest park designer of all time. And you could tell. His park was a wonderland. And it was in front of our new house. In the back, on the other side of our backyard fence, was another masterpiece: a low-slung house of gorgeous simplicity and huge windows designed by Frank Lloyd Wright. So I was sandwiched between two amazing pieces of design. What's more, I woke up every morning to the sound of lions roaring, elephants thundering, and peacocks mewing (yes, peacocks sound exactly like crucified cats trying to meow two words—"help me").

The walk to school was nearly a mile—the length of the Lewis and Clark expedition by eight-year-old standards. I was just as welcome socially in my new neighborhood as I'd been in my old one. One day the boys who made fun of me at school were in an empty lot dividing up into teams for a ball game, palavering over who would be on what team. Then they saw me coming. They literally picked up their gloves, balls, and bats and headed off to find another place to play, one where I would not be able to find them. The same crew also blackballed me from their informal after-school social club.

But I had an undeniable magnetism. As I took the long walk home, clusters of kids would trail me, pounce from behind bushes, pummel me around, and toss my school books in dog shit.

Nonetheless, I was spoiled rotten. I locked myself in my bedroom from the age of ten and read two books a day—starting with all thirty-eight Oz books (as in *The Wizard of...*). The Oz books assured me that every day Glenda, the Good Witch of the South, would take out her magic crystal, put away her Georgia accent, and scan the world looking for little boys and girls who deserved to be whisked to the Emerald City. I wasn't doing particularly well in Buffalo, so I combed the pages of Frank Baum's *oeuvre*, concluded that Glenda did her international youth inspection every day at precisely four, managed to sneak a Big Ben alarm clock out of my parents' bedroom, and locked myself in my room every afternoon, where I squeezed my eyes shut for a half an hour at 4:00 p.m. and pleaded with Glenda to send me a magic carpet, a couple of flying monkeys, or just an airline ticket, and let me lick her toenails in gratitude. Apparently, the demand for Jewish children who hiked their pants up to their armpits was not big in the Land of Oz, so I never passed the kingdom's admission requirements. Glenda didn't even grant me her consolation prize—the pills that allowed Oz's inhabitants to get A's on all their report cards without studying.

Thus, I gave up on the country that had been so hospitable to Dorothy and Toto, and, at the age of ten, turned to outer space. There was no room for me on the earth, so I felt that there might be a spot for me on some cozy dwarf planet. It was the TV show *Tom Corbett Space Cadet* that clued me into the possibilities of extraterrestrial living.

Then something miraculous happened. One day I was sitting in the new, big Tudor house alone. I was still ten, and I was in the living room, which even at three o'clock in the afternoon, was darkened by thick velvet curtains closed so you couldn't see the view of Frederick Law Olmsted's astonishing greenery. I knew every book on the room's shelves. They'd been in exactly the same location ever since we'd moved in two years earlier. Who knows if any of these tomes had ever been read. Then a book I didn't recognize, a book that had never been on the shelves, appeared in my lap. It was one of those rare books that grabs you by the collar, yanks you into nose-to-nose contact, and announces, "Listen up, I'm talking to you."

What message did this nameless book shout into my face? The first two rules of science.

Rule one: the truth at any price including the price of your life. To illustrate its point, the book told the story of Galileo. And it got it wrong. It portrayed Galileo as a man so wedded to his truth that he'd have been willing to go to the stake and be barbecued for it. Complete with hot sauce. Sorry, that was Giordano Bruno, who stuck to his opinion that there was life on other heavenly bodies so stubbornly that he was roasted like a Cajun hot dog in Rome's Campo de' Fiori, complete with a leather bridle gagging his mouth to keep him from uttering heresies. Why the gag? To avoid polluting the aural canals of the godly crowd, a mash of the pious who had gathered to see precisely what entertaining variations on your basic writhing Bruno would perform as the flames reduced him to a blackened straggle of meat. Galileo, on the other hand, made a deal with the Pope, who happened to be an old acquaintance. Mr. Galilei swore that everything he'd ever written was false. In exchange, he was allowed to live. But to live under house arrest in Florence for the rest of his life.

That was the sordid reality. But I was lucky. The book portrayed Galileo as a man of courage willing to be poached, toasted, and broiled in Mozzarella cheese and marinara sauce for his insights. That rang some newly sprouting longing for heroism in me. So in a statement about truth, there was an irony. The untruthful version was more useful than the facts.

Rule of science number two: look at things right under your nose as if you've never seen them before, then proceed from there. Look for things that you and everyone around you take for granted and hold those invisible realities up to the light. Question them. And question something else invisible, your own assumptions. To illustrate rule two, the book gave the example of Anton van Leeuwenhoek, the man who invented the microscope. Van Leeuwenhoek looked at pond water and saw a world of life that no one had ever suspected. He saw what he called animalcules, tiny beasts that we call microorganisms.

But there was more. More that the book dared not mention. Van Leeuwenhoek's most courageous move in the "look at things right under your nose" department was this: he looked at human sperm under the lens and discovered that it, too, was a puddle of animalcules. Then he wrote about that fact to the Royal Society in London, the brand new Vatican of science. Where do you suspect that van Leeuwenhoek got fresh sperm? Yes, he had the courage to confess an act of masturbation. To the Royal Society. That takes balls. For more reasons than one.

Masturbation would also play a role in my future, thanks to the Boy Scouts of America. Yes, all of them. But that's a topic for later.

The two rules of science hit me to the quick. They roiled, churned, and glowed in me like the lava in a seventy-pound volcano. They became my religion. And they gave me something I'd never had, playmates. My new companions were men of science who could not send sentries down the driveway or pick up their bats and balls and go someplace else. Why was this gang of playmates—the great scientists of history—unlikely to reject me? Because most of its members were dead. They no longer had the energy to shoo me away.

So I read every adult science fiction book at the local library (they weren't supposed to let anyone under eighteen touch 'em, but the librarians took pity on me). After my first year reading two books a day, I was older and wiser and eleven, so I realized that no saucer people were likely to rescue me from life on Lake Erie. But the books were addictive. Men and women frequently engaged in something that hinted at sex. Not that I knew what sex was. But sometimes your hormones understand things that your brain has not yet figured out. What's more, the sci-fi protagonists did this mysteriously exciting unknown act on strange planets that were nothing like the town where I'd been beaten up by my peers since the age of four. And on top of that, the books taught you about neat stuff like the Doppler Shift, this fetching little dress that Christian Doppler wore during his night life in the beerhalls of Prague. No, I'm kidding. The Doppler Shift is a blush in the color of light from distant stars. Apparently, some astral bodies embarrass easily.

I soon moved on to real science, along with a few things like the *Federalist Papers* tossed in for good measure. This meant that I read books under the desk at school, never paid attention to my teachers, and had no idea of what a gerund was, or of the difference between Kansas, Katmandu, and canned asparagus. In other words, I was doing abysmally in school, but my parents had read Doctor Spock's *Baby and Child Care*, the hot parenting book of the late 1940s and early 1950s. Spock, a real honest-to-goodness medical doctor, did not have pointy ears and flit through the skies on the starship *Enterprise*. That Spock would not be invented for another thirteen years. Spock (I'll leave you to figure out which one) advised that you never hang your offspring from the rafters in the attic by their pinkies. And he sternly warned that you should avoid drawing and quartering your children, even with pen, ink, and sharpened coins. Even if you had a spare kid in reserve. So my mom and dad let me get away with this in-class form of truancy. I mean, how could my dad, who had flat out exited the school building altogether, complain?

Meanwhile, my teachers liked me almost as much as my peers did. My hand-eye coordination was a sight to behold. In first grade, where you do a lot of writing, drawing and filling in workbook quizzes, I was the last one to finish every single classroom assignment. There was one exception:

the day I finished second-last. The teacher was so startled that she gave me a gold star. For real.

With my best interests at heart, the concerned pedagogue called in my mother and explained that I was mentally retarded. So my mother took me off to a specialist for psychological testing. What this sage concluded, my mother has never confessed. But, apparently, he felt the corned beef hash that God had dumped into my cranium contained the appropriate proportions of meat and potatoes, because I was not exiled to an institution for children who drool.

My popularity among peddlers of learning grew as the years went by. My mother recently presented me with a gift-wrapped box of memorabilia in which she'd kept all of my grammar school report cards. Why she preserved them, Lord alone knows. Each document contains the exasperated rantings of some teacher who obviously could not tolerate having me in her class. After all, teachers are humans like you and me. They are starved for attention. And I was so epoxied to my books that I failed to give them even a glance.

But these little incidents, along with the fact that my parents were constantly at each others' throats, may help explain why I was forced to defend myself by seeking solitary confinement in my bedroom as the chief carbon dioxide generator in a micro-environment of small mammals, fish, and lizards. It may also explain why the summer camp kidnap didn't work.

THE SUMMER CAMP KIDNAP— AND HOW IT BACKFIRED

My parents weren't entirely pleased to have the front corner bedroom taken over by a child from another planet. Not only that, they were somewhat disconcerted that in a house kept so neat that no one was even allowed to sit on the couch but guests, this visitant from God-knows-what-slum in the solar system was turning 1,800 cubic feet of bedroom decor designed to make the bridge club die with envy into a cross between a biology lab, a miniature zoo, and a facility for the manufacture of high-grade, small-animal manure.

Yes, my bedroom was a sanctuary, but it was also a barnyard bedlam inhabited by: a gaggle of guinea pigs hell-bent on overpopulating the planet; ten white mice who thought they were engaged in a procreative race to outdo the guinea pigs; an extremely tolerant cat who came to accept interspecies pluralism as a natural way of life; a slime-infested, five-gallon pickle jar in the back of the closet, a container in which I raised paramecia, amoebas, and other invisible beasts kind enough to perform nautical maneuvers under the lens of my brass-barreled 1930s professional medical microscope; and 140 guppies who amused themselves by leaping out of their tank in the middle of the night, committing suicide on the hardwood strip beyond the edge of the brown shag carpet, and, as they flipped noisily about in the darkness, terrifying me into thinking that my room was filled with ghosts. Then there were half a dozen snails eating the algae on the inside of the aquarium's glass walls, two miniature catfish swallowing mouthfuls of sand at the aquarium's bottom and spitting the grains out again, an assortment of angelfish, blue gouramis, neon tetras, and whatever else the tropical fish store was selling cheap that month, plus a lizard who found the whole place so unendurable that he literally hanged himself from the leash on which I'd allowed him to run around the dresser top during the day while I was away at school.

Not everyone loved the animal population as much as I did. One year, when I was about eleven, I became curious about raising lizard eggs. I'd read in a book about reptiles and amphibians that you could get these eggs for free from your local pet store. After all, the lizards insisted on laying them. And the pet store owners didn't know what to do with them. So you could probably cadge a few before the owners threw them out. Or threw you out. Whichever came first. The book turned out to be right. I went down to my local pet emporium and came home with an egg. I nestled it in peat moss, kept it slightly moist (or was it slightly dry...I forget). Fortunately, I was not required to sit on it. Then I waited for something to happen. But nothing did. Or so it seemed.

Three weeks later, as I trudged up the driveway after a hard day of reading books under the school desk and being beaten up on my way home, our maid was running from the house screaming that she would never come back again. There was, she shouted over her shoulder in panic, a monster in my room. I entered my den of natural history to see what was up. There was an empty, leathery little egg shell in the peat moss. Whatever had been in it had experimented with the novelty of adhesive feet by crawling up the nearby wall, crossing the ceiling upside down, and finding itself a comfortable, eye-level spot smack dab in the middle of the wall on the opposite side of the room—the one place where the cleaning woman had never seen an animal before. And there he clung, head down—a real beauty: two inches long, a lovely green, his brain cage twice as big as his body. My first (and only) lizard hatchling.

Fortunately, the maid forgave me for terrifying her with this two-inch-long reptilian monstrosity. She even continued the hopeless task of trying to clean my room.

◆

IT WAS MY FATHER and mother's most profound hope that if they simply exerted enough effort, they could make those terrible antennae on my head go away. So every year or two they came up with a new plot to turn me into a human, the kind who plays baseball and plans furtively for months to find a way to get his hands up—or down—the front of some girl's blouse. (I would later learn, after leaving home, that you could skip the whole blouse-and-bra stage of adolescence by simply accompanying a girl to bed—where she was usually kind enough to show up without a collection of fasteners, clasps, and buttons. But that, too, is a tale for later.)

None of the plans for my normalization ever worked. But my dad and mom were persistent. The worst of their schemes to entrap me in normalcy was summer camp—a high-security penal colony for undersized inmates. There may be no barbed wire fences or machine-gun-toting guards, but if you try to escape you'll either be eaten by raccoons or sent back to your sneering counselor, who will make you do something humiliating like cleaning out the urinals with your teeth. In summer camp, my parents reasoned, they would *force* me to abide by eleven-year-old standards and practices: baseball and the blouse business, which, with any luck I'd pick up from listening to a densely packed cabin of horny pre-teens.

I was anything but happy about this strategy. In fact, I would have preferred an all-expense-paid two months in Sing Sing. But there was no fighting it. My parents were much bigger than I was. And at my weight, I could easily be dragged anywhere.

So I packed about two hundred sci-fi paperbacks into a suitcase, put a few changes of underwear with my name sewn in the back into a trunk big enough to be a condo, and went off determined to continue pursuing my own interests.

My parents' grand experiment was not a success. There was no way the camp authorities could get me to play baseball. The reason went far beyond my basic lack of interest in the game, or my technique for catching the ball, which consisted of closing my eyes and sticking my hands up in front of my face to protect my nose. When it came time to decide who would be on which team, the other kids, the same ones I'd grown up with in grammar school and who'd always done their best to keep me at least a mile and a half from their social activities, competed over me like major league owners over the next Babe Ruth. But the object of the bargaining was to make sure I *didn't* land (God forbid) on the team the negotiator was speaking for.

At first a counselor or two tried to be liberal and make sure I was wedged onto some unfortunate squad. But when it became obvious that having me in the outfield turned a viciously competitive, high-skilled sport into a Marx Brothers movie with an intolerable number of pauses for mending broken film, the authorities went along with the kids, and I was allowed to "sneak" back to the bunk and read my books in peace.

What's worse, I ran into a very appealing snake in the woods, made a cage for it, and planned to take it back to my bedroom menagerie. When I introduced my mother to the prospective houseguest on visiting day, she screamed.

What's even worse, about the only kids I could relate to in those days were four or five years older than I was. So I hung out with this fifteen year old fellow-camper who, because he was from New York City, was *sophisticated*, a man of the world and a budding bohemian. There were no bohemians in Buffalo, so this was a whole new experience. My new friend taught me all about a subversive form of music called jazz, whose every trill of improvisation was a clarion call, as he explained it, to freedom. It was the first seed of a Venus flytrap which some years later would nearly eat my parents alive.

When I returned to my bedroom animal refuge in Bisonburg, my antennae were longer than ever. What's more, I began squandering the family fortune on vast quantities of music by Mingus, Miles Davis, and Lord-knows what other drug addicts, in addition to my growing diet of Bartok, Stravinsky, Beethoven, and Vivaldi. Why, oh why, thought my mother in her silent prayers, won't he listen to Elvis?

◆

MEANWHILE, I HAD ACQUIRED an ambition truly worthy of someone judged mentally retarded by his first-grade teacher. I wanted to be Albert Einstein. I first discovered that he and I were similar when I was ten years old and spent an hour roaming the empty house from basement to attic in a frantic search for the scissors. Then I found that someone had cagily hidden them in my left hand. A bit of deductive reasoning led to the conclusion that the culprit was...*me*. Thus, I realized that I had all the equipment necessary to be an absent-minded professor. Which is to say, I was prematurely senile.

Einstein, of course, had been plagued by the same problem. He'd shuffle off to the Institute for Advanced Study at Princeton University wearing bedroom slippers and pajamas, and his poor wife (his second one; wife number-one had become tired of this nonsense and gone off to find a husband with a brain) was forced to sprint up the street carrying shoes, socks, pants, a shirt, a winter coat, and whatever other relevant items she could find in the closet. "Albert, Albert," she'd shout, trying to get her perpetually preoccupied hubby's attention, "You forget something." Poor Albie had forgotten to get dressed. Which is why half the time he delivered his lectures in a fitted sheet.

In high school, I would discover yet another curious Einsteinian characteristic. I could master the concepts of advanced mathematics with only a few hours of bashing my head up against the nearest wall, but couldn't do arithmetic—at least not in a manner that allowed the results to resemble reality. So I'd get ninety-nine on all my homework assignments. Why no one hundreds? I'd absorbed the principles of each problem in my own very peculiar way, head bashing. But in carrying out the addition and subtraction, I'd invariably added one and one and gotten three, so all of my answers were bizarrely off base. Einstein, it seems, had the same difficulty. He'd stand at a blackboard for an hour scrawling complex equations that only three men in the known universe could understand. Then, when he was finished, some visiting six-year-old in the back row would raise her hand and point out that the professor had added two to three and gotten six.

But my ultimate attachment to Einstein did not come when I discovered that he and I both dressed like unmade beds (when we remembered to dress, that is). It came when I was in eighth grade and some young wench in my class who'd made a point of ignoring me all year (just as all the other females had) brought a whole new phenomenon into my life—eye contact. Her pupils did something no girls' had ever done before. First they swiveled in my direction. That was a shock. Then they locked onto my irises. That was electrifying. It set my entire nervous system into overdrive. What impelled her to do something so violently against the laws of nature? What motivated her to walk up and actually open a conversation? "I told my mother," she said, "that you understand Einstein's Theory of Relativity."

Now, look, I had absorbed huge globs of advanced science at this point, but the Theory of Relativity wasn't one of them. However, I wasn't about to admit it. After all, I couldn't catch a ball. I couldn't quote a sports score. The one thing I could claim was having some sort of a brain. What sort, not even the animals in my room knew. So I wasn't ready to give up the one title my classmates had glued to me like a "kick me" sign—the "sickly scientist." Which means that the minute school was over, I jumped on my bike and pedaled two miles to my local library, a small, white, single-story building dwarfed by six-story high elm trees. I suspect the library building was small because books had not yet caught on in Buffalo.

The librarians knew me better than my mother did. They were the ones who had let me loose in the forbidden zone, the adult books, the sci fi books with petting and heavy breathing, when I was ten. "Give me everything you've got on the Theory of Relativity," I said. One of the pair went back into god knows what shelves, returned, and slid two books by Einstein across the desk. One was not just fat, it was obese. The other was slender. It may have been on a diet. I grabbed both of them, put them in the clamp on the back of my bike, and pedaled frantically for home. I was on a deadline. I had to understand the Theory of Relativity by 9:00 a.m. the next day or be deemed an idiot. I took the books up to my bedroom and closed the door so I could concentrate.

The animals were vaguely curious, but none of them volunteered to help. And help was what I needed. The overweight book contained approximately sixteen words of English per page and 425 mathematical formulae. Yes, 425 equations per page. Equations that might as well have been cellulite. Math formulae have always been beyond me. But the overweight tome was the book I tackled first. Why? I'd learned that if you slog through something you don't understand a bit, by the time you get to the end, you've understood something. Even if only at the level of your gut.

So I attacked the bulging book at 4:00 p.m. By 8:00 p.m., I'd only gotten through fifty pages. And I hadn't understood a thing. Now remember, I was on a deadline. I had two hours left before my mom would order lights out and sleep. Two tiny hours in which to understand the most elusive theory of the twentieth century. So I gave up and turned to the slender, blue, cloth-covered book.

The overweight book had been written by Einstein and two collaborators. The skinny one was written by Dr. Einstein all by himself. What struck me most about it was its introduction.

In 1915, when Albert Einstein finished his General Theory of Relativity, it was said that only three men in the world could understand it. Cambridge astronomer Arthur Eddington told of being at a party in Europe. Some foreigner from a second-class Eastern European country, a scientist Eddington knew vaguely but considered insignificant, came up to him and said, "Congratulations. You are one of the only three men on this earth who understands the theory of relativity." Eddington answered, "Yes, there's me and Professor Einstein, but who is the third?" The man talking to Eddington had been referring to himself. But Eddington snootily blew him off. And Eddington was so proud of that fact that he told the story over and over again. Eddington's tale is where the notion that only three men understood Einstein came from. By 1955, the number said to understand Relativity had rocketed to seven.

But Albert Einstein was opposed to the sort of snobbery that Eddington had displayed. Genius, Einstein wrote in the introduction to his skinny blue book, was not the ability to be obscure. It was not the ability to come up with a theory that only seven men in the world could comprehend. It was the ability to express that theory so simply that anyone with a high school education and a reasonable degree of intelligence could understand it. In other words, it was the ability to render the most difficult concepts understandable to even the village cretin. Which was what Einstein was hoping to accomplish with his sveltely skinny book. He only asked one thing from his reader—that as he turn the pages, he try not to drip saliva on the print. I apparently was precisely the sort of drooling cretin that Einstein was looking for.

With his introduction to this skinny little blue book, it felt as if Albert Einstein had reached out though the printed page, grabbed me by the shirtfront, put his nose up to mine, and said, "Shmuck. Listen up. To be a genius, you have to be a writer."

When I finished the book that night I'd gotten a handle on the General Theory of Relativity, but the Special Theory of Relativity, which is where the hot stuff is located, still eluded me. In fact, I'd understood it. But I didn't believe that what I'd understood could possibly be what Einstein had meant. So I was forced to slog back to school the next morning prepared to tell the girl who had shown such faith in my intellectual prowess that I hadn't mastered relativity after all. Fortunately, she had received so much ridicule for speaking to me the previous day that she never came within 50 yards again. So the secret of my ignorance was safe.

However, Einstein's words had given me three lifetime goals: to become a scientific thinker, a genius…and a writer.

◆

WHILE I WAITED FOR my genius to flower (it never did), I made one tiny concession to normalcy. I believed in God until I was about twelve, and prayed fervently to Him for higher bowling scores. My classmates were landing 200 games, but my numbers were down in the 80s. Gutter balls were my specialty. Every variety of gutter ball you can imagine—from the raucous, sloshy one that rocks back and forth in the runnel and threatens to escape and jump to another lane, to the highly-disciplined, straight-as-an arrow kind that zooshes at high speed into the dark at the far end without threatening a single pin. Then I began to have doubts about the Lord of the Universe (my bowling scores never went up). But I stifled my disbelief because my Bar Mitzvah was coming and I didn't want to miss out on the avalanche of presents.

Once the critical ceremony was over and my father had bankrupted himself on a party that rivaled the ones thrown by the Shah of Iran, a bowling party where all the kids I'd been rejected by in grammar school showed their commitment to consistency by ganging up in foursomes and rolling murderously heavy balls toward ten poor, innocent pins, but not inviting me into the games—yet once I had put all the checks from relatives too lazy to buy me useless objects in the bank, I felt free to rethink things and came to the conclusion that I was, guess what? An atheist. Which led to a revelation.

I dared confess my utter disbelief in god to myself on roughly August 5, 1956. A month later, the Jewish High Holidays rolled around. My parents insisted that I go to temple with them. In fact, dodging this obligation to my tribe was to my mom and dad utterly unthinkable. They managed to bully me into putting on a form of Western clothing that I loathed—a suit. That wasn't easy. A dress suit is supposedly clothing. But in reality, it acts as your very own portable, personal prison. Try lifting your arms above your head to catch a falling squirrel in a suit jacket, and you'll see what I mean. Or try gulping. Your necktie will throttle your Adam's apple, strap it in to the upper reaches of your throat, and will threaten to crush it if it dares to move. I don't know how my parents convinced me to tie a variation on a hangman's noose around my neck and shove my arms into the sleeves of a restraint device disguised as formal attire. But that wasn't the end of my nurturers' accomplishments.

They also managed to shoehorn me into their blue, four-door Frazier, a long-forgotten car named after industrialist Henry J. Kaiser (more about him later). And they succeeded in driving me the two miles to Richmond Avenue without my opening the door at a red light and bolting for home. But when it came time for me to exit the car and walk the block to Temple Beth El, a building so old that all of the classrooms in the basement smelled like urine, they ran into a difficulty. I refused to leave the car. I wanted nothing to do with a long and boring ceremony whose efficacy in persuading a non-existent entity to treat you gently for the next twelve months I didn't believe in. So my parents opened the car door and literally tried to haul me out by my ankles. While they shredded my socks, I held on to the solid door frame that Henry J. Kaiser's laborers, using legendary American craftsmanship, had made of sturdy steel.

From this wrestling match came an epiphany. Yes, we atheists can epiphanize. Flares of static electricity can illuminate the dark corridors that crease and wrinkle our brains. The starring epiphany of the moment? There were no gods in the skies above the eight-story-high elm trees of Richmond Avenue. And there were no gods below Richmond Avenue's cement pavement. Yet there were gods in this scene. Yes, gods. Real gods.

Where were these deities? Or, to be more specific, where was my mishpacha's thunder-maker-of-choice, Jehovah, the gray-haired mountain of muscle and fury in a beard and a bathrobe who allegedly lived above the clouds and kept a double-entry bookkeeping account of your life and mine? The Ruler of the Universe was deep inside of my dad and mom. So deep that my parents were using my ankles as handles in their efforts to drag me to the house of the supernatural.

There is a tradition in science. It comes from the men I'd latched onto as mentors when I was ten—Galileo and Anton van Leeuwenhoek. Their legacy? Break the rules. Look for the unexpected. Turn the tables. Step outside the traditional perceptual frame. Galileo was a consultant to the arsenal of Venice on next-generation armaments. The techno-geek heard of a miracle military device that a Dutchman named Hans Lippershey had invented in Holland. It was a tube that allowed the Dutch to see the armies of their arch enemy, King Phillip III of Spain, at a distance so great that in the past it had invisibilized incoming marches of men intent on mass murder. In other words, with the spy glass you could see your enemy before he could see you. The spy glass was based on a clever use of another high-tech gadget—the lens. Galileo gathered information on this newly-invented gizmo, a tube with a lens at each end. Then he made one of his own. And he increased the magnification of the spy glass by a factor of ten. He turned it into the telescope.

Because the spy glass had been invented to see armed men marching in your direction with ill intent, the instrument was used horizontally. Galileo's breakthrough came from breaking convention. He decided to turn an optical instrument made for flat and level viewing in another direction. Instead of training his telescope on the horizon, Galileo turned it to the skies. The night skies, to be specific.

Now this was downright crazy. Everybody knew what was in the ebony heavens. Aristotle had described it. And Ptolemy had confirmed it. The heavens were filled with God's perfection. I mean, they were the heavens. As in "God's in His heaven and all's right with the world." The skies were the living room carpet of the Almighty. And God was perfect. So were his heavenly furnishings. Aristotle decreed that the circle was the most perfect of geometric forms. So in heaven, it was circles all the way. Perfect spheres rotating in perfect circles. A direct reflection of the aesthetic preferences of a geometry-obsessed Creator. In other words, by pointing his telescope up, Galileo was committing an act of heresy. He was peeping-tomming into the private apartment of the most perfect of all beings. Sort of like installing a spy cam in the bathroom of the woman you idolize. Or going through the underwear drawer of your dad. What did Galileo spot up there in the skies? A moon that looked broken and craggy. And planets that behaved less like Aristotle's perfect circles and more like stones. From that observation and its consequences came a Pope so upset that he gave Galileo ten years of house arrest for heresy.

But what had been Galileo's biggest screw you to the Almighty? And his biggest contribution to science? Changing the direction in which he pointed the lens. Forgetting about eye level and aiming his telescope up.

Then there's Anton van Leeuwenhoek, who fiddled with the same next-tech gizmo sixty years down the line—the lens. Van Leeuwenhoek was a draper. He was in the fabric business. The lens came in handy for examining the quality of the cloth he was about to sell. It helped him see how tight and regular the weave was. Van Leeuwenhoek's big innovation was like Galileo's. It came from noticing the norm…and stepping outside of it. It came from breaking the rules. Galileo had pointed his lenses up. Van Leeuwenhoek pointed his lenses down. Down at pond water. Down at blood. Down at his own spurt of semen. And, like Galileo, van Leeuwenhoek discovered an unexpected world. Galileo discovered that the sky was filled with stones. Van Leeuwenhoek revealed that the micro-territory down here on earth was riddled with "animalcules." As you know, he uncovered the hidden world of what we today call "microorganisms."

My parents' passionate belief gave me a job, a mandate, a mission. So did Galileo and van Leeuwenhoek. If the gods were not in the scud of clouds across the sky and not in the muck beneath our feet after a big rain, then where were they? Deep, deep inside. Inside of all of us. Including inside of atheists like me. And, no matter what your beliefs are, inside of *you*, too. My job? Turn the lens not up, not down, but *inside*. Train it on the inner world and its passions. Illuminate the realm where the spirits reside. Find the gods inside. And in finding the source of deity, I was certain I'd find the forces of history. But *why* is a subject we'll save for later.

Meanwhile, let's give credit where credit's due. Turning the lens to the world inside wasn't original. The guy who had set the standard for this sort of thing was Sigmund Freud.

And finding the gods inside also had a precedent, a forefather.

When I was fourteen, I heard about a book called *The Varieties of the Religious Experience*, a 1902 work by the father of American psychology, William James. This sounded like the ringing of the bell of a kindred soul. The brass walls of my identity resonated to the very sound of the title. There was no Amazon.com in those pitiful, primitive days. So it took me four months to hunt down a copy of the tome. But when I got it, it was another one of those volumes that reaches a hand out from the flat paper of the pages and grabs you by the collar of your shirt. James laid out the extreme experiences of folks like Saint Teresa of Avila and George Fox, the man who founded the Quaker movement in 1652. James saw a deep validity in whacko visitations that, under ordinary circumstances, would be deemed what he called "psychopathic."

For example, Saint Teresa was a nun, a bride of Christ, in Spain in the 1530s. Lying in her monastic cell, she would feel Christ coming through the walls, penetrating her body, and filling her with rapture. Or she would be caught up to heaven in an out of body experience, an ecstatic experience. Here's her description of one of her mystic raptures:

> *I saw an angel near me, on the left side, in bodily form...He was not tall, but short, marvelously beautiful, with a face which shone as though he were one of the highest of the angels, who seem to be all of fire: they must be those whom we call Seraphim...I saw in his hands a long golden spear, and at the point of the iron there seemed to be a little fire. This I thought that he thrust several times into my heart, and that it penetrated to my entrails. When he drew out the spear he seemed to be drawing them with it, leaving me all on fire with a wondrous love for God. The pain was so great that it caused me to utter several moans; and yet so exceeding sweet is this greatest of pains that it is impossible to desire to be rid of it, or for the soul to be content with less than God.*

"What empire is comparable to that of a soul who," she writes, "from this sublime summit to which God has raised her, sees all the things of earth beneath her feet." But these moments of mystic madness, explains James, can be harvested. They can turn those they visit into some "of the most powerfully practical human engines that ever lived."

Somehow men and women like Saint Teresa turn madness into truth. Or at least that's how William James saw it. So where are the gods? In the margins just outside of sanity, in the dark outskirts of the psyche where lunacy lies. Your psyche and mine.

James had no scientific explanations for experiences like Saint Teresa's. He simply laid them out on a lab bench, explained that they were specimens that went to the heart of something powerful and profound, then left his samples of "the religious experience" in the pages of a book for fifty to five years waiting for—*guess who?—you*. Or, to be more specific, *me*. Waiting for you and me to approach the puzzle of truths that can be milked from delusions. Waiting for us to analyze mystic raptures with scientific tools that did not exist in James's day. Which is where drugs would someday come into the picture. But not for another six years.

◆

To my parents, the whole thing was one unending nightmare. I not only bore the family name, but I was dragging it through some very strange mud. My mom seldom spent time with me. She was busy running organizations. But every once in a while, she did something truly remarkable. I took a liking to Johns Hopkins University when I was ten because I'd heard it was called the Johns Hopkins University of Science. And science was my main thrill in life. So my mom helped me get my hands on a catalog from the place. When I was twelve, she took me to a used-medical-equipment store and bought me the brass barreled professional medical microscope with Zeiss lenses that shimmered itself into this narrative a few minutes ago. She never bought me toys. But when I was still twelve, I begged her for the cash to send for a build-it-yourself computer kit. She gave me the money on the spot. Alas, what a disappointment. It turned out to be a kit for a Boolean Algebra machine. A symbolic logic contraption. Heck, it wasn't even binary. Real computers would have snickered and behaved as contemptuously as Sir Arthur Eddington had to that hapless Eastern European upstart who had presumptuously claimed to understand Einstein.

To make up for the Boolean humiliation, my mom introduced me to the son of a friend of hers, a kid three years older than I was with whom I co-conceived a real computer that won a few local science awards.

Then, when I was still twelve, my mom realized that one of her distant relatives was the head of research and development at a company that made futuristic engine valves for the first planes to make it to the edge of space—the X planes. Her relative spearheaded R&D at a company whose name sounded like the bleat of a queasy cow—the Moog Valve Corporation. Despite the ludicrous name, my mom persuaded the poor man to give me private tutoring sessions in weird scientific and engineering concepts. But when this genius of the fluttering valve saw that I didn't seem to grasp the significance of cycloids, he gave up on me. Perhaps he shared the opinion of my first grade teacher that I had rusted Brillo pads where my brains should have been.

My mother, in another of her periodic fits of helpfulness, scored an even greater success. She dragged me off to converse with the head of the graduate physics department at the University of Buffalo. Remember, I was twelve. There is no reason on earth why a savant of this magnitude should have wasted time with me. My mom must have twisted arms like telephone wire to get me this audience. My guess is that the august graduate department head had grudgingly granted me five minutes in his busy schedule smashing atoms until they screamed. But the session lasted an hour. Why? Because the two of us—the department head and, yes, I— dished into the hottest issue in the science of the day—Big Bang versus Steady State theory of the universe. It was 1955, the year when Steady State ring leader Fred Hoyle was certain that he was about to demolish George Gamow, the leader of the Big Bang Gang. Hoyle knew with absolute certainty that within a year, Gamow's Big Bang would be ridiculed, and within two years it would be utterly forgotten.

The outcome of the showdown between Hoyle and Gamow hinged on the interpretation of that cosmic smudge you've heard about in earlier pages, the phenomenon that makes the light of some stars blush bright red—the Doppler Shift. And Christian Doppler's Shift was what the department head and I laced into with gusto and glee. Meanwhile, my poor mom sat in the professor's tiny waiting room with his assistant and a copy of *Colliers Magazine*. The five minutes allotted to a snotty twelve year old dragged on and on. At the fifty-nine-minute mark, my mother was grinding through a magazine she loathed, the *Readers' Digest*, searching for jokes that wouldn't make her wince. When the physics department head and I finally emerged from our session, the fellow towered over me, put his hand on my right shoulder, and told my mom not to save for my grad school education. I'd get a fellowship in theoretical physics, he declared, at any school in the country. It wasn't until I was forty-eight years old that I discovered she'd saved the money for my graduate education anyway.

By then, it was too late. I'd acted on the notion that my only grad school funding would come from fellowships. More about how that flipped me off the academic track and into twenty years of adventure in the world of Michael Jackson, Prince, Bob Marley, AC/DC, Aerosmith, KISS, Queen, Paul Simon, and Billy Joel later. Be patient with me.

◆

DESPITE OCCASIONAL HEROIC EFFORTS to support me in my oddnesses, my parents made one final attempt to inject me into the mainstream of society. One final crash-program to make me normal. And, boy, was it sneaky. My parents decided that my problem was entirely nasal. I've mentioned in passing that I had this schnoz of rather unusual proportions. Were it not for extraordinarily powerful neck muscles, I'd have been forced to carry the thing around in a wheelbarrow. What's worse, as an air passage, it was a failure. This would have left my lungs seriously undersupplied...if it hadn't been for my big mouth.

One night my despairing father and mother had a brainstorm. "*Of course* he's a social reject," they said, clapping their hands to their foreheads. First off, boys didn't like me because I was incompetent at sports. Why? The Nose. How could I possibly see around it to catch a ball? And as for my lack of popularity with girls, the difficulty once again was obviously nasal. If only these sylphs and nymphs could see past my breathing apparatus, they'd be entranced by the sweet charm of my marginally crazed face. So my parents sent me off to a medical specialist, supposedly to correct my peculiar breathing (not to mention my daily nose bleeds, a result of the frequent occasions on which my classmates mistook my snorkel for a punching bag).

"Aha," said the proboscis expert, "the child has septal spurs." This sounded like good news to me. Despite its many drawbacks, at least my nose might someday allow me to get maximum speed out of a quarter horse. No, said the doctor, these hideous distortions of my nasal passages would have to go. Then my parents cautiously revealed their hidden motive. Since I was going to have my nose sliced open like a hot dog roll, my mother cooed sweetly, wouldn't it be nice if we could get it trimmed down in size? At first, I huffily refused. I had my integrity to think of. What's worse, I was already a ninety-nine-pound weakling. Without the twenty-pound nose, I couldn't even qualify for that! But my protests were of no use. When I woke up after the operation, most of what I'd formerly thought of as my body was gone. Oh, sure, the arms and legs were still there. But where was my nose?

For weeks I walked around with my head in bandages, looking like The Invisible Man after his magic formula wore off. Finally, the day of the great unveiling came. The doctor unwrapped my head. I looked in the mirror and saw, to my horror, an unfamiliar elephant. "Nothing to worry about," said the surgeon, pointing to my trunk. "The swelling will go down in about two weeks. But," and his voice turned icy, "you will have to be *extremely* careful. Your nose is still plastic." Apparently, this didn't mean my schnoz had been molded in a Chinese toy factory, but that it was as easily reshapeable as a lump of spackle. "Under no condition," the doctor said, "are you to engage in contact sports." This was one order he could count on me to follow. Folks with athletic skills felt that the less contact with me the better.

So for ten days, I conscientiously avoided the baseball and football teams that wouldn't allow me within five blocks of their playing fields and waited for the inflated organ to shrivel to its new size. Smaller than a salami. Then, one day, I made a mistake. I washed my face. The problem was not the water.

The half-bathroom that served as an extra convenience on our first floor was big enough to sit down in—but barely. After doing the usual unspeakables, I stood up, went to the sink, carefully soaped and watered my frontal features, then turned around with my eyes shut to reach for a towel. Not a good idea! The bathroom door, which opened inward and was almost the size of the room itself, was ajar. And, alas, not a mason jar. As I pivoted clockwise, my nose smashed into the hinged slab of lumber. The door consulted the laws of physics, concluded that two objects could not occupy the same place at the same time, and decided that my nose would have to move. Move it did…all the way to the far left-hand side of my face, where it shook hands with my earlobe. As I stepped back, the nose bounced wildly across my windscreen, seeking its original position. It missed, and snapped to the right, reaching the far side of my cheek. After a few more rubbery bounces from one cheekbone to the other, it finally settled in the middle…more or less. But it was no longer the carefully sculpted key to social acceptability that my doctor had labored for hours to create. The pieces had reassembled themselves in a jagged crescent arching sideways from my eyebrows to my upper lip. The incident was a sign from the Almighty I didn't believe in. There was no way in Hell he wanted me to be normal.

THE CASE OF THE FAMILY SNATCHING

My best friend from grammar school was literally an egg-head—not only was he a complete intellectual doofus like yours truly, but his head bulged like a Martian's to make room for a couple of extra brains. Suddenly, in ninth grade he went off to a formerly all-white high school and they integrated the place. My pal with the double dome turned to gambling and ran high-stakes poker games on the ping pong table in his basement. Obviously, the ghetto influence at work.

My parents sent me off to another local high school, one that had been integrated for eons. It was a gargantuan place designed by the folks who brought you the wistful architecture of Leavenworth Penitentiary, with 750 freshmen in the incoming class. In homeroom, I sat next to this tall black kid, and he was one of the nicest people I'd ever met. I liked him a lot. The feeling seemed to be mutual. Not something I was accustomed to from my peers. We probably would have become good friends, even though we hadn't a stitch of interests in common. But I felt as if I were stuck in a penitentiary (could it have had anything to do with the architecture?). Then, after seven days of torment, my parents revealed that they'd gotten me into a small, ultra-progressive private school. Since I looked as if someone had hung me upside down on a dungeon wall for the last week without food or water, if I really wanted to, and if I promised to study, they said they'd let me go. Hmmm, studying. That was something I'd studiously avoided…by reading.

But you wouldn't believe how relieved I was. Parole! After only a week!! So I made the promise—yes, I would try to pay attention in class and do my homework. In other words, I would try to end my real education—those two books a day under the school desk.

The private school—the Park School of Buffalo—turned out to be a godsend. For the first time in my life, the teachers actually tried to make me fit in, even if the other kids still thought I should go back to the planet I'd come from. Yet they voted me head of all kinds of committees, I guess on the theory that an extraterrestrial perspective might add something to the student government. And eight years later, one of those committees would play a role in a sexual scandal in a galaxy far, far away...Vermont. But, again, we'll get to that later. The bottom line: I ceased to be a social bag of dirt for the first time in my life. At least partially.

Despite the fact that I was so uncoordinated that I couldn't even roast a marshmallow, much less kick a soccer ball, Park School insisted on awarding me bogus certificates for athletic achievement. Coach Herb Mohls must have had tears in his eyes every time he was forced to sign one of these things. I wonder who was holding the gun to his head.

And besides, I took the promise to study seriously. The idea of having to go back to Penitentiary High was terrifying. So I became...a shoolaholic!

◆

SINCE I HAD A hard time identifying with my father and mother—who had scads of good qualities, but were involved in a poisonous relationship whose acidic contents kept splashing onto me—and since my father and mother didn't share my interests or represent my aspirations (neither of them, for example, showed signs of premature senility)—I groped around for families I could adopt. That is to say, I mercilessly hunted down ersatz parents. I only bagged two pairs.

The first were the Pressman's. The father of the two Pressman kids, Dr. David Pressman, had been a student of Linus Pauling back in the days when Pauling was working on the stuff that won him a Nobel Prize. Then, for Lord knows what reason, Dr. Pressman moved to Buffalo and became head of the biochemistry department at the Roswell Park Memorial Cancer Research Institute, which at the time was the biggest organization of its kind in the world. He probably came to our cesspool on Lake Erie because Roswell Park gave him the money and staff to do pioneering work on immunology, outside-the-box work that would become the basis of much of today's medical science.

Dr. Pressman's son, Jeff, as I mentioned a few minutes ago, was an extraordinarily gifted kid who became my best friend in something like sixth grade. Not that he was happy about it. There was always this phantom notion in the back of his head that if he could only ditch a geek like me and improve his football, he could be normal. But, frankly, Jeff didn't stand a chance. With his aforementioned bulging skull, the odds that by learning to tackle he'd somehow come out looking like Gregory Peck were on the slim side. I was the best he could do in the way of semi-human companionship, so we spent a lot of time together. And, like a leech, I latched on to his parents.

His father never showed any great affection for me, though he did take me along on family outings. And he apparently respected my scientific obsessions, because when I was sixteen he got me into a summer internship program at his cancer research institute without my having to apply. He even bucked the fact that I was technically too young to meet the requirements. What's more, he assigned a short, barrel-shaped young biochemist to be my mentor and to make sure I didn't smash too much lab equipment. And that mentor would change my life.

His name was Phil Fish. He had grown up in Boston. When he was first asked to move to Buffalo, he'd been shocked. Buffalo, in his mind, was a city in the Wild, Wild West. A town in which dime store Indians still sold cigars on the street corners. Nonetheless, Roswell Park had lured Phil into what he'd imagined was the land of prairie grass, tumbleweeds, and bulls with anger management problems. But Phil would teach me a lesson. And he would help me discover a small part of my mission in life. How?

Phil took me to his small and windowless office. In it was a built-in desk that went lengthwise from one wall of the room to the other. On that desk were six stacks of books, each roughly seven books high. And every one of these tomes was in German. Explained Phil, "I'm synthesizing a single molecule. To do it, I have to read all of the books on this desk. The three piles of books on the right are books I've finished. The three piles on the left are books I'm going to have to read before I can synthesize the molecule we're looking for. The whole process will take me five years." Something hit me.

Phil Fish was a scientist whose specialization was so narrow that his work made any big picture synthesis impossible. Phil's dilemma reminded me of something I'd been reading a few months earlier, when my high school headmaster had arranged for me to take a course in philosophy at the University of Buffalo. The entire course had been dedicated to two philosophers—Aristotle and Nietzsche. Nietzsche had transfixed me. Most men, he'd said, huddle in the valley, protected by the walls of the mountains on either side. But they seldom see the sun. In the morning, their village is in the shadow of the mountains in the east. In the afternoon, their town is in the shadow of the mountains in the west. They only see the sun at noon. Sounds like my predicament when I'd been locked by a child gate into a dark corridor at the age of two and a half. But, says Nietzsche, occasionally a rare individual, an *Übermensch*, an over-man, a superman, leaves the protection of the village, climbs to the tallest mountain's peak, stands on the pinnacle, and dances in the sun.

In fact, Phil's labors hinted that there are two kinds of scientists. One is a gopher. He is so specialized that he digs a hole and can only see the dirt ahead of him and on either side. He can't see the landscape. I never wanted to be that kind of scientist. Scientist number two is like an eagle. He soars over the landscape and tries to see how all the specializations fit into a big picture. I loathed the idea of becoming a gopher. I wanted to be the eagle. Or like an Übermensch equipped with wings.

I'd soon discover that most scientists are stuck with the role of gophers. And that there is no role for the eagles. There is not even a formal name for what the eagle does. But the goal of flying over the landscape and discovering how all the puzzle pieces produced by specialists fit into a big picture would become a central thread of my life.

A mission is not something chiseled into you by a supernatural force. It's an aspiration woven into your passions by key emotional experience in your first twenty years of life. A mission is an aspiration that you choose to pursue. Phil Fish had helped me find a part of mine.

◆

PHIL FISH, IRONICALLY, WAS hungry for the big picture. And, of all the absurdities on earth, I tried to give it to him. There were a bunch of older kids in Roswell Park's student program, kids who would soon troop off to august institutions like MIT. One was the kid I'd co-conceived a computer with at the age of twelve. He, Phil Fish, a close friend of my fellow computer conceiver who was also in the Roswell Park program, and I convened in the Institute's cafeteria for lunch every day and brainstormed. Wildly. Multi-disciplinarily. The process was so exhilarating that when work ended at five, we went to one of the kid's big house in a nearby town, Clarence, to sling ideas around like pizza dough until the wee hours.

During the course of these summer brainstorming sessions, I was sumo wrestling with a mystery in the physics of 1959, the CPT problem, the Charge-Parity-Time problem, which goes like this. If matter and anti-matter are created in equal amounts at precisely the same time, why is there so much normal matter in this universe and so little anti-matter? Thirteen point seven billion years ago, at the instant of the Big Bang, did anti-matter consider the raw stuff of our universe beneath contempt and march off with its nose in the air, settling in some gated community where it could keep the low-life particles of normal matter from knocking on car windows and asking for spare change? Tackling this brain boggler for two months straight, I spewed forth an entire cosmological theory complete with an explanation for the beginning, middle, and end of the universe. And this theory implied one minor prediction—that at a certain point, the migrating herds of matter in this cosmos—flocks of matter like galaxies—would gain a distaste for each other's company and, like your mate after a fight or vast herds of bison spotting Buffalo Bill loading his Remington .44 revolver, would begin an ever-accelerating sprint for the exit. Today that accelerating sprint is called dark energy. And it's one of the biggest puzzles in theoretical physics. But the Bloom Toroidal Model of the Universe, alias The Big Bagel, the result of these summer-of-1959 thrashings, explains it. And predicted it thirty-nine years before its discovery.

However, I was sure that Big Bagel theory was comic-book science and would never hold up in a court of mathematics. So at the end of the summer, I put it away and didn't talk about it for thirty years. But fifty-one years later, in roughly 2010, Big Bagel theory would be declared "rigorous" and thoroughly mathematical by one overly-generous cosmologist, the University of Pittsburgh's Martin Bojowald. A man whose charity outshines that of Mother Theresa. More to the point, my dogfights with the puzzles of physics managed to keep our tiny Roswell Park verbiage-production group spellbound—or at least awake. Entertaining intellectuals in those days was easy. Remember, we didn't have Netflix.

It also allowed Phil Fish to immerse himself in something that his single-minded pursuit of a single molecule denied him—the big picture. The connect-the-dots that soars over the scientific landscape like an eagle. It got Phil out of his gopher hole.

And the urge to be an eagle would soon play a role in shaping The Sixties.

◆

AFTER THE ROSWELL PARK adventure, I lost touch with Jeff Pressman and his dad. Jeff eventually moved on to Princeton, wrote a brilliant book in his first year of grad school proving that for every $100 being spent on federal programs for the poor, only a dollar made it to anyone impecunious, then killed himself. Probably because he was a liberal who'd been forced to a conservative conclusion. Not to be topped, his father, who seemed to have everything to live for (among other things, his wife was ebullient and gorgeous) killed himself, too. So adopted family number one disappeared. And I must admit that I was anything but happy about it. But Jeff's dad had left me with a gift—a destiny.

When I moved to Park School in ninth grade, I met a tall, bespectacled lad named Jon Hyman. He was even more on my wavelength than Jeff Pressman had been. For one thing, he was capable of tripping over a chalk mark on the sidewalk. For another, we were both into geopolitics. And we were fascinated by science. When the *Scientific American* recommended taking apart a pocket watch and putting it back together as an exercise in philosophical thinking, we made a mess on the Hyman's dinner table as we tried to get the microscopic parts of $4.98 timepieces to balance while we managed to delicately lower the top plates into which each wobbling pinion had to fit. Both of us failed in this act of finger-flagellation.

To top it all off, in class we made nuisances of ourselves by frenziedly passing notes. But these were not the comments on the latest classroom mammary developments that ordinary males shuttle back and forth. Ours were more phallic—specifically, they were designs for rocket reentry vehicles that could avoid being burned up while penetrating the delicate folds of the upper atmosphere.

About the only thing I think we failed to share was my obsession with poetry. As you'll see in a minute, I devoured anthologies of modern verse from cover to cover and gave public readings of T. S. Eliot and Edna St. Vincent Millay at a seedy jazz bar downtown…usually after the audience had wisely left for the night. And the poems I recited would change my life.

But Jon more than made up for his poetic failings with a mathematical gift that was breathtaking. Plus, his parents seemed to represent my every goal in life. His father had all the warmth of a rock carving on Mount Rushmore. But he was a Harvard grad who headed the law school at the University of Buffalo. And his wife was a Radcliffe alumna with far more than the usual ice-cream-scoop of cerebral neurons. What's more, she was extremely attractive, warm, always smiling, and—though she didn't believe in this kind of stuff—could probably heal by the mere laying on of hands.

Jon's sisters were two of the most gorgeous and vivacious creatures you've ever seen. And, to top it all off, the whole family lived on the backside of my block. So, like a barnacle gluing itself to a ship, I made the Hymans my second substitute family.

My immersion in the Hyman homestead left its footprints all over me. It shaped my political attitudes, sculpted my tastes in music (for example, I learned that holding an LP by the edges was an indispensable symbol of intellectual status), and reshaped pieces of me like putty. Except, of course, for my nose, which even with the aid of plastic surgery had proven beyond redemption.

So far, all of this sounds bucolic, doesn't it? Nothing here to disturb the sheep munching grass in the Western New York countryside thirty miles from my house. But it was, in reality, the raw material for a rather explosive cocktail. To find out why, I'm afraid you will have to read on.

SEIZED BY POETRY

Wе're about to hit pay dirt—sex. But first comes something that sex hides within like a termite in the Trojan Horse—meaning.

Yes, believe it or not, this is a book about a quest for meaning. And the manhunt for what's worth living and thrilling for in this volume would have lacked its compass and its astrolabe without, well, without Galileo Galilei, Anton van Leeuwenhoek, William James, and Albert Einstein. But three other mind-noodlers were crucial to this squirrely Odyssey in pursuit of purpose. All of them were poets.

◆

YOU RECALL THAT I was fifteen years old and attached like a tattoo to the Hyman household. But another bunch had me in their telescopic sights: the muses. Yes, all nine of these epitomes of gorgeousness who tweaked and twiddled brains from their remote control HQ on Mount Olympus had apparently decided to grab me by the hair. Lord knows, no one else wanted me. And my hair was so shortened by the demon barbers of the 1950s that it wouldn't have made a convenient handle for anyone else. Like, for example, a real girl. So at fifteen, for reasons utterly unknown, I was seized by poetry. First came the rhyming couplets of A. E. Housman, the man whose sprightly syllables may well have inspired Dr. Seuss.

You've probably run across this bit of Housman's work. And when you did, I hope that your insurance company covered the damages:

When I was one-and-twenty
I heard a wise man say,

"Give crowns and pounds and guineas
But not your heart away;
Give pearls away and rubies
But keep your fancy free."
But I was one-and-twenty,
No use to talk to me.

When I was one-and-twenty
I heard him say again,
"The heart out of the bosom
Was never given in vain;
'Tis paid with sighs a plenty
And sold for endless rue."
And I am two-and-twenty,
And oh, 'tis true, 'tis true.

Remember that one?

My Housman obsession lasted a year. I wrote an infinitely long piece of poetry of my own in a style influenced by Housman. OK, it was only five pages. But it took twelve months to perfect, and my dad, who had never noticed any of my previous deeds, assuming there were any, loved the poem. I suspect he was the only one to read it.

Then I tripped across a poem almost as long by a woman named Edna St. Vincent Millay. How? It was probably in a big, fat, brown paperback anthology laying in ambush for me in the tan shag rug of my bedroom, disguised as a carnivorous pack of loops of wool. But that anthology became one of my most treasured companions. And it had the guts to do more than merely throw me off balance and threaten to disarrange my nose for the second time.

This book had the gumption to restrict itself to modern poetry. You know the sort, Ezra Pound, E. E. Cummings, and other charlatans who refused to put capital letters at the start of their sentences and who exiled commas and periods, forcing them to pair off and become semi-colons in international nuclear agreements or to go to the punctuation purgatory where unwanted apostrophes and occasional flyspecks are tortured by sadistic characters of the Chinese alphabet.

Buried somewhere in mid anthology was a four-page poem by a woman named Edna St. Vincent Millay. She had been sainted by her parents, who were so insensitive to the grief that kids with strange names undergo at the hands of other kids that they named her after a hospital, a hospital that had just saved her uncle's life—New York's St. Vincent's. Millay had written an epic bit of verse when she was an older woman—sixteen years old, a year or two older than me—and living in Maine. Or as Wikipedia puts it, "living in poverty." Yes, that would be Poverty, Maine. What's worse, the four-page epic of verse misspelled its own name—"Renascence."

Renascence purported to be the musings of a young woman in a clearing on a mountain top. She lies face-up in the dirt, grass, and weeds, then looks straight up into the sky. But all she sees as she stares into the heavens is how narrow the space is between the trees on either side, and how claustrophobically small the slice of blue between the sharp-elbowed branches is. She feels cramped, hemmed in. Then she has a strange experience. In her imagination, she leaves her body and travels the world, whiffling through the air without benefit of a single bolt, panel, or Yorkshire-terrier-sized coach seat from Boeing, seeing into the hearts and souls of a man who's starving in Capri and a hundred passengers going down in a ship at sea. What grabs her attention the most? The sufferings and missteps.

All sin was of my sinning, all
Atoning mine, and mine the gall
Of all regret. Mine was the weight
Of every brooded wrong, the hate
That stood behind each envious thrust,
Mine every greed, mine every lust.

But that was not exactly how Edna's words struck me. To me it seemed as if the imagination of her girl in a mountain clearing soars over the world and sees into the radically different emotions and impenetrably alien senses of reality of folks from cultures all over the planet, people who would regard your way of seeing things and mine as exotic and unreal. One way or the other, when the heroine of Renascence returns to her own body, her visual gifts have changed. Her perceptions have expanded. She is still staring at the same small patch of sky. She is still hemmed in by the same aggressive branches and imperialistic trees. But in what she views, she now sees an infinity.

In her words:

The world stands out on either side
No wider than the heart is wide;
Above the world is stretched the sky,
No higher than the soul is high.
The heart can push the sea and land
Farther away on either hand;
The soul can split the sky in two,
And let the face of God shine through.
But East and West will pinch the heart
That can not keep them pushed apart;
And he whose soul is flat—the sky
Will cave in on him by and by.

That poem hit like a bus slamming into an oil truck. And it felt familiar. Remember the second rule of science? Look at things right under your nose as if you've never seen them before, then proceed from there? That's a command to see the infinite in the tiniest of things. Edna St. Vincent Millay said that to accomplish that infinite vision, you have to radically expand your empathic powers. You have to be able to feel the emotions of people who are insanely different than you are. In fact, you have to immerse yourself in emotional extremes. Reason and logic are not enough. You need to trek into the passions. You have to scuba-dive deep into the abyss of feelings. You must adventure.

Sometimes instructions like these cut to the quick. They restructure your ideals. They rearrange the ground plan of your soul. They insert themselves like malware in your brain. But unlike malware, you welcome the bits of programming inserted by certain key experiences, and they guide you for the rest of your life. That's what Edna St. Vincent Millay's "Renascence" did for me. And what Millay would soon do for the quests at the heart of The Sixties.

There was yet another piece of poetry rattling around in the dark cave of my skull, a bit of verse that must have been horny as hell. How did I know? It appeared anxious to have sex with Edna St. Vincent Millay's "Renascence." Maybe because Edna was only sixteen. It went like this:

> *To see a World in a grain of sand,*
> *And a Heaven in a wild flower,*
> *Hold Infinity in the palm of your hand,*
> *And Eternity in an hour...*

That was William Blake, a lunatic in the eighteenth century who swore he saw "God put his head to the window." Like a baseball smashing through? Or did God just peek, look for naked ladies, and move on? But Blake harvested his lunacies—his visions—to make poetry and pictures. How very William James.

Those two poems grabbed me, from the roots of my nearly scalp-level haircut to the stones in my gizzard. (Do we humans have stones in our gizzards, or is that just chickens? Chickens in our gizzards?) OK, even the dumb clucks in my gizzard were standing on end to these two poems. Which end they stood on, the head or the feet, it was hard to know.

Meanwhile another piece of poetry was trying to worm its way into the dark cave of my skull where it would be safe from the chickens. And, boy, did it have a hard time. My English teacher was determined to hammer T. S. Eliot into us. Eliot's poems—in particular "The Wasteland" and the "The Love Song of J. Alfred Prufrock"—appeared to me to be deliberate frauds. Eliot's technique, I was convinced, was to construct impossible-to-understand poems, poems that were incomprehensible for a good reason: they had nothing to say. But Eliot draped that nothing in so many words of Greek and Latin, and so many references to the canon of English Literature that they conned you. If you confessed that you didn't understand Eliot, you revealed yourself as stupid and folks edged away from you at cocktail parties. Whatever cocktail parties were—celebratory aggregations of alcoholic roosters? But if you said that T. S. Eliot was brilliant, everyone thought you were smart.

Eliot, I was convinced, was using the emperor's new clothes strategy to make himself appear to be a genius. He was, I was certain, the most sophisticated tailor of invisible costumes on seven continents. Or the most fraudulent bard. But to level my accusations of charlatanism and to do it believably, I had to read Eliot's poems. Over and over and over again. And that wasn't easy.

The bigger the investment of time you make in something, the more it holds you and won't let go. And the more you hold on to it.

One day I dipped into a twenty-five-year-old book called Axel's Castle by Edmund Wilson, a critic whose insights had influenced folks like F. Scott Fitzgerald. And in two meager paragraphs, Wilson made Eliot's meaning clear. Clear as one of those glass walls you occasionally try to walk through, convinced that they aren't there. Or that I occasionally try to walk through.

Thanks to Wilson, one of Eliot's poems, "The Love Song of J. Alfred Prufrock," turned into what Edna St. Vincent Millay's "Renascence" had recently become—a personal anthem, a wake-up call, a motto posted on the inside of my forehead so my cerebral cortex could see it every morning when it woke up. What was Prufrock's message? Why was it so galvanizing? And why would it be essential to the soul of an era that had not yet arrived…The Sixties?

You have a limited amount of life energy, said T. S. Eliot in "The Love Song of J. Alfred Prufrock." You also have a limited amount of time. And you have an inner sense of the heroic, of the things that you will someday do to become the you that you have always imagined yourself to be. You have an inner sense of the things that would make people of the opposite sex, in particular, look up to you. And possibly even lust for you. But you put those heroic deeds off. You procrastinate. You tell yourself that there will be time in the future to accomplish them. Instead, you do the things that are easiest for you. You do small, ordinary things. Then you wake up one day and realize that it's too late. You no longer have the strength or the time to go after your real goals in life. The result? You lead a pathetic, inconsequential existence.

The bottom line? If you have something important to do, something heroic, something you feel will define you, begin it now. Today. Here's a bit of how Eliot put it. If you don't adventure, you wake up one day and realize that:

> *No! I am not Prince Hamlet, nor was meant to be;*
> *Am an attendant lord, one that will do*
> *To swell a progress, start a scene or two,*
> *Advise the prince; no doubt, an easy tool,*
> *Deferential, glad to be of use,*
> *Politic, cautious, and meticulous;*
> *Full of high sentence, but a bit obtuse;*
> *At times, indeed, almost ridiculous—*
> *Almost, at times, the Fool.*
> *I grow old...I grow old...*
> *I shall wear the bottoms of my trousers rolled.*
> *Shall I part my hair behind? Do I dare to eat a peach?*
> *I shall wear white flannel trousers, and walk upon the beach.*
> *I have heard the mermaids singing, each to each.*
> *I do not think that they will sing to me.*
> *...We have lingered in the chambers of the sea*
> *By sea-girls wreathed with seaweed red and brown*
> *Till human voices wake us, and we drown.*

From these three poems emerged a mission. To expand your ability to see the infinite in the smallest things, you must mount safaris into every outlandish extreme of human emotion, every strange twist of alien culture. You must undertake scientific expeditions into the most overlooked but important corners of the human experience. You must adventure! And you must start these adventures in the fringe and beyond it today. Now.

As you're about to see, these three poems were more than just words to me. I would act on them. Over and over again. And the results would be as maniacal as the visions of William Blake. What's more, those three poems would be essential to the spirit of The Sixties.

◆

THEN CAME YET ANOTHER piece of literature, Jack Kerouac's *On the Road*, which had been published when I was fourteen. I was late to read it. By the time I got around to it, it was two years old...and I was sixteen. But it advocated the very heroic deed that I needed—grabbing whatever internal-combustion-engine vehicle you could get your hands on and vrooming from New York State to California. So I told my parents I was going to drop out of high school. In my junior year. What was my grand goal? I would get on a motorcycle and cross the continent, exposing myself to random escapades. T. S. Eliot and Edna St. Vincent Millay, I was certain, would have been proud.

There were only, well, umm, two or three problems.

- I didn't own a motorcycle and the funds from my bar mitzvah, $315, wouldn't allow me to buy one.

- I had no idea of how to ride a motorcycle. And I was the only person my age in the entire city of Buffalo, New York, without a driver's license.

- Oh, and one more thing. Without a lot of coaching from gas station attendants, I had no idea of which direction was west.

My parents, in desperation, asked for the aid of my English teacher, the man responsible for pouring T. S. Eliot into my head. This august, New England–born-and-raised pedagogue approved of my plan of dropping out of eleventh grade, but he had a better idea than the motorcycle. An idea that didn't require a driver's license. He would arrange a stint for me in a lumberjack camp in Oregon.

The thought of all that armpit sweat made me treesick. So I called off my plans for cross country adventure. Temporarily. As you will see.

However, "Renascence" and "The Love Song of J. Alfred Prufrock," became so urgent to me that I would go to Buffalo's only jazz hangout late at night, and wait until the musicians came in after their gigs at weddings or nightclubs and jammed for their own benefit until they were exhausted. Then I would go onstage reciting these poems to the three people still left in the audience. In fact, I would recite them to anyone who would listen.

Why was I reading these poems at the top of my lungs to anyone willing to endure them? It would take me thirty years to figure that out. But here's the conclusion: I wanted to galvanize others. To wake them up. To prod them into action. That was the easy part. But here's the flipside that it took me forever to understand: the person I needed to wake up the most was...me.

I would follow these poems' dictates for the rest of my life. And thanks to those three pieces of verse, a very strange life it would be.

◆

ONE MORE TINY INCIDENT would carry me, barreling like a *Mad Max* dune buggy, toward the infinite in the tiniest of things, not to mention toward the Olympian plateaus and dirt roads in the sky, the contrails of the gods inside.

Park School had a brilliant set up, a structure that made room for more than just the gorgeous kids whose looks and Pontiac convertibles made the knees of the school's maidens buckle and their wells of anticipation grow moist and ravenous. It worked like this. The most popular male in a class would be voted class president. The second most popular would be voted vice president. The most popular Jew would be voted class treasurer. And the most popular girl would be voted class secretary. Then all four of them would do nothing for the rest of the semester. At least nothing pertaining to their duties. What they did on dates was still beyond me.

But during the first week of classes, we were told that in October the school would have a fair to raise money. OK, sounds good. Well, think again. We'd be divided into teams of eight. Each team would have to conceive a booth for the fair. A booth whose amusements folks would pay genuine, real, green, full-faith-and-credit-of-the-the-United-States-backed money to experience. So our first week of school, eight of us were locked in a room to conceive some dynamite form of sure-fire entertainment. Yes, seven normal, healthy, reasonably good looking kids.

And me. Now a strange thing happens when you get a group of popular, rambunctious, well-adjusted, normal kids into a room to accomplish a goal: they are immobilized. Yes, they are stumped, stomped, stymied, and speechless. Not to mention just a tad humiliated. Why? When it comes to accomplishing something more than buying a case of beer and an illegal bottle of scotch or two, they don't have a clue.

OK, I'll admit, when you put them into a room together, each kid gives a little speech to mark out his territory. Or hers. And that done, these healthy, hearty specimens of Americana lapse into a befuddled silence. So if you happen to be a blabbermouth and your motor lips can machine gun the faintest semblance of an idea of what to do next, suddenly you are it. The others realize that if they vote you the chairman of their committee, they can all go back to heavy petting and you will take care of the rest. Which means that I may have been the most unpopular kid on the entire thirty-four-acre campus of the Park School of Buffalo, but I when it came to getting something concrete done, I was suddenly elected to high office. Not one of the popularity offices, mind you. Those were strictly off limits. But one of the practical offices.

Now Park School began every day at 8:00 a.m. with a gathering of the entire student body. Yes, all the freshmen, sophomores, juniors, seniors, and the entire staff. Three of these assemblies were programmed by the faculty. And two were put together by students. A very particular group of students. The students on the Program Committee. Which means that the Program Committee was not a glamor job, a job where you showed off the fashionable, Brylcreemed wave at the front of your crew cut, strutted your well-cut chinos, flashed your pearly teeth, then did nothing. It was one of those ghastly jobs where you actually had to get something accomplished. So in my junior year, an unusually young age for the task, I was elected chairman of the Program Committee.

And the Chairman of the Program Committee had one more responsibility other than just programming. He was also the MC of all five morning assemblies. Which meant that for the first two months on the job I was knotted in fear, staggered by stage fright, paralyzed by the idea of going before 350 students who hated me, opening my mouth, and actually shoving terrified syllables past my teeth with my tongue. Then I got used to it. In fact, going in front of an audience and shoveling syllables became like breathing.

Emceeing must have terrified everyone else at Park School, too. How do I know? In my senior year, my fellow students voted me head of the Program Committee for a second year in a row. Surely it was not because they liked me. In fact, there was a brand new clue to their distaste for my existence. I starred in many of the school's plays. The ones that didn't require singing—a skill that I handled with the fine-tuning of a fingernail screeching across a chalk board. One night when we'd finished performing Sophocles' *Antigone*, we had a cast party. It was at a bar on Main Street. I was clueless about bar behavior. I still am. Minutes into the celebration of a play in which I'd just performed the male lead—Creon, the ruler of Thebes—it became obvious that the rest of the cast would be far more comfortable if I wasn't there. By unspoken popular demand, I edged my way out of the bar and went home. I was not welcome at the cast party of a play in which I'd been the star.

Nonetheless, a week or two later, the juniors came to me with a request. They were going to have a dance. Could I please find some way of advertising it to the assembled multitudes in the morning assembly. Little did they see the irony. Kids all over Buffalo made it abundantly clear that if there was something resembling a terpsichorean gathering anywhere in the city, I was kindly invited to park my feet as far away as possible— say, Cleveland. What's more, I had learned from a year in dance class—a humiliation we'll get to in a minute—that I was so clumsy at the basic ballroom steps of the late nineteen-fifties—the box step, the fox trot, and the waltz—that if you put 300 girls on any dance floor anywhere in the world, I could step on all 3,000 dainty, nail-polished, female toes with just a few swift, tripping movements of my dress shoes. Do I have the math on the number of podiatric digits right?

And the juniors wanted me to advertise their dance? I mean, really! But I said yes.

So I picked a piece of music, put it on a record player at the back of the stage, then went center stage with absolutely nothing planned. And let loose. Moved. Wriggled. Jiggled. Writhed. Whumped. Bumped. Jumped. Stumped. Whipped my shoulders up and down, Let my arms fly. Wriggled and squoonched my facial muscles. Interpreted the music in a way that apparently no one had ever seen before. I looked like a Loony Toon drawn under the influence of something that would not appear on the scene for another two years—LSD. Yes, I looked like a cartoon drawn by Chuck Jones (of Wiley Coyote, Pepe Le Pew, Daffy Duck, and Tom and Jerry fame) himself. On a night when his brain was chemically whipped, beaten, mashed, boiled, and fried.

This maniacal spasm of movement had consequences. It did something strange to the audience. Three hundred fifty people who hated me—700 spite-filled eyeballs worth—had a look I'd never seen before. The ocular orbs of the girl who hated me the most were zeroed in with disbelief. Six hundred and ninety-eight other irises were glued with an intensity I'd never seen. Talk about eye contact! Pupils dilated—they grew wide. Yes, 700 of them. Faces went limp. Three hundred and fifty physiognomies flaccidified. Everything that those spell-bound students had, were, and felt was concentrated in their gaze. And that gaze was lasered onto the least likely object in the room—me.

The power of those 700 emotionally-focused fovea sent a strange force coursing through me. It was as if the energy of the individuals in the auditorium had merged into one big collective thundercloud, as if that cloud had aimed its bolts straight through the core of me, as if those ribbons of lightning had slammed up my backbone from my tail to my throat on their way to a transformer just above my head, a transformer in which the voltage was converted into something bigger, stranger, and more powerful, then was channeled back down through me as if I were a coaxial copper cable, zapped out to those 350 transfixed faces, then sizzled from them back to me again for further amplification.

Meanwhile, I had an out of body experience. No kidding. I was on the ceiling watching this whole thing from above. And what I saw was a reverberatory circuit. A circular flow amping up a high-watt current. And transmogrifying it. Utterly. A feedback loop of human spirit. A feedback loop of naked soul. When the music was over and my fit of dancing ceased, the crowd did something it had never done before in my three years at the Park School and that it never did again. Not for football players, homecoming queens, or exchange students just back from Italy. All 350 Park Schoolers surged down to the foot of the stage, picked me up off the proscenium, put me on their shoulders, carried me out of the auditorium door, and transported me up the sidewalk to the building where our classes were held.

Ecstasy is a funny word. It means standing outside of yourself. And the dance-trance was ecstatic. It was one of those *Varieties of the Religious Experience* that William James had attempted to capture. An experience of the sort that he couldn't explain. In fact, accidentally fire-balling on the stage at Park School would prove to be a massive clue to the gods inside.

I had heard the mermaids singing each to each for five brief moments. And they had sung to me.

◆

How WILL OUR HERO find satori, discover the meaning of life, and get the girl? How will he do it by following the instructions of the three murderers, the dictates of the three poets, a clue or two from William James, and by adding in a lesson learned from clams and seagulls? In other words, how will he do it by accidentally helping to start The Sixties? For the answer, dear reader, please plow on.

SEX TRIES TO ENTER THE PICTURE
BUT CAN'T SEEM TO DRILL THROUGH
THE FRAME

Well, you've read this far, and I know it wasn't easy for you. Frankly, the only reward I can think of is the saga of how I shocked my teachers, horrified my parents, sought spiritual enlightenment, found sex instead, and helped start two revolutions, the Sexual Revolution and the Drug Revolution. Two of the movements that would define The Sixties.

We will begin with a prologue—the pathetic narrative of my early love life.

You're aware of the fact that at about the age of ten I withdrew totally from my parents' perpetual combat and built a world of my own in my bedroom. The place was so self-contained that you probably could have removed it from the rest of the house and launched it into orbit, and I wouldn't have known the difference.

I slathered the walls with arcane posters showing the lift-off velocities of every rocket ever built by German rocket scientists pretending to be Americans from Alabama, and I wouldn't allow a soul in except the reptile-repelled maid.

OK, I admit that there was one other guest permitted in this sealed-off sanctum: the girl next door. She was willing to accept the fact that I did strange things like anneal wire to make electrical coils (that never worked), soldered together my own transistor radio (that never worked), made cold cream from scratch by following the list of ingredients in a book of industrial formulae (my mother refused to use it), and built the computer I mentioned many pages ago, the one that carried out symbolic logic operations (this one *did* work, but all the other computers laughed because mine, as you recall, used a form of math called Boolean Algebra, and no electronic processing device in its right mind could take a name like "Boolean" seriously). The girl next door was also willing to tolerate my blither about cosmology, topology, quantum physics, microbiology, and other such unearthly nonsense. Needless to say, none of these achievements are considered admirable in eighth grade—at least not by your baseball-obsessed peers and the girls who swoon over them.

However, the girl next door was unavailable for anything but wrestling matches and chess games because she was an older woman (by six months) and besides, she was two grades ahead of me in school (she'd been leapfrogged over her age group a couple of times) and had her eye out for much more mature men—like fifteen year olds. This was agonizing because when I hit sixteen, I fell in love with her. So much in love that when she took a month-long summer trip to the musical festivals of Europe, I made her give me the list of every hotel she'd be staying at, then wrote her a six-page, typewritten letter every day. No dice. She was still hooked on mature, sophisticated men—seventeen year olds.

Then there were our games of chess. Chess was the pastime of the truly brainy. Since braininess was my only claim to fame, I insisted on learning how to play. That proved a huge mistake. Even after months of practice with the girl I loved but could not have, a lady bug could have beaten me with her wings tied behind her back. In fact, when I finally met three really bright kids, all three could lick me in five moves. They could even whip my butt while I played with the chess board and pieces on my bedroom floor in clear sight, and my opponents laid on the bed looking up at the ceiling, playing the game in their heads. So I clearly was about as bright as a door knob. How in the world would I be an Einstein?

The answer: genius is not just a matter of the talent you're given. It's a matter of the persistence with which you apply what you've got. And of your willingness to see in ways that others don't dare conceive. But that answer would take eons to make itself apparent.

Meanwhile back at school, where the process of playing kickball with me as the ball had frequently made me the center of attention among my male comrades, I was incredibly popular with the girls. To show you just *how* popular, let's take a brief flashback into another parental attempt to make me normal: dance class. Yes, if I could only dance, my parents reasoned when I was thirteen, I would be human. And I'd learn the social graces: Grace Kelly and Grace Burns. So in eighth grade they packed me off to dance class at the ritziest temple in town. Yes, every Friday night for a year I'd stand alone on the boys' side of the room, rejected by every girl in viewing distance, while my peers found partners and danced. Every once in a while the instructresses would take pity on my miserable state and dance with me. The number of mashed toes that emerged from this process must have been staggering.

Then came the end of the year, a chance to celebrate all the box steps, fox trots, and waltzes we had learned. So the dance instructors planned an elaborate formal ball at the snootiest Jewish club in town. There was only one small problem. Arithmetic.

When we arrived in formal attire, there were one hundred and eighty-one of us pubescents eager to ape the ways of adults. One hundred and eighty-one, you'll notice, is not an even number. In fact, like me, it's odd. Very odd. Which led to a problem. There were ninety girls in the room. But there were ninety-one boys. Some luckless boy was doomed to be the odd one out.

To pair off couples for the preparatory dinner, the name of each of the boys was written on a scrap of paper, crumpled like a spit ball, and thrown into a bag. The girls drew spit balls of paper at random. Ahhh, egalitarian democracy. Ahhh, the spirit of fairness. How they shine! What the pedagogues of dance failed to account for was the force of the market. Supply and demand. Disgust and desire. And the intensity of female competition. The thirteen-year-old girls tossed the principle that all pubescent boys are equal in the eyes of their creator into the coat closet, and began a half hour of horse trading, haggling, and swapping the random swatches of paper like crazy. When all the bargaining, cajoling and begging was over, one male name was tossed back into the bag. Guess whose it was? I'll give you a clue. It was me! Yes, a democratic, free market process had proven unequivocally that I was the least wanted male in the room. And just possibly the least-wanted male in the city.

As you can imagine, this led to a rather full social calendar. I was denied invitations for every party, sporting event and informal gathering ever conceived in the Buffalo of the 1950s. And my dating schedule—well, I could write an entire comma about that.

In high school, things didn't get much better. There was an occasional girl—undoubtedly some social misfit with a slight indentation in that part of the brain responsible for maintaining sanity—who got a crush on me. But I didn't pay attention to any of them because I was madly infatuated with Marge Walls, who was two inches taller than I was and thought of me as one of her best friends and a person she put on an intellectual a pedestal… then left there to go out with college basketball players.

About the only relief in this dreary landscape of sexual abstinence was the field trip my class took to the Cambridge School in Massachusetts. My best friend, Jon Hyman, and I conceived a skit mocking the Kennedy-Nixon debates. I forget which of us played which part. But when the skit was over, I found myself mobbed by Cambridge School groupies, all of them extremely fetching maidens, each one hoping to spend the rest of the evening with me doing whatever teenage boys and girls of that age did with each other. Actually, I had no idea of what that might be. The only sex book that Jon and I could get access to was an anthropology text we smuggled from his father's library, and its most explicit phrase, repeated quite frequently, was "quick encounter in the forest." What one did during that brief and leafy interlude, God alone knew.

So I didn't pick one of the girls in the flock and settle my attentions on her. I conversed with the entire crowd. The result? Eventually that crowd melted away. Leaving no girls whatsoever. Surely there was a lesson here. Like you have to know when to stop multi-tasking and focus? But whatever it was, it eluded me.

Alas, I couldn't have taken the gaggle of feminine admirers back from Cambridge to Buffalo, even if they had chosen to stick around. And there was no chance of transferring to Massachusetts. So that single evening was pretty much the beginning and end of my life as a high school sex symbol. Four years of school, four hours of glory.

The result, as you can imagine, is that I was totally unprepared for college. I went off to Reed, in Portland, Oregon, which at the time had the highest proportion of Rhodes scholars in the country and the highest median SAT's, higher than Harvard, Yale, and MIT. Reed was the school that would in the distant future produce one of the most famous dropouts on the planet, Steve Jobs. Hot stuff, huh? For some reason, the institution's proportion of virgins was not noted in its catalogue.

When it came time for dormitory accommodations, I was thrown into a two-room suite with three other guys...all men of the world. One was a junior who wore an ascot, smoked a pipe, was going steady with a girl, yes, a real, actual girl, and gave broad hints that he and she were "doing it" on a fairly regular basis. Another was a sophomore who'd transferred from Caltech. He was no Robert Redford, but he exuded *savoir faire* and sexual experience. What's more, he could play the guitar like nobody's business and work wonders with every folk song ever catalogued by a Lomax Brother. As girl-bait in those bohemian days, this was better than owning a dozen Porsches. My third roommate was a freshman like myself, but he was from New York, so he was no fool and had done things most eighteen year olds from backward burgs like Buffalo can't even figure out how to dream about.

This bunch and the guys across the hall showed off their macho credentials by hanging around the dorm on Saturday afternoons sipping fine wines out of pseudo-crystal glasses, spitting out sports statistics, and topping each other with tales of sexual conquests. I hated sports and had no sexual conquests. What's more, I found women far more attractive than hairy specimens of my own sex. Even if these men were marinated in a fine wine.

So while my comrades paraded the stories of their triumphs, I went off each weekend to the girls' dorm and horsed around with blonds from North Dakota who had grown up on turkey farms but who had the brains of future Nobel Prize winners and the bodies of Playboy Bunnies.

This practice brewed a strange resentment amongst my roommates. Like there was the Saturday afternoon they spent telling tales of all the gorgeous *femmes* who had found them irresistible and who had wrestled them into bed. Somehow none of them seemed to notice that they spent so many of their weekends telling these ever-escalating anecdotes that none of them had had a date in months. Not even the guy who was going steady.

When the afternoon was over, I walked into my dorm room, having missed out on the male bonding. What's worse, my neck was covered with diminutive red elevations. It seems the girls at the female dorm had decided to spend the day practicing the production of hickeys. And I was the practice hickey-ee.

There was a strange look on the faces of my dorm-mates as they put two and two together and came up with five. It was the scowl of an incipient lynch mob.

Gradually, the Caltech lad who could sing 4,000 folk songs fell in love at a distance with an incredibly alluring female, the kind legends are written about, Trojan Wars are launched for, and in whose praises the balladeers pour forth verse after verse. She was so utterly above the sphere of ordinary mortals that the aspiring Casanova hadn't mustered up the nerve to introduce himself to her yet. But he had a plan. A plan he perfected in top secret meetings with two of his three roommates. Note that this secret cabal of strategists did not include me. In fact, they shut their mouths about their plot whenever I entered the room. Months later, I would find out what they were scheming about the hard way. As you will soon see.

Here's what the trio was planning. The annual Christmas Ball was looming in the distance, the biggest event on the Reed College calendar. The only celebration in which Reed College students tossed aside their jeans and work shirts, dressed in tuxedos, and played the F. Scott Fitzgerald routine to the hilt. My guitar-twiddling, folk-singing roommate had bought a pair of tickets to the ball and was busy planning the perfect moment to invite the face and body that had launched a thousand of his fantasies, the most-desired woman on the Reed College campus, Mademoiselle X.

About the same day my roommate and his two dorm henchmen were purchasing tickets to the Big Dance and hatching plans for the romance of the century, I—who had not even learned how to hold hands with a girl, much less put my arm casually around her shoulder and attempt to kiss— marched off to the cafeteria for lunch. Now, the Reed College cafeteria had a strange social pattern. Males would sit with males. Females would sit with females. Much as students of opposite sexes might have yearned, burned, and prayed for each other's attentions, they were terrified of sitting next to a person of another gender over a meal. But, as I said, I preferred women to men. And I didn't have a clue about how to be normal. So I defied the rules and seated myself wherever the most interesting-looking young ladies were planted. That was where I felt the most at home.

On this particular day, there was a lone co-ed at a table all by herself. She obviously liked hanging around with other women about as much as I

liked being stuck with other men. So I took my tray filled with *drek du jour*
and plopped myself next to her.

The year was 1961. This wonder of the lunch table had dark hair and
even darker eyes. We began to talk, and she turned out to be amazing. She
had hitchhiked—something I'd wanted to do ever since I'd read Kerouac,
but had never dared attempt. What's more, she claimed she could easily
clamber to the top of any tree in sight, and could climb brick buildings from
the outside. In fact, on nights when she missed curfew and the entrance
to her dorm was locked, she explained how easy it was to scramble up the
facade of the building and enter through the window of her third-floor
room. The lady wasn't fibbing. Later, I would see her accomplish this feat
on numerous occasions. And, oh, what a difference her ability to out-climb
a kitten would make for me!

She also had her elegant side. She designed her own formal gowns,
sewed them together from scratch, and made all the other girls on campus
drop dead with envy (the major cleanup problem after one of the school's
rare dances was picking up the green-tinged female corpses). She had
developed a crush on her high school headmaster at the age of fifteen, and
after six months of diligent effort had seduced the man, thus beginning an
affair that had lasted four years, and actually still seemed to be bubbling
under the surface despite the distance between them (he was stuck in Long
Beach, California, where she'd grown up, and was still foolishly living with
his wife and a son older than our heroine). What's more, she had a brain
that would have made the folks at Mensa salivate with envy. This astonishing
and stunning-looking woman knew French literature I'd never heard of, like
all the plays of Jean Anouilh. She could tell you their plots in a way that
made your jaw drop. She was intimate with more poetry than anyone I'd
ever met. And everything she talked about came alive with a sparkle.

She was bewitching. She gave the impression that other listeners, sitting
at her feet in an effort to catch her every glistening word, had accidentally
been turned into toads.

What started as a casual conversation turned into one of those sessions
where your pupils seem glued together with those of the person you're
talking to and every one of your nerves comes to the surface, wriggling in
some sort of orgiastic dance as you reveal things you've never dared confess,

discover excitements you share in common, and are caught in a mutual trance. I told her I wrote poetry in voluminous quantities (my high school English teacher had hated my poetry—once I got out of my Housman phase and into Samuel Beckett, it had become too modern for him; my high school math teacher, on the other hand, seemed to like it…but he was from Egypt, so what did he know). She wanted to see my literary output. When we finished lunch, we went over to my dorm and I picked up a handful of the stuff. Then we planted ourselves on a huge lawn under a tree and the wild conversation continued. She loved the poetry. I was hypnotized by her vivacity. When the night's curfew fell, we were still together, blurting out revelations. We had missed all of our afternoon classes. Then we parted to our separate dorms. But not until after I saw her scale the brick wall to enter her third-floor room.

Early the next morning, I was sure I would never see her again. I was worth less than the seared, browned remains of one of Walt Whitman's blades of grass after a terminal drought, and she was an entire spring meadow in bloom. Surely she had realized the mistake of talking to me the minute our conversation had ended the previous evening, had fled to the bathroom, and had induced vomiting to eject whatever foul taste of me was still in her system. It was 8:30 a.m., and I was packing my book bag for my first class when she showed up at the entrance, twenty feet down the stairs from my open third-floor dorm room door and said she had accidentally left something in my room. When she invaded the quarters that I and my roommates shared, she and I started talking again and couldn't stop. We missed our classes again. All of them. There was a rainstorm. We sat on the campus lawn madly talking through it, imagining that we were raging against the forces of nature like King Lear. She climbed the highest tree on campus just to show me she hadn't been kidding about her Spider-Man claims. By the time we should have been forced to leave each other, it was dark, and curfew had arrived again. Curfews didn't matter to her. She snuck me into her dorm room. I spent the night.

Now mind you, I had never, as I've mentioned, gone through the normal motions of petting, though several girls, at one time or another, had tried to involve me in the sport. But I wasn't in the mood for a learning experience with the only women who seemed insane enough to lust over my twiggy form—the young ladies of the Weight Watchers set. So Jimmsy Law, the miracle sylph, and I didn't do anything suspicious. We merely slept in the same bed, fully clothed, with her curled up against me, her head on my arm, my arm going to sleep, the rest of me staying awake, unwilling to move my numb limb from beneath her exquisite temple even though I knew this meant they would have to amputate it in the morning (my arm, that is, not her head).

The next morning, she showed me a trick. There was a trap door in the ceiling of the hall outside her room. The men's and women's dorms were in one long Victorian building divided into seven separate units, some set aside for males, others for females. There were no connecting doors, and the male and female sections were hermetically sealed off from each other...or at least they were supposed to be. But the trapdoor led to a cramped attic in the tiny triangle—the claustrophobic A-frame—beneath the peaked roof. The attic was not meant for mere mortals. It was filled with piping, insulation and narrow boards spanning the beams for the convenience of maintenance men and of any Flying Wallendas who might drop into Portland, Oregon. I hoisted myself up to the attic, crawled across the boards, found the equivalent trap door in my own dorm, and dropped down into the corridor outside my room. My roommates wondered where I'd spent the night. I didn't tell them.

From that point on, Jimmsy and I were inseparable. Every night, I crept across the boards in the attic to Jimmsy's dorm and went through the platonic ritual of tormenting my left arm in her bed. The only hint of sex came from the adjoining chamber where her roommate slept. The roommate had a boyfriend—a philosophy major who had already graduated from school but continued to hang around—and he apparently snuck into the dorm every night, too. But what the roommate and her philosophical companion did with their mattress sounded frightening. All I heard were several hours of shrieks, moans and screams. Obviously Jimmsy's roommate was being tortured to the point of death...and was enduring this agony over and over again. Surely we should save her...or at least give her a painkiller. When I expressed my concern to Jimmsy, she reassured me that they were not reenacting the Inquisition. However when it came to exactly what they *were* doing, I was still very confused.

Then Jimmsy sprang a major proposal on me. Christmas vacation was coming up. She had arranged to rent a house off campus instead of going home to see her parents. She asked me to come live with her for the treasured two-week holiday break. This was a little sticky. Because of the expense of trips from Oregon to Buffalo, I hadn't seen my parents for Thanksgiving. They were looking forward to my return at Christmas. In fact, they were consumed by the desire to spend a few weeks with their long-lost son. If they missed the chance, maternal suicide seemed a likely outcome. But when the tides of opportunity knock, even those who hate having water flood their apartment are fools not to open the door. I accepted Jimmsy's offer.

When I got back to my dorm that afternoon, I finally confessed to my roommates where I had been passing my nights and told them where I planned to spend my Christmas vacation. That look of the lynch mob crossed their faces again. But this time, it had a new twist. That's when I found out the identity of the gorgeous and unattainable girl my older, far more-sophisticated, master-of-the-folk-song roommate was planning to ask out for the Christmas dance—the girl who had snared his heart and for whom he had laid four months of careful plans to make his own. It was Jimmsy. And I, the klutz who knew nothing about sex, couldn't discuss football, never had a single carnal adventure to brag about, and even had the audacity to evade the libidinous bragging sessions by hanging out with GIRLS, had through some ghastly accident of fate, some practical joke perpetrated by a particularly nasty gaggle of gods, landed this heavenly vision first! What's worse, I'd done it by accident!!!

The lesson: sometimes action is more important than planning.

◆

I WROTE TO MY parents to tell them I wouldn't be coming home. They were shocked, flustered, flummoxed, and furious. It was only 1961. The high point of the Sexual Revolution—the Summer of Love—was six years in the future. And the phrase "living with a girl" was not yet in circulation. So when my folks figured out that I was going to cohabit with a person of the opposite gender, their gall bladders threatened to throw stones, their hearts murmured ominously of shutting down the valves, and even their bunions put in a special request for aid to Dr. Scholls.

Nonetheless, when classes ground to a halt, Jimmsy and I moved to a modest shack with a kerosene heater, kerosene lighting, and other luxuries that would have made the Jukes and Kallikaks—the Appalachian mountain folks who wore tattered clothes, married their sisters, and shredded each other with gunshot in perpetual backwoods feuds—feel thoroughly at home.

It didn't take her long to seduce me, though that first time was a little bumpy. I was in an arm chair. Jimmsy sat, as she had often done, on the floor between my legs, the back of her head on my crotch. As she wove one of her entrancing tales, she took my hand and slid it down her blouse. She wasn't wearing a bra. It was clear from the audaciously skyward tilt of the object in my hand that she didn't need one. The experience so stunned my fingers that the blood drained from every organ above my navel. So I have no idea of how we preceded from my armchair to the bed. In fact, there's very little I can recall except this: while we lay there wriggling and such, all my male classmates from high school came swimming to the forefront of my consciousness, dried themselves off, sat in an amphitheater behind my forehead, and watched. I was so self-conscious that I could perform tolerably, but only up to a point. This meant that I had an erection that lasted three hours. But with the eyes of all those Park Schoolers looking over my shoulder, I couldn't ejaculate. This led Jimmsy to the erroneous conclusion that I was the most virile lover she had ever encountered. I didn't have the heart to tell her the truth.

A few nights later, a girlfriend of Jimmsy's came to the door crying, sobbed that she was having terrible troubles, and asked if Jimmsy could please go walking with her for ten minutes to comfort her. Jimmsy, who would have helped a trapped mosquito if it asked politely enough, promptly put on her winter coat and stepped out to implement an emotional rescue. I had a horsemeat roast (it was all we could afford) in the oven, and it was due to reach the peak of succulence in a quarter of an hour. I reminded Jimmsy to come back before it could overcook.

Fifteen minutes went by, and Jimmsy didn't return. Another half hour, and still no Jimmsy. Two hours passed, and my beautiful sexual savior seemed to have been swallowed up by the Northwest Pacific fog. Finally, afraid for her safety, I jumped on my bicycle and pedaled off into the dark to see if I could find her. By midnight, no luck. I pedaled back, dispirited, to our hovel. The roast was ruined! Then Jimmsy finally returned.

She'd been kidnapped. The supplicant with the urgent problem had lured Jimmsy to the street corner, then she and a bunch of male cohorts had stuffed the momentary love of my life into a car and had taken her, protesting that the roast was due out of the oven any minute, across town. They'd dragged her up the stairs to a dingy apartment whose living room was dominated by a Fu Manchu–like presence—my frustrated, folk-singing roommate. For the next three hours, this picture of sophistication begged Jimmsy to leave me and to come live with him. He told her what a fool, an ass, and idiot I was. He revealed the fact that I didn't know how to sip wine and recite football scores. I was a misfit. He was everything a girl could ever dream of. Whereupon he whipped out his guitar and began to show her his stuff.

The trick didn't work. To get out of the place, Jimmsy threw him a sop. She agreed to accompany him to the Christmas Ball. She knew I didn't want to wear a tuxedo, and this would give her a chance to show off the latest gown she'd designed and built. Then she persuaded the kidnappers to put her in their car and drive her back...to me.

Jimmsy and I had two extremely interesting weeks off campus. I finally learned what some of the shrieking and moaning from the dorm room next-door had been about. But my devotion swelled beyond the limits of female endurance. I was ripped apart emotionally by even a separation of half an hour. My neediness was unendurable. Two months after the vacation, Jimmsy dropped out of school and went back to Long Beach and her old headmaster. He left his wife, his kid, and his job. The last I heard, the two of them were married, and he had a new position as a professor at the University of Oregon. In Eugene, the town where I would soon meet the murderers. I hate the idea of a man busting up his family like that. But I know why he couldn't resist.

Thanks to Jimmsy, I'd been ushered into a movement that, as yet, had no name: the Sexual Revolution. And that Revolution was about to become one of the key currents of an era that was also nameless: The Sixties. But that's not the only current of the Sixties into which I'd stumble before it got its name.

When I returned to school from vacation, I discovered I was being reassigned to a new dorm. My three roommates had gotten together, visited the dean, and petitioned him to send me as far away from them as possible—preferably to the septic tank of a monastery in Tibet. Their grounds for this request? We were, they said, "incompatible." Thus was I tumbled onto the path recommended by a Frenchman who had fried his brain when he was seventeen years old and served it up to us with a light burnt butter sauce in his poetry. The Frenchman—Arthur Rimbaud—called his recipe for *Cervelles au Beurre noire*, "the deliberate derangement of the senses." I would soon outdo him in deliberate derangement by baking my brain in a light cactus marinade.

THE CHEMICAL CONEY ISLAND
OF THE MIND

My God, we're three thousand pages into this book, and I'm still working up to how I met the woman the murderers insisted that I should. (Believe me, the entire tale above eventually turns out to be relevant.) I promise, I'll make it up to you. Trust me.

But first we have some elementary chemistry to take care of—to wit, my role in co-founding the Sixties drug culture.

My adventure with Jimmsy was one sign of a sexual revolution bubbling beneath the surface in 1961 and 1962. A revolution of private parts set free to interpenetrate. A revolution that, six years later, would lead to the aforementioned Summer of Love. I mean, in my father's day, if you slept with a woman, she wasn't a woman anymore. She was a tramp or a prostitute. Jimmsy was something new. A woman who experimented with sex audaciously, but who stayed on her pedestal. And the birth control pill was about to take the pedestal approach that Jimmsy pioneered mainstream. But more about that later.

I have to confess that my contribution to the drug culture had a slightly different character than most, a character determined largely by my anal-retentive nature. It all started when I was in high school, and the whole thing was Henry Luce's fault.

Henry Luce was the titan of American magazine publishing in the mid-twentieth century. One Oxford University Press book called him "the most influential private citizen in the America of his day." Luce created the very first weekly news magazine—*Time*. Luce also put together the very first big-format, glossy, weekly magazine to cover the news with photos—*Life*. He crafted the first slick-paper business monthly magazine,

Fortune. And he created the first weekly, slick-paper sports magazine, *Sports Illustrated*. In a sense, Henry Luce also created two other things: The Sixties…and me.

As you'll recall, I had scarfed up two books a day in my grammar school years and I had discovered that my calling in life was as a workaholic when I entered high school. From ninth grade on, I labored at homework until ten o'clock every night, including weekends. Not that it did any good—my head was as porous as a pellet of Kevlar, and the facts just wouldn't stick, even though I tried every form of mental adhesive known to man. But in my spare time, I downed several magazines from cover to cover, including a subversive left-wing rag called *The Reporter*, the much more acceptable *New York Times News of the Week in Review*, and *Time* magazine. *Time* magazine was the one that would change me. In fact, *Time* would not just change me, it would alter America.

For unknown reasons, the facts from *Time* actually accumulated in my otherwise information-resistant skull—so much so that my best friend (the aforementioned Jon Hyman) and I annually tied for first place in the *Time* magazine current events quiz, which was a great relief to the accountants back at the *Time Life* headquarters in Manhattan because they only allocated one prize per high school, and with two winners, neither got any awards whatsoever, thus saving at least seven dollars a year with which the corporation could pay for another glass of Mr. Luce's Chateau Lafitte Rothschild.

Now all of this should make parents proud and teachers beam like flashlights filled with Duracell bunnies. But the exercise in ultra-respectability backfired terribly. Like summer camp and dance school, reading *Time* magazine should have turned me into a normal human being, capable of carrying on casual chatter with the sort of commuters who do the daily run from Greenwich, Connecticut, to Manhattan and make the world of advertising and finance run like clockwork. But, unfortunately, my alien metabolism picked up the information and transmogrified it in ways that would unleash tidal waves of stress hormones in the circulatory systems of my high school teachers, and would make my parents wish they'd been born in a nice, incurable coma.

You see, Henry Luce had made a discovery in the nineteen fifties that had added great quantities of extra lucre to his fortune. If you could spot a weird bohemian trend out there in America somewhere, no matter how small and marginal, you could give it a name, write it up every week, and turn it into a national movement. This would allow you to produce great piles of indignant verbiage and long strings of lurid tales condemning a generation lost in lust and rebellion, thus satisfying the hidden needs of the men in the gray flannel suits who read your publication. These flannel-shackled souls could steep themselves in your tales of free love among the despicable bohemians. Thus, they could vicariously throw off the manacles of convention for a few minutes a week. And they could justify their fascination with sex by registering outrage at the socially destructive barbarians who had the gall to wallow in sexual freedom. Then they could go to their conference rooms and spend the day yessing the boss and return home at night to be bawled out if they'd forgotten to pick up the milk.

In the mid-1950s, Luce had discovered a scruffy group of semi-derelicts named Allen Ginsberg, Jack Kerouac, Gregory Corso, and Lawrence Ferlinghetti. It was only four guys—along with whatever nubile young women (or nubile young men, in Ginsberg's case) they could tempt into their unmade beds. But given a little push from the armies of Luce typewriters, this unkempt quartet could be made to look like an invading army. Luce and his underlings snatched a name coined by *San Francisco Chronicle* columnist Herb Caen and shotgunned it to the masses—the beatniks. And all hell broke loose.

In Buffalo, New York, where I was growing up, there was nothing resembling a genuine beatnik anywhere in sight. Sure, we had more Poles than Warsaw. But beatniks? Not even one. But that would soon change.

Meanwhile, the nice, gray-flannel-suited models of masculinity that *Time* attempted to pump into my brain each week made no impression. It was the beatniks I identified with. They were the ones who provided a voice for the incoherent mutterings of my sixteen-year-old soul. So I turned the magazine's coverage into a do-it-yourself, make-a-bohemian-in-the-comfort-of-your-own-home course. One week *Time* reported that during a party, Corso, Ginsberg and Ferlinghetti had listened to records of Bartok and Stravinsky. So I ran over to Jon Hyman's house and borrowed all of his father's treasured Bartok and Stravinsky LPs. The next week, Corso, Ginsberg and Ferlinghetti sprouted sandals. So I scoured my hometown, whose inhabitants consisted almost entirely of burly steelworkers wearing steel-toed Sears work boots, for a pair of these peculiar footpieces. I was forced to obtain a set from a Catholic craftsman who turned out costumes for parochial school pageants centering on the Nativity. The next week I showed up in class wearing open-air footwear.

A week later, *Time* had the fabulous beatnik foursome sitting around jabbering about existentialism and Zen Buddhism. So I bought a paperback or two on Zen, became a sloppy pseudo-expert, and immediately set my sights on satori, the ultimate Zen state of bliss.

Yet another week went by, and *Time* reviewed Jack Kerouac's *On The Road*. That's when I told my parents that I was going to drop out and ride a motorcycle across the country in search of the Spiritual Ultimate. And that's when my father turned purple, vomited, threatened to leave me an orphan at any moment, then fainted. My mother was trying to choose between apoplexy and hemlock. All thanks to *Time* magazine and its Wizard of Odd, Henry Luce.

Since I was ten, everybody had known that I was going to be a college professor. Because of the two books a day I stuffed into my cranium, there were always crumpled pages sticking out of my ears. That, and the fact that I combed the *Scientific American* from cover to cover, giving it a clever poodle cut, meant that I was on a clear path to some sort of academic ivory closet.

Now with Kerouac and Corso choreographing my hormonal tango, my future as a college professor was turning from a dream into a nightmare. It looked like I was going to be trapped in the world of abstraction, separated from reality, prevented from ever putting my feet on the ground and feeling what it was like to walk around for myself. The prospective imprisonment was intolerable. And ten years later this discontent would have consequences. Big ones.

Then my parents made a strategic error on a multi-megaton scale. They decided to take the family for a summer vacation...to Cape Cod. Unbeknownst to them, perched on the tip of that very tame cape is a rather untame little village—Provincetown—which is exactly where my naive father and mother had booked accommodations for two entire weeks. Little did they realize that Provincetown was an artist colony. And artist colonies were filled with a genuine article I'd never been exposed to in the flesh before—living, breathing, honest-to-goodness beatniks, beatniks imported from the heartland of the species, from Beat Central, from New York's Greenwich Village.

When we hit the shores of the Atlantic, I was in hog heaven. I promptly befriended a middle-aged gallery owner from Jane Street (one of those narrow alleys in the depths of the West Village), who excitedly introduced me to all of her artist friends. And suddenly, there I was, a sixteen-year-old neophyte showing up in my benefactor's gallery every afternoon to discuss existentialism, Zen Buddhism, Bartok, and Stravinsky with the best of them.

This terrified my father, who was convinced I was becoming a homosexual. So as soon as our two-week reservations at our beach-front cottage expired, my parents hauled us out of this Gomorrah-on-the-Beach breathing sighs of relief that could be heard all the way to Kansas.

When high school resumed, my immensely improved bohemian regalia, complete with authentic beatnik sandals from a store in Provincetown, sent typhoons of terror through the cerebral lagoons in my teachers' skulls. One French teacher who was particularly fond of me actually took me into a walk-in closet, closed the door, and—trembling as she asked—stuttered out the horrified question, "A-a-a-are y-y-y-you a b-b-b-beatnik?" Frankly, I don't remember my answer. But I was flattered.

Now none of this actually meant anything much, except that my feet were getting a lot more ventilation, and when winter came I'd occasionally lay down in the snow (with galoshes on), stare at the moon for an hour or two, and try to meditate my way into Nirvana, which, if I'd lain there any longer, I'd probably have achieved, since frostbite would have turned my brain a heavenly shade of green. But the whole experience, along with one more vital ingredient, was my preparation for bigger things to come.

The second indispensable additive to the explosive mixture that I was about to become arrived from yet another source which should have been pounding great spikes of respectability into my head. I am speaking of the British Broadcasting Company, the BBC. You see, Buffalo may be bereft of most high cultural advantages. But it was on the outskirts of a potent cultural diffusion zone. Buffalo was on the border with Canada. And in Canada, they have this radio network called the Canadian Broadcasting Company, the CBC. The CBC didn't have much of a budget, but it *did* have high cultural pretensions. And where is the ultimate home of culture? London. So the CBC bought huge patches of programming from the BBC. And I listened to the resulting imports of British sophistication like crazy.

Theoretically, while *Time* was fitting me for a gray flannel suit, the BBC should have been training me for dark pinstripes and a bowler. But when your brain is warped, the respectable stuff never makes a dent. Instead, I was impressed primarily with a bit of utter lunacy called *The Goon Show*—a sort of radio father of *Monty Python's Flying Circus*—featuring Peter Sellers and a bunch of limeys named things like Spike Milligan, yes, Spike, carrying on as if they'd spent too much time swimming in a pool of mescaline.

Which leads us to the second great contribution that the CBC made to my life: a series of lectures by the highly-regarded author and master of intellect Aldous Huxley. When I was twelve, Huxley published a new book called *The Doors of Perception*. His erudite radio exegeses on the book's revelations, delivered in the clipped accents of the English aristocracy, were about his discovery of a wondrous new chemical that would have made *Alice in Wonderland*'s hookah-smoking caterpillar envious, a chemical that had surfaced in the Navy's Project Chatter, a diabolical series of experiments to see if you could concoct a potion that would drag—and drug—secrets out of prisoners of war without the use of torture. The chemical failed to be the secret weapon with which to get enemy prisoners blabbering, but it proved to have another use. For centuries, unfortunate Zen students had not experienced enlightenment until their generous Zen masters had humiliated them for fifteen years, then tossed them off a porch and broken at least one of their arms. But this miracle alkaloid opened the human mind to all the wonders that those crazy Zen recluses had been forced to dig up the hard way. I am referring to mescaline. The stuff in peyote buttons.

Up to this point I had never had a glass of beer, never been closer than five feet to a tumbler of liquor, never smoked a cigarette, and never even used a four-letter word. I just dressed in peculiar foot gear and had a mind chock full of bizarre jigsaw puzzle chunks.

The jigsaw pieces came together when I finally left home on the three-day-and-night train trip to Portland, Oregon, and Reed College. In addition to its stratospheric median SATs, and a set of courses tougher than the ones they casually toss around at Harvard, Reed was home to an environment known as one of the most "progressive" in the country, complete with an art class whose teacher was the most popular on campus because, instead of teaching anything about art, he devoted his entire lecture time to Eastern mysticism. He danced perilously close to the volcano's edge—to Zen Buddhism and satori.

It was at Reed, as you'll recall, that Jimmsy Law introduced me to the secret of sex.

What's more, Jimmsy introduced me to this stuff that you could buy in flat boxes about the size of a medium pizza box at a mere ten dollars per carton from some mail-order Indians in New Mexico. It was called peyote, and it wasn't even illegal yet. Unfortunately, the Reed kids had some misimpressions about how to take the stuff. They noticed that it tasted as appealing as a slatternly vegetable's menstrual fluid. So they baked it, shredded it, and put it in gelatin capsules. Very clever. Also very dumb. It meant that you could have gotten a more effective buzz by taking two aspirin and calling your doctor in the morning.

But this 1962 chemical misstep was about to kick start something new—the drug culture, a pillar of The Sixties.

AEROBICS FOR THE GONADS

When we last said good-bye to our hero (that's me), he had gone off to college after a high school career so sexually ascetic that it would have shamed a monk, then had landed—with no preparation—in bed with the one girl on the Reed College campus whom every man over the age of thirteen in the state of Oregon was hoping to sandwich between his sheets. After two weeks living with *me*, her brain—an astonishing specimen of brilliance—was so mangled that she fled, thus leaving me once again alone in the world.

And from that alone-ness would emerge two things: the currents of an embryonic drug culture, and another equally embryonic movement. A movement that would someday be named by, guess who? Henry Luce.

◆

THERE I WAS, IN isolation at Reed College in the dark gray, perpetual mist of Portland, Oregon, in January of 1961. And isolation in a gray mist, it would turn out, was the perfect place for the mutant intellectual seeds planted by Luce, Jack Kerouac, Allen Ginsberg, and Gregory Corso to germinate. The Jimmsy incident resurrected the old itch for finding the ultimate in mystic enlightenment. What's worse, in a dramatic demonstration of the fact that college courses can be dangerous to your health, I was a hot shot at Gallic literature and was taking a semester's worth of French Surrealist poetry and prose. I don't know if you've ever read this stuff—but Mallarmé, Baudelaire, Rimbaud, and that guy who wrote *Ubu Roi* were utterly mad, which fit my state of mind perfectly. Rimbaud, as we saw earlier, recommended a "systematic derangement of the senses," which went beautifully with all the Zen trash I'd absorbed. And with William James's awe of insanity in *The Varieties of the Religious Experience*.

I overlooked the fact that this sort of wisdom had killed off Rimbaud's creativity when he was a mere twenty-one, and I began to follow my Zen/beatnik/surrealist hodgepodge of gurus into the thorny undergrowth of the human mind.

Eastern mysticism instructed you to detach yourself from the things of this world so you could dive past all the outer layers of the onion and get directly to the small green sprout of spontaneous awareness that comes straight from the center of consciousness. Or from the universe or the Godhead or whatever. Since I'd been tossed out of my dorm room anyway, I decided to shuck my connection to material things. They were mere defense mechanisms, artificial vanities, designer jeans for the ego, trapping you in the superficial, shielding you from the reality pulsing at the center of *is-ness*.

So I did a little analysis of the "artificial patterns," the defense mechanisms, with which I'd propped up my ego over the years, and decided to discard them one by one so I could follow the yellow brick road to Enlightenment. First of all, I'd toss away any identification with a single room. After all, what is a habitation, anyway? It's a place where you smear your vanity all over the walls, erecting a shell of devices that hide you from your spontaneous self. Every poster or painting that you put up, every book that you squeeze onto a shelf, and every record album in your LP rack is secretly designed to impress the next pretty girl who walks in, stupefying her with the superiority of your taste and your intellect. Your room is as superficial as the exoskeleton of a dead cicada and as ego-driven as the scent markings of a horny dog. It's a barricade against the unpredictable energy of the universal mind. You've gotta get rid of it!

So instead of settling into the new dorm room that the college authorities had generously assigned to me, I made myself a bedroll and did my dives into the land of Morpheus on the concrete floor of the library basement, on the linoleum floor of a dormitory social room, and wherever else I could sneak floor space without anyone noticing.

Why didn't anybody trip over me and complain to the authorities about this obstruction in the path, you may well ask. Fact is, I'd noticed that I leaned on another artificial crutch—going to sleep at the same time every night. When you're stuck with the interminably dull 1,200 pages a week of Ficino, Averroes, Hobbes, Locke, Falafel, and the other obscure and confoundedly convoluted writers whose books Reed fired at you like cannon balls, you can barely keep your eyes open, and the idea of a slow death by blowtorch begins to sound like relaxation. So what do you think of as the ultimate escape? Bedtime!

Under the new spiritual regimen, escapes were *verboten*. Bedtime had to be eliminated! So I slept at a different arbitrary hour in every twenty-four-hour solar cycle, napping for no more than 180 minutes at a time. And I did all my snoozing long after others had passed the precipice of the REM state. That's why no one ever caught me napping on their linoleum tiles. I was catching cat naps at three am. What a victory. I had removed one cosmetic layer from the face of reality!

Then there were meals. Looking forward to breakfast, lunch and dinner was just another way to dodge the bullets of boredom. Regular feeding times had to go. I took to eating at unpredictable hours. One small step for man, one giant step for Zenkind.

These were the sort of spiritual athletics that monks everywhere from Nepal to 4th century Egypt had competed with each other to master. Remember Simeon Stylites, who sat on a fifty-foot-high pillar in the Syrian desert for the last thirty-seven or so years of his life way back around 450 AD? How in the world did that man get his food? How did he handle personal hygiene without toilet paper? In the category of physical abasement and self-denial, I was definitely going for the Olympics. (I can see it now—Gold Medal winner in Lunatic Asceticism for 1962: Howard Bloom.)

The whole thing worked just the way that Rimbaud said it would. After two months of this discipline, plus a few other spiritual aerobics I invented on my own, I was capable of having full-scale hallucinations in the middle of class… without the use of drugs! Fittingly, I had most of them in my surrealism sessions, where each word on a page would conjure up its own color, globular shape, and melody in my brain, then go dancing around like something Disney had been too frightened to concoct for *Fantasia*. I also dozed off a lot during lectures, though I was still acing my exams, maybe because Vishnu was on my side. *Gesundheit*.

Meanwhile, you may recall from our former episode that as I had lain with Jimmsy in her bedroom with my arm about to drop off in the days before this spiritual quest began, her roommate was in the sleeping chamber next door with her boyfriend.

I held this pair in awe. Not only were they older than I was, they were infinitely better stocked with worldly wisdom. So far above me did they seem that I had never even dared approach them to say hello.

But, one day, when I shambled into the cafeteria at about three o'clock in the afternoon to get some breakfast, Jimmsy's roommate—Carol Maynard—and the man who aided her in her shriek-fests—Dick Hoff—were sitting at a nearby table. Shyly I averted my eyes, knowing that to them I was lower than a bottom-feeding shrimp in the Marianas Trench. To my utter surprise, they tried to make pupillary contact. What's more, they got quite acrobatic and actually waved, summoning your lowly peon to their table.

I clued them in on what I'd been up to and their jaws dropped, rolled around the floor and lodged in a corner. After they'd reinserted their wandering mandibles, we began to converse. Several days later, we became inseparable. Surgery would have been useless. So when my Western Culture program reached Immanuel Kant and I discovered that I couldn't understand a single sentence of the man's twisted syntax, the moment seemed opportune to finally live out the ambition I'd been nurturing for years and drop out of school, devoting myself full time to traveling like Jack Kerouac and searching for satori.

I made one small mistake. I called my parents to tell them what I was doing. They were vacationing at the Fontainebleau Hotel in Miami, a once-in-a-lifetime splurge. But that treat came to an instant end with my phone call. They caught the next plane from Miami to Portland. Yes, they traveled a distance of 2,708 miles, a slashing diagonal across the North American continent. And they left behind one of the biggest gifts they'd ever given themselves. To save me.

The phone call had appalled them. But when my mom and dad arrived they were even more horrified. The long ringlets of hair standing on end like shocked electric eels, the bare feet, the general mien of tunneling into a whole new universe of bohemianism. It curdled their blood like cottage cheese. So my mom did some sleuthing, found the most prestigious psychiatric institute in Portland, laid out a bundle of my dad's cash, and sent me for three days of psychiatric testing. When all the TAT tests and ink blots were over, I was summoned to the office of the man who ran the institution. He sat behind his desk, leaned back in a strangely relaxed and open pose, and announced, "According to your tests, you are marginally psychotic and I should institutionalize you." News that at a later point in this story, I would have welcomed. But there was a but. A big one. He leaned across his desk with intensity and went on, "I think you're the sanest person I've ever met. You are on the hunt for something important. I wish you luck in what you are doing. And, frankly, I wish I was you." William James, who saw the deep truths in insanities, would have been proud.

So I had received, of all the strange things, an official permission to drop out. My parents went back to vacationing, this time by driving down the Pacific Coast to California. With my mom looking out the window of the passenger seat wondering if each hitch hiker by the side of the road was her son.

Wherever I was about to go, Carol Maynard and Dick Hoff wanted to come along, which meant that Carol would have to drop out, too. The three of us decided to hitchhike to Seattle, where Carol had some friends who would put us up. This is how I, who, despite my heavily self-conscious coital bliss with Jimmsy, had never had a full-scale date, never smooched, necked, petted or performed any of the steps preparatory to a proper physical education, took my next step as one of the accidental pioneers of The Sixties' Sexual Revolution.

◆

ACTUALLY, DICK HOFF was the real revolutionary. Hoff was about 6'1" in an era when that was so tall it could have induced altitude sickness. He had a body that Adonis would have drooled over. And he possessed a strange face that was covered with acne scars, but was illuminated by a smile unlike anything you've ever seen.

There was something unearthly about Dick. He'd been raised an only child by a single mother. What influence that had on the way he turned out, Lord alone knows. But he was the only person I'd ever met who had genuinely never in his life felt guilt, depression, humiliation, or any other psychological pain. Everything and everyone he saw delighted him. Any activity he'd never tried or place he'd never been or emotion he'd never had intrigued him. He wanted to experience them all. Edna St. Vincent Millay would have loved him.

Hoff took such overwhelming pleasure from the mere act of waking up in the morning that the emotion illuminated him like a beacon. The result? Despite the fact that his skin had more craters than your average moon, females of all species could not take their eyes off him. One glimpse sent their hormones racing. When we walked down the street together, strange women passing on the sidewalk locked their eyes on him, swiveled their gaze through me as if I were invisible, forgot what they were doing, and altered their routes to follow him. The most gorgeous and intelligent ladies of any town he happened to pass through developed hot flashes, their thighs trembled, and they fantasized uncontrollably about getting him into their beds. And into even more intimate locations.

All of this despite the fact that Dick complemented his pitted countenance by dressing in a rather abnormal manner. He wore net shirts that showed off his insanely perfect upper musculature. His jeans had worn out at the crotch about a century earlier and he never donned underwear, so his pelvic appendages had a tendency to tumble into broad daylight. He never wore shoes.

But he capered down the street like some tall, woodsy male sprite straight out of Ovid. The mere act of taking a walk got him so blissed-out that he'd jump high in the air, wrap his hand around the upper reaches of a lamp post, and swing down in circles. No matter how odd he appeared, you couldn't gaze at him for more than ten seconds without realizing that he took the same joy in life that a baby radiates when it sees a new ceiling fan. And the impact was way, way beyond charismatic.

At any rate, the three of us, Hoff, Carol (Jimmsy's former roommate), and I all headed for the highway and hitchhiked from Portland, Oregon, to Seattle, where we put up in the basement of this guy who was teaching anthropology at the local university and finishing up his PhD on the previously mentioned penis cones of the South Pacific. Peculiar extremes of sexuality seemed to be the house's motif. Sharing the lower bowels of the basement with us was the aforementioned drag queen who could have put Marie Antoinette to shame. I mean, when it came to ball gowns and tiaras, this man knew how to dress!

Carol and Dick kept up their regular bouts of copulation, raising enough noise to seriously undermine the nice, white house's foundations and to make me realize that whatever I'd learned about sex in my apprenticeship with Jimmsy was not even beginner-level.

So I stuck to my own areas of expertise: seeking spiritual enlightenment, and telling anyone who seemed the least bit interested the story of how and why I was doing it. Hoff had his effect on people, I had mine. Women wanted his body. And folks of both sexes seemed to want my brain. Or at least my hunt for the spiritual ultimate.

By some strange accident, I was morphing into a pre–New Age Elmer Gantry. You remember Elmer, a fictional evangelist from a Sinclair Lewis novel, an ex-college-athlete whose preaching was so electrifying that his frenzied fans multiplied, made him famous, and gave him sexual access to nearly every woman in town. I wasn't going anywhere near Gantry's sexual magnetism, but I was apparently neck and neck with him in oratory. When I talked about stripping the artificial layers from a carefully hidden nugget of bliss buried at the bottom of the soul, people found it hypnotic. Don't ask me why. As you've seen, I didn't know a thing. I didn't have a single answer. But I had questions. And I was a fireball of conviction about my quest, about my carefully thought out path to the alleviation of my ignorance.

Like there was the time many months later when I was hitchhiking through LA. The folks I was with took me to MacArthur Park, where there were dozens of madmen standing on soapboxes, orating their tonsils out about Marxism or the Second Coming of Christ or whatever else had twisted their cerebral ropes into a slip knot. Some intelligent-looking fellow walked up to me in the crowd of listeners and said that I looked like a character out of Dostoyevsky's *The Idiot*. Not the highest compliment in the world, I suspect. But my first grade teacher would have concurred. The amiable stranger quizzed me about what I was up to and started to drag the story of my spiritual mouse hunt out of me.

Without quite realizing it, I slipped into messianic mode. And by the time I was finished, all the Socialist Utopians and Second Coming advocates had been abandoned. The entire population of the park was clustered around the least likely humanoid in the place—me—trying to clasp, grasp, and wrestle with my every word. It was embarrassing. I didn't even have a soap box!

But I suspect that the spell-bound audience really hung on every syllable because they wanted to know how a Russian with the brains of a boiled cabbage could speak English.

◆

By the way, Dick Hoff harbored another habit I forgot to mention: wandering around indoors without clothes. He'd get up in the morning and shamble past me stark naked. Since I considered male genitalia the ugliest thing hung on a creature since turkey wattles, I found this utterly shocking. What's more, Hoff left the bathroom door open when he went, and continued grinning and carrying on his conversation as if nothing unusual was happening at his nether end. This made my hair stand in horror and look around for some new body toward which to migrate. But within a couple of weeks, Hoff had me wandering around like an accomplished nudist. And I, like Hoff, gradually came to regard bathroom doors as mere impediments to a good chat.

All of this would make a contribution to two revolutions that were still in the distant future: the sexual and the drug upheavals that would soon distinguish The Sixties from all other decades, marking off the period the way that black and white splotches brand a Guernsey cow. Our contribution was a prelude, a preamble, the first faint stirring of what would emerge two years later under the aegis of Timothy Leary, Ken Kesey, and The Beatles. How? As I said, wherever we went, women flung themselves at Hoff's feet, or at body parts slightly higher if they could manage it. And Dick couldn't resist new experiences, like exploring the anatomies of girls he'd never had the pleasure of before. What's more, Dick had no suspicion that his travel-and-bed companion, Carol, was vulnerable and depended on him. His feel for her griefs was blinded by the fact that he'd literally never been vulnerable, never been hurt, and never been dependent. So he would frequently disappear for a few hours with some delicious lass who had newly thrown herself across his path. And Carol would agonize.

One night we were visiting a party thrown by a clump of University of Seattle students in our temporary neighborhood and Dick quietly went *poof.*

Carol and I finally got tired of waiting, decided to go home to our Seattle basement, and hunted for Hoff. But we couldn't find him. Eventually we knocked on the door of an apartment across the hall belonging to a girl who had been at the soiree earlier in the evening and had mysteriously disappeared at about the same time that Hoff had become invisible. Hoff answered the door in the buff, smiled delightedly, and explained that this girl had the silkiest skin he'd ever felt and would we mind going home without him.

Carol and I trudged out into the darkness. I knew that Dick meant no harm. This was simply part of his impulse to taste everything in life at least once, even if his lollipop of the moment nestled between moistened labia. Carol had a harder time accepting it. So I tried to calm her down and make her feel better. Finally, we passed a storefront housing a closed-up artist's studio. Turned out that Carol had lived with the artist once, he had gone out of town, and she knew how to get in despite the fact that the place was locked. So we sidled somehow through the back door.

Carol didn't want to walk all the way back to our place—another mile or two away—and decided we should bed down at her old lover's place for the night. But there was just one bed, and an awfully narrow one at that. We both climbed in. I had no particular hopes that this arrangement would turn into anything physical. As far as I could tell, Carol found me about as appealing as a blister.

Well, there we were in this bed whose sheets hadn't been changed since the Vikings discovered Greenland, and I was squeezing my body into sixteen square inches of space and trying to sleep, when Carol turned around and aimed her soft, round face at me. Her translucent green eyes were exaggerated in size and appeal by a street lamp's light filtering from the sidewalk through the dusty plate glass display window. The question she cooed was totally unexpected: "Do you find me sexually attractive?"

What had we here? I admitted very timidly that I did. I mean, the girl had this kind of kittenish appeal that no one with a body temperature over zero could possibly ignore. What's more, I explained that she was very tactile, which means that any male would have a hard time keeping his hands off her.

Carol had popped one of those questions that Emily Post will tell you demands polite reciprocity. So I asked her if she found *me* appealing, knowing full well that in all probability the only way she could tolerate having me around was by taking a steady dose of Dramamine. Her answer: yes, she did. I had, she said, a certain cat-like appeal. This was such an insult to the feline population that I could hear a meow of protest ricocheting around the globe. But she was apparently serious. So serious, in fact, that it was only a matter of minutes before we had each other's clothes off. (It would have been a matter of seconds, but as I've implied before, I have the hand-eye coordination of a petrified tree.)

That's when I discovered that every art has its virtuosi. Jimmsy Law had been a pleasure, a delight, and a figure who deserves the immortality of Helen of Troy. But Carol Maynard could do things with her internal musculature that no anatomist had ever imagined. The girl was more than just an artist. It's a shame that she performed all of her gymnastics within the narrow confines of her abdominal walls.

It took me decades to realize Carol's motivation. She had been discarded by the man she was in love with—Hoff. Yes, only temporarily, but when you're in love, seconds are eternities and minutes are agonies. She needed to prove that she was still attractive. And I was her litmus paper. I was her proof.

There was a crucial lesson in Carol's embrace: sex comes with more than mere physical pleasure. It is packed with emotions. Emotions that sometimes go to the very heart of who and what we are.

◆

THE BUFFALO BOY WHO'D never had a date had just gained his second lesson in *The Joys of Sex*. But there would be more to come.

After a month in the gender-challenging basement in Seattle, Dick decided we should go to Berkeley, thus theoretically leaving the fog of the Pacific Northwest and heading for the California sunshine. We packed and prepared to catch a freight train south. That's when I came down with a cold, got left behind, was forced to hitch-hike to the San Francisco Bay on my own, and was scooped up in Eugene, Oregon, by the three fatherly murderers you may remember from our opening chapter. The kindly men in the black Hudson who delivered sermons on the need for meaning despite the fact that they occasionally amused themselves by punctuating skulls with periods and commas of lead.

It was roughly 7:00 a.m. in some numberless morning in May of 1962 when my generous threesome of homicide specialists from Vancouver let me out on the shoulder of a San Francisco highway. The sun was glorious, and the plants by the roadside were unlike anything I'd ever seen. In the lands to which I'd recently traveled—Buffalo, Portland, and Seattle—a blade of grass was a skinny affair. Broad to catch the sun. But flat and playing-card thin to save on cellulose. A proof of nature's pinch-penny ways. What passed for grass on the shoulders of San Francisco's freeways showed no interest in thrift. At least not in saving on lignin. These grasses were built for a different sort of saving. Which meant that California blades of highway grass were not the ribbons of green that Walt Whitman would have recognized. They were fat, rubbery stubs, like long ink erasers. Their sole challenge was apparently not just to snag the photons flooding from the solar orb. Their second job was to hog up as much water as possible on the rare occasions when it rained, and to hold that water in fat, stubby storage tanks so that it would be available during the long and inevitable seasons of drought—the dry seasons. It was a shame to walk on plants that were working so hard to overcome a tricky challenge. But I had no choice.

We had no cell phones or Google Maps in those primitive days, so I have no idea of how I did it, but early in the afternoon, I rendezvoused with my gang on Berkeley's main drag, Telegraph Avenue, just a fast automobile's sneeze from San Francisco. Hoff, Carol, our penis-cone anthropologist from Seattle, and his girlfriend had not found a place to stay. So we marched up and down Telegraph Avenue, a thoroughfare awash with coffee houses and bookstores, looking for signs advertising vacant apartments. Lord knows how we planned to pay the rent. We were close to penniless. But, alas, we had no luck. Finally, in desperation, we pounded on apartment doors and asked the appalled inhabitants if they knew of any vacancies. Or we would have pounded on apartment doors. If the first knock had not turned out to be so darned lucky.

Yes, the first door on which we politely used our knuckles was on the second floor above a store in a Telegraph Avenue building three blocks away from the Berkeley campus and just one block from Cody's bookstore. The hinged slab of wood was opened by an enviably handsome nineteen-year-old. His hair was raven black, his complexion and face the fair-skinned and ruddy cheeked sort generally reserved for Dickensian heroes once they've overcome their poverty and become radiantly rich.

To our surprise, he invited us in. Entering involved the kind of maneuvers used by seventeen clowns to squeeze into a Volkswagen Beetle. There were quite a few of us, and not much of him. Or not much of his habitation, that is. He was the possessor of a single room filled nearly to capacity by the slender girlfriend, draped across two floor cushions. The first one of us who figured out how to breathe explained our plight. We needed a place to live. The face of the young man lit up. "Why," he said, "don't you stay here?" The fact that the only way we could fit was by Scotch taping ourselves to the ceiling was not an obstacle to our eagerly saying yes. We were desperate.

So we spread out our sleeping bags, sat on each other's shoulders, and began to chat. It soon became obvious that our host, William, was quite a lad. He was a Berkeley student, and a top-flight one at that. What's more, he was a cello virtuoso with the sophistication of a young Mozart. And he had enough charm to be elected president in the country of his choice.

Shortly after we moved in with William, someone I'd met on the street came to the apartment and told me I had a call. This was a little strange, since William had no telephone. The call, it turned out, had come in at the pay phone of a gas station two blocks away. Lord knows how my mother had located me. Remember, we had no GPS in 1962. But sleuthing is one of her gifts. I suspect her powers as a peeping tom and policewoman of the cosmos may have played a role in shaping my fear of women. A fear that will reveal its significance in a bit.

◆

HOFF ATTRACTED MORE FEMALES and I attracted more followers, which means that we were aching for enough space to periodically expand our rib cages and un-hunch our shoulders. A month later, we managed to find a place big enough to inhale in. It was a big, pink condemned house three blocks away from Telegraph Avenue and a short walk from the Berkeley campus. The fact that it could collapse at any minute didn't bother us. We had faith in the quality of American workmanship.

William abandoned his apartment and followed. And when we transferred across the bay to San Francisco, he once again came along. William's disposition was so upbeat that he was indispensable.

Keep William in mind. He is the lad who will teach us the lessons of San Diego, including one of the reasons that romance so often ends in a mangle.

◆

SAN FRANCISCO WAS FAMED at the time for guess what? Its role as the West Coast headquarters of the Bohemians of the Decade. This was my big chance to finally meet the spiritual saints I'd been reading about all these years—the masters of existential *angst*, the pioneers of poetic revolution, the frontiersmen of the new nihilism, the beatniks. A day or two after I arrived, I hitch-hiked across the Bay Bridge and headed for San Francisco's North Beach, home of Lawrence Ferlinghetti's famed City Lights book shop, where, according to *Time* magazine, Allen Ginsberg, Gregory Corso, and Jack Kerouac passed their afternoons howling at the lostness of their generation. I couldn't wait to prostrate myself at my heroes' dirt-encrusted feet.

Ferlinghetti's shop was exactly where it was supposed to be. But its only inhabitants were one drab clerk, a false hope for customers, and shelves packed with eccentric books. I asked the clerk where the beatniks were. He looked as if he'd never heard of a beatnik, and gave no answer. I staggered out to the sidewalk wondering what sort of natural disaster had desolated my shrine. What sort of intergalactic specimen collectors had beamed my idols up into the skies. I stood in place on the concrete in front of the bookstore, perplexed. Finding the beatniks had become a task at the core of my very being. And now it had been yanked out like a 150-watt, brightly-shining light bulb. Not unscrewed, but yanked, leaving an appallingly empty socket. And darkness. I looked up the street to my left and down the street to my right to search for scruffily enlightened characters. None were in sight. Finally, a respectable San Franciscan pedestrian spotted me standing there dumbstruck by dither, my face pretzeled by quandary and said, "You look disturbed about something. Can I help you?" I explained to the kind Samaritan, "Yes, I'm looking for the beatniks." He rolled his eyes up into their lids, scratched his head, thought appallingly hard, then said, "They disappeared about a year ago. Don't know what happened to them. Have you tried Colorado?" Searching an entire state, alas, was beyond me.

The beatniks were gone! It was clear that if Carol Maynard, Dick Hoff, and I wanted to be part of a movement, we were going to have to start our own. Which seemed to be what we were doing. Totally by accident.

◆

WITHIN A MONTH, THERE were roughly a dozen of us, all running around totally naked on the first floor of our flamingo-pink hazardous house with visions of satori somewhere in the back of our minds. In fact, we got so used to nakedness that it was hard to remember that normal folks wore clothes. Which meant that we were tempted to go down to the local supermarket in our birthday suits. It took a lot of effort to remind ourselves that this was a bad idea.

We were on the house's first floor. Someone we scarcely knew was on the second floor. But when he threw a party one evening, he was kind enough to offer us an invite. For supermarkets, we needed pants, skirts, and shirts or blouses. But for a party in our own building? Surely this was informal. Surely this was come as you are. So we did. When we entered and began to introduce ourselves to the strangers in the room, they backed away. The living room in which we were attempting to be warm and sociable had been clogged with people when we first entered. But within minutes, we were the only ones in the space. Everyone else was crowded into a bedroom where we were not. And they were disturbed. Finally, they sent an emissary to tell us that our nakedness was not welcome, and could we please leave. How the inhabitants of a nudist colony manage to remind themselves that humans shock easily, I do not know.

Despite this, our reputation was apparently spreading, because folks came from as far as Virginia to join us. Which is how Sylvia of the Red Hair, whom you will meet shortly, entered our lives.

◆

Now, IF YOU'LL RECALL, this whole epic started as a subplot on how I made a miniscule contribution to the start of something that would soon grow big, the Sixties drug culture. So if I haven't utterly parboiled your patience, in my next four chapters I will give you the succeeding adventure, in which, if we're lucky enough to get that far, some graduate biochemistry students at Berkeley discover how to manufacture a mysterious chemical used by the military to make cats desperately afraid of mice, then put drops of it on sugar cubes. The budding test-tube wranglers wrap the enhanced sweetener in tin foil and sell samples to their friends, thus threatening to allow small rodents to subjugate the human race.

NO RIGHT TURN ON A GIRL
WITH RED HAIR

Our fame was apparently spreading like an avian flu. You know the kind, a virus that cleverly sneaks into the guts of a migrating bird, travels a thousand miles in the avian's innards, waits for a stopover at a farm, exits the fliers' intestine by means we cannot mention in a family publication, and inserts itself into a hungry pig, then seizes on the nearest human, and takes its next big leaps using airlines with engines instead of beaks. One day, ambling into our illegal pink abode in Berkeley, California, came a couple of virtual foreigners. They were refugees from the genteel society of Virginian aristocracy who had gone off to the University of Virginia, where folks of their particular crust (upper) were expected to indulge in fraternity pranks for four years, do an inordinate amount of drinking, and emerge as lawyers, politicians, and pillars of the community.

The pair that showed up on our doorstep—a young man and his girlfriend—had failed to find the meaning of life in a beer bottle. So they'd dropped out of school, tucked their spare jeans into the trunk of a classic, red MG open-topped sports car, headed the vehicle in a westerly direction, and ended up in the general vicinity of the Pacific. How they'd heard of the band of humans to which I belonged and how they'd dug up the address of our big, pink, condemned house in Berkeley, God alone knows. But one morning, there they were, determined to visit, or perhaps even to fall in with our wayward deeds. Little did I realize that through one of them, I'd trip across the generation of Bohemians who had come before the beatniks, a generation so antique that Henry Luce had not even dignified them with a name.

The distaff member of this couple was particularly impressive. She was slim but shapely—with flaming red hair that fell to her waist. She was clothed in jeans, a motorcycle-style denim jacket, masculine boots, and swore with a hammer-hard authority that would have shocked a truck driver. Frankly, she scared me to death.

The two of us managed to successfully stay at opposite corners of every room in which we found ourselves for a week or two, until one night, six or seven of us—including her and her boyfriend—decided to crash a movie. We had no money, hadn't seen a film in years, and one of my favorites, an Alec Guinness thing with great gobs of music by Prokofiev—*The Horse's Mouth*, had come to town. So we all trooped off to the parking lot outside the local theater to wait for intermission, when the exit doors would open and we could sneak in the back way. Unfortunately, the neighbors saw us, called the cops, and we had to split. This left us with no way to amuse ourselves.

But being resourceful, we pinch-hit. We went off to a laundromat and decided to shock the patrons by taking Sylvia (the girl with the long red hair), who pretended she was a corpse, and stuffing her into the dryer. Just as we had gotten Sylvia's limp upper half into the machine and were about to slip her lower extremities in, a very tall man in a business suit tapped one of us on the shoulder and asked us sternly whether we needed any bleach. He was, he explained, the manager.

We all ran very fast. The main body of the mob sprinted out the front door. I dashed out the back with one other person following close behind. I didn't pay much attention to who it was until we got to our big, rosé, condemned domicile, sat down in the living room to catch our breath, discovered we were utterly alone, and looked each other in the eye. My fellow escapee had been…Sylvia. The woman who terrified me. And there was no one around we could use to avoid each other.

Well, it was a long night. God knows where the rest of the crew had disappeared, but they didn't show up. I was still panicked by this stainless-steel lady. But when it became obvious I wasn't going to be able to dodge conversing with her, I defended myself by doing something utterly despicable. I analyzed her personality. Piece by piece I took her apart, displaying the disassembled components before her eyes and explaining how they worked together to make a finished, ultra-tough human being who used a fist-like pose to hide a carefully-concealed vulnerability, a need to curl up like a kitten in the protective hand of someone she felt was stronger than herself. It was nasty, fiendish, and I apologize, but I was young.

At any rate, we were still there talking (or was I lecturing?) when the sun latched its first dim, green fingers of light around the sill of the horizon and threatened to haul its full body through the window of the sky. As the light acquired the pea-soup quality of very early day, a strange transformation hit Sylvia. Her dagger-throwing eyes went soft. The hit-man hardness in her face relaxed. Her I-can-whip-your-ass muscular posture melted. Then came the ultimate shock. She swore she was in love with me. My God, what had I gotten myself into!

◆

SYLVIA DECIDED THAT SHE and I should go off together. Which we did. At that point in my life, I wasn't particularly adept at saying no. We hitch-hiked the 403.8 miles or so down to San Pedro, the port south of LA. Which gives you a precise measure of the distance that at least one man will go to have sex. Our passionate love affair, which had been entirely one-sided and based on some illusion of me that Sylvia had concocted in that peculiar night of escape from the laundromat, lasted about five hours. I was not a commanding giant who would take five hours to focus on her emotional interior and analyze it on a daily basis, then take her to bed when she unclenched. That had been a one-time-only self-defense maneuver. Who cared? She was far more interesting as a roommate and a friend than she'd been as a nemesis.

Remember, it was the early summer of 1962, two years before anyone would recognize that we had left the 1950s and entered a strange new period of history, The Sixties. Sylvia and I started body-surfing in the Pacific waves five blocks away from the room in which we slept by day, and hanging out by night at a seedy little bar straight out of a pre-beatnik fantasy, which is where I met a living embodiment of 1940s bohemianism, a man about to teach me new lessons in meaning and the unseen range of human possibilities. New lessons in the hidden infinities hinted at by Edna St. Vincent Millay, T. S. Eliot, William Blake, and William James. His name was Ed. And he was a blessing.

THE COWBOY AND THE INDIAN

No search for the spiritual ultimate is complete without a visit to a Native American wise man. I had mine six years before Carlos Castaneda's books about a flying Mexican peyote eater would make the practice fashionable: in the early summer of 1962. Though in California, it is difficult to tell summer and winter apart.

My opportunity to absorb the wisdom of those who show their love for nature by sleeping in fur blankets yanked from unwilling buffaloes came when Sylvia and I marched off to the aforementioned pre-beatnik bar, a bar even Tom Wolfe and Ken Kesey never imagined in their wildest dreams. And a strange place for a kid who didn't drink, but I fit in for other reasons which will make themselves apparent shortly. It was, as you already know, the hangout of a lost generation of bohemians. I qualified highly here, since I hadn't worn shoes in eight months, even in the snow, my hair was down to my shoulders, and I got lost easily. What's more, since every hair on my cranium was curly, it fluffed itself into what would later be known as a Jew-Fro, so my coiffure stood at attention about a foot above my head.

To make matters worse, the Beatles hadn't shown up in the United States with shockingly long hair, so anything more extensive than a crew-cut was considered un-American. In fact, a male with long hair was something people had never seen...except on portraits of Jesus Christ. And he had straight hair. I did not. So my coiffeur resembled the wig worn by Harpo Marx. The result? Kind-hearted folks would literally stop their cars in the middle of the road and stare. Then they'd jump out and generously offer to beat the shit out of me, gang rape me, tie my heels together, attach me to a fender, and drag me to the nearest barber shop...twenty-seven miles away. Fortunately, I was always able to talk my way out of being turned into a well-tenderized and neatly-groomed sack of meat.

But back to the bar. Just to give you the flavor of the place, every night at 2:00 a.m. when her professional duties were over, the town Madame, a woman of fading but stately beauty, would glide up in her eighty-foot-long Cadillac to find the companionship of folks she could count on as friends. One of these was a man who rapidly adopted me as a semi-son.

The guy who took me under his wing was a big, genial man in his forties, Ed. He'd grown up in New York, and if I'm not mixing things up terribly, said he'd been sired by an extremely authoritarian rabbi, which is a bit strange since he looked about as Jewish as Clark Gable. At any rate, no matter what his father's religious persuasion, Ed couldn't take being bossed around all the time, and at the age of fourteen he ran away from home, followed Horace Greeley's advice, and headed west. How he traveled, Lord alone knows, but soon he found himself in the vast lands of sagebrush and tumbleweed, where men are men, sheep are nervous, and fried bulls testicles are a munchie on a par with popcorn (which, I should think, would give the bulls even more anxiety attacks that the ewes).

So, Ed bravely strode into whatever ranch seemed to be hogging up the roadside and asked for a job. They probably gave him one sweeping up the cattle droppings in the barn. But Ed wasn't the kind of guy to let a humble beginning get him down. Before long, he was the best darned cowboy you'd ever seen. He could rope a calf, ride a bull, chew two packets of Marlboros, and tell the difference between a horse and a hearse. Just to show he was REALLY a cowpoke, though, he couldn't handle the difference in spelling between the two.

Ed became so good at what he did that from time to time he'd go off to Mexico for a season and sign up with the gauchos, the cowboys south of the border. These virtuosos can lasso a bull with dental floss and get the damned hulk of beef to brand itself, then to convince the next bull in the pasture to step into the caballero corral and show how macho he is by tattooing himself as well. This is why gauchos can take siestas: they trick the cattle in to doing most of the work. At any rate, Ed was able to out-gaucho the gauchos at their own game (gin rummy), and won a reputation everywhere from Juarez to Argentina.

Breaking in wild stallions became his specialty. He could stay on a bucking bronco's back longer than a stripe sticks to a zebra. Then, one day, he was being tossed up and down on the vertebrae of some ornery untamed brute (no, it wasn't his boss' wife, it was a horse) and was about to give it the surprise of its life, the final dramatic coup that would turn it once and for all from a fiery individualist into a meek mount fit for women, small children and elderly quadriplegics. That's right, he was about to go through the old ritual of breaking a bottle of cold water over the beast's head, a technique that totally confuses even the most blood-hungry horse and leaves it staggering around begging for someone to tell it where to go next and whether the prospective passenger would like a receipt at the end of the ride. Then it occurred to my friend Ed that he had left New York because his father was breaking *his* spirit. Now he was about to break the spirit of this magnificent wild thing. He couldn't do it.

He jumped off the bucking beast and explained his philosophical position to the befuddled creature, who had just been getting enthusiastic about tossing Ed like a shot put, then stomping him into sewage. As Jonathan Swift will tell you, horses understand these things a lot better than we do, so the stallion was sympathetic. They shook hooves, went off for a drink, and traded the stories of their lives.

We won't go into the horse's sad tale here, since we're trying to stick to the story of Ed. But let's just say it isn't easy being a colt during the Depression.

The upshot was that Ed gave his saddle and a jar of Adolf's Meat Tenderizer to a blind and homeless man who hadn't eaten for months, then moseyed off into the sunset and became a union organizer back in the days when management used negotiators who ironed out the fine points of a contract with Tommy guns and lead pipes. Ed was arrested for organizing union protests, led a jail breakout, tore the door off of his cell, was welded (yes, welded) back into the cage with thirty other freedom-hungry criminals, led a hunger strike, and learned all the words to "We Shall Overcome," a brand new song at the time.

By the time I met him, he owned a pickup truck and not much else, having spent about six months of the year prospecting for gold in the mountains of Northern California, which gave him just enough money to make it through the rest of the year, then loafed, passed his evenings at the bar, and occasionally took a long-distance vacation traveling as an illegal passenger on freight trains. The last time I heard from Ed, he was spending a month at a cushy New York State resort called Attica Prison after being caught fixing up first-class accommodations for himself and a friend in a boxcar. The state was hoping the free room and board would convince him to change travel agents.

Remember the Sixties was not just a time of revolution for the sexual organs—for their right to stand up and speak for themselves. And it was not just a time for new potions to discombobulate the brain. It was a revolution in the horizons of the human soul. The kind of revolution that Edna St. Vincent Millay preaches in *Renascence*. The kind of revolution that T. S. Eliot urges you to begin today. The kind that William Blake and William James admired. It was an era of mind expansion. And Ed did his best to expand mine.

Ed sensed in me a kindred soul (though certainly not a kindred body; with my hand-eye coordination I couldn't even hang a lasso on a coat rack, much less use one to trip a calf). So he decided to educate me in what freedom of spirit was all about.

First he drove me to a place called Watts Towers, a five-story-tall contraption made out of scrap metal, concrete, and the bottoms of thousands of old pop bottles that an Italian immigrant had spent his whole life building in an impecunious residential district of Los Angeles just to show how high even the souls of the poor could soar. Ed was particularly proud of the fact that when the city decided to supposedly conduct a stress test and sent its wrecking crews out to the unauthorized monument, the contraption was so structurally impregnable that the biggest bulldozers the town fathers could muster didn't even dent the towers' finish—or so I was told.

Then Ed drove me further south to San Juan Capistrano to visit an Indian friend of his. The friend was a Native American anthropologist who had gone off one summer to do some research on the Southwestern mesa where his ancestors used to roam. First he'd discovered that to feed himself, he was going to need to shoot some rabbits. But whenever he fired a gun, every rabbit on the mesa heard the bang and high-tailed it for the nearest burrow (if they'd been Mexican rabbits, they'd probably have headed for the nearest burro, but that joke is so far beneath contempt I won't even mention it). So he made himself a bow and arrow, which solved the noise problem, much to the chagrin of the rabbit population.

Next he found that whenever there was a downpour, it soaked him to the skin, and his clothes took hours to dry, threatening him with pneumonia. But there was a solution! If he stripped down to a loin cloth, he ceased to be waterlogged in seconds. So he diapered himself in chamois.

Finally, since there were no barbers in sight, his hair grew and got in his eyes when he was rabbit-hunting. So he ripped up some cloth and made himself a headband. By the end of the summer, he'd gone whole hog and returned to the ways of his ancestors. Then came September, and he had to put his clothes back on and return to fighting for tenure. But he'd learned a lesson from it all. Listen to your great, great grandparents. Sometimes ancestors are not as dumb as they look. But don't always depend on your great grand-elders for advice on how to dress if you want to impress your department head.

Together, Ed and his anthropologist friend gave me one more gift. Ed described what it had been like to go on a hunger strike during his post-labor-protest jail experience. After day three without food, something remarkable happened. Ed felt invincible. He was soaring with a mightiness of mood he'd never before experienced.

The anthropologist had dipped into the same sort of thing. His ancestors, he explained, had gone on spirit quests to find their true identity. And their adult name. They had left the tribe late in their teens, plunged into the wilderness, and had starved themselves until they were visited by a vision, a vision that gave them their sense of self and their title: Running Bear, Dancing Elk, Humble Horse, Flying Buffalo, Pitiful Prairie Dog, etc. When the anthropologist had discarded his rifle and clothes and had gone back to the ways of his ancestors, he, too, had begun a spirit quest. To achieve it, he'd fasted. And like Ed, his clarity of mind and his sense of power had soared. So I, too, wanted to fast. It was the Edna St. Vincent Millay and J. Alfred Prufrock thing to do.

For the next two or three days, I ate nothing. Then something strange happened. Ed was hungry. He took me to a restaurant. I read the menu. And I looked at the dishes that diners up and down the rows of tables were tucking into. They looked delicious. Now here's the weird part: I was able to taste each item with a sharpness that actually eating the food would never have delivered. Others in the restaurant were limited by two things.

They were forced to choose just a small number of items from the menu. And after the first two or three bites, the pleasure of a dish's flavor leached away, abducted by what psychologists call "habituation." Meaning even the most remarkable dish becomes ordinary by the fourth fork-load. But I didn't have those obstacles. I could taste everything that I saw on the restaurant's twenty tables. I could taste items represented only by words and pictures on the menu. Which means that my eating choices were vast. And I didn't grow tired of the flavors. They stayed sharp and delicious.

The lesson? The spirit can be more vivid than the flesh. You don't always need to physically possess something to enjoy it. Sometimes simply knowing it exists is enough. Like the Hubble Space Telescope. You've never seen it. You can't tuck it away in your closet. You can't feel its metal with your palms. Yet you carry what it sees around in your head day after day. It has given you a cosmos. And you carry that cosmos around in the creases and wrinkles of your brain.

The realm of the human spirit is vast. So is the potential universe of your mind.

THE FINE ART OF NUDE CLIFF HANGING, or FROM MUPPET TO MOUNTAIN MAN IN ONE EASY LESSON

I'd eaten everything in the restaurant without any artificial stimulation. Aside, that is, from organic, one hundred percent natural starvation. But far more powerful tools for the exploration of the soul were about to enter the scene—those bizarre things Aldous Huxley had pontificated about on the BBC: psychedelics.

When a month had passed, Sylvia of the red hair became bored with me. Never again had I attacked her and pulled her apart. Never again had I given her intense hours of emotionally charged attention. Attention is the oxygen of the human soul. And I was not the oxygen-giver she'd hoped for.

What's more, I had learned all that I could from San Pedro, like how to be very polite to policemen when they pick you up for looking like a suspicious character and when they threaten to show you exactly how limber your limb bones can be. For example, one evening at dusk, I was getting the daily exercise recommended by the President's Citizens-Advisory Committee on Fitness of American Youth and attempting to enlarge my muscles by running the two miles from our apartment to the bar. And I was cheating. The whole run was downhill.

In those antediluvian days, the word "jogging" had not yet been invented. Nor had the upper middle class rituals that go with it—$2,000 designer shorts cleverly camouflaged to look casual, fitness apps, fanny packs, armbands for your iPod, and a discreet supply of artificial smiles to wear when it feels like your spleen is about to burst. Which means that a nineteen-year-old youth running on a residential sidewalk in the gloaming meant just one thing—robbery. Even if that youth had bare feet and hair that looked like an explosion in a coiled telephone cord factory.

A police car rounded the corner just uphill. It came halfway down the street, drew even with me on my left, and cruised at my precise speed. What a coincidence. Then the officer on the passenger side rolled down his window, ordered me to stop, and both men in blue emerged from their vehicle. They were considerably larger than I was. You could have squeezed two of me into one of them. The opening move from these keepers of the peace was a generous offer to augment my aerobic lope by helping with a bit of stretching—a necessity if I was to retain maximum flexibility. Their suppleness-enhancer of choice? Spread-eagling me against their car and frisking me. How could I possibly refuse their kindness? Before they could make me assume the position, I countered their verbal suggestion by telling them my tale. I was a poor college student who had dropped out of school on a spiritual quest. Yeah, really? Then they grilled me on the most criminal suspicion that my words aroused. How long had it been since I'd seen my mother? When I confessed that it had been almost a year, they were seized by nurturing instincts. They tried with all their might to persuade me to go back home and see my family before my mother's heart could crack like a glass egg and leave shattered shell fragments all over the interior of her torso. And they were right about one thing: maternal wisdom matters.

As your mother will tell you, manners mean everything, because by the end of fifteen minutes trying to save me, the officers of the law asked if they could buy me a cup of coffee. I didn't drink coffee, but I appreciated the offer.

◆

THE TIME HAD COME to leave San Pedro and head back to the Bay Area. Trailing me as I left the town in which Sylvia of the Red Hair was seeking new men to terrify, was an eighteen-year-old who had become hypnotized by my tales of seeking the spiritual holy grail and had insisted on leaving his summer job at the post-office, his future as a college student, his horrified middle-class parents, and, so far as I could see, his sanity. Why? I'd met him at the bar where I'd run into Ed. The eighteen-year-old had a strange problem. His life, as he explained it, was filled with wild adventures. He'd worked on a merchant marine ship, crawled through African jungles, lunched with polar bears in the Arctic, discussed existentialism with seals, wallowed in Wittgenstein with walruses, sipped rare wines with sea otters, and a whole lot more. There was only one problem. None of his tales were true. They were symptoms, outcroppings of his extreme dissatisfaction with an embarrassingly ordinary life. In reality, as you remember, he had a job at the post office. Apparently, he had never heard the message of "The Love Song of J. Alfred Prufrock"—if you have something heroic to do, something that defines you, start it now. Today. And unfortunately for him, he got that message, but not directly from Mr. Prufrock. He got it from me.

So he kicked himself in the gristly tissue cushioning the posterior of his pelvis and set out for real adventure by leaving his parents and attaching himself to, well, poor choice, but, ummm, to me. His real-life adventures would begin much more rapidly than he imagined.

◆

THE TWO OF US set out for the open road early in the evening, and sure enough were blessed with instant luck. A brand new blue Chevrolet, the all-American kind that in those days—before a luxury automobile was downsized to fit on a charm bracelet and manufactured in Germany or Japan—could do 120 miles per hour, pulled over and offered us a ride all the way to SF. Well, actually, it wasn't the car that made the offer. It was the kid inside, a nineteen- or twenty-year-old in a genuine cheap suit, rumpled as if it had just been yanked out of a laundry bag and wanted to get back in and hide. He had an open shirt collar and no tie and said it was his dad's car, and that he'd been attending a business convention in San Diego. Now as you may recall, in those days, I was the only person from Buffalo, New York, over the age of 16 who had never gotten a driver's license. But I loved to stomp my left foot on an accelerator. Miracle of miracles, the driver said he was tired, and asked if one of us would mind taking the wheel...he wanted to take a nap. I couldn't wait to sidle into the pilot's seat, which I did with the swiftness of a chameleon's tongue.

Then our host, yawning from the back seat, asked if we'd mind pulling the car into a filling station and putting some gas in the tank. He'd pay for the fuel, he said, but someone had stolen his wallet at the convention and his cash was all gone. My post-office runaway friend and I pooled our spare change, pulled into a station, and purchased two dollars' worth of nourishment for the machine.

When the attendant asked us to turn off the engine, we discovered that we couldn't. There were no keys. We asked our genial friend, who was laying so low in the back that you'd have thought he was auditioning to be a carpet, where the keys *were*. "Oh," he whispered, "they were in my wallet when it was nabbed."

The gas jockey kindly agreed to dole out a few drinks to our thirsty gas-guzzler despite the fact that its eight pistons were still spitting internal bursts of flame. And despite the fact that we could only afford two dollars' worth of fuel.

Then we set off on our travels again, glorying in the realization that it was 2:30 a.m. Why? Because this meant that the six-lane highway was almost totally empty, and I could methodically test the technical limits of the engines they shoved into Chevys in 1962. Frankly, it wasn't a bad little V8. It cruised comfortably at 115 mph. I didn't take it much above that speed. After all, I was driving illegally, and I didn't want to push my luck.

Our only bad fortune came when we were barreling down the tarmac and some vehicle bore down upon us from behind flashing ominous red lights. "Oh, my God," I thought, "the cops." So I hit the brakes like a sledgehammer, decelerating at a rate that nearly tossed our heads through the windshield. This was not, it turned out, a wise move. The thing behind us had no ability to slow down at a commensurate speed. As our rapid descent in velocity brought the vehicle on our tail to within about thirty feet of our back bumper, I finally made out in the rear view mirror exactly what it was—a Mack truck bigger than Darth Vader's death star hurtling toward us at 120 miles an hour. It had red-lighted us as a signal to move to the right and let it pass. Thank God Chevys in those days could accelerate. I smashed the gas pedal half-way through the floorboards and we gathered momentum fast enough to avoid becoming just another squashed bug on the Mack's already insect-littered grill.

We hit the San Francisco area just as the sun was coming up and all the early-morning commuters were emerging to park their cars on the highway. By the light of the dawn, we could see that the grass on the hills on either side of the road, grass that had been a promising green when I'd headed south from Berkeley to San Pedro with Sylvia, had lapsed into its default color—brownish gold. In California, it seems, grass is green for a maximum of two weeks a year. Then it goes through the sort of thing that Keats was lamenting when he wrote:

> Oh what can ail thee, knight-at-arms,
> Alone and palely loitering?
> The sedge has withered from the lake,
> And no birds sing.

Sure enough there were no birds in sight. Or lakes. That may be why the blades of grass I'd first seen when exiting the car of the murderers on my descent from Seattle had been so balloonish, so insistent on imitating tiny water tanks. Is the yellowish tan of the hillsides on the West Coast the real reason they call California the golden state?

But we made it through the frozen molasses of morning traffic, finally dropped ourselves off at my tribe's new location, and thanked the guy in the back seat profusely for the ride. New location? Yes, my clan had by now abandoned its big, pink lair and found new quarters in the heart of San Francisco's black ghetto. The super-slum neighborhood of choice was called the Fillmore District, but Bill Graham wouldn't discover it for another three or four years. So at the moment, my companions were the only people in the neighborhood whose faces had the reflective qualities that make your cheeks and chin clearly visible at night. The rent for the new abode was dirt cheap because the spacious seven-room apartment was on the third floor of a building whose first two stories had been burned to a fine ash, leaving only six columns of questionable strength holding up the higher floors and a stairway that wobbled in the wind, but, with care and mountain climbing equipment could convey the intrepid to the two surviving stories, the two remaining apartments in the sky. I had not yet seen this new nest.

It was only as we were climbing the swaying stairs to the new apartment that I began to put two and two and two together about our ride in the muscular Chevy. As usual, when I added two and two, I got six (arithmetic has never been my strong point, as you'll recall from the collection of flaws I shared with Albert Einstein). The guy with the V8 engine had no money, no keys, and had made damned sure he wasn't driving the car. In fact, while he made himself respectable by wearing a suit and looking inconspicuously horizontal, he positioned this guy at the wheel whose overgrown hair and shoeless approach to sartorial elegance would have made him highly suspicious in the eyes of guys in blue uniforms. Me. The car was stolen!

And here I'd been flying it across the desert at slightly subsonic speeds *without a license.* If we'd been caught, the car's "owner" would simply have claimed that *he'd* been the hitchhiker, we'd picked *him* up, and if there was a theft involved, surely WE must have been the ones to pull it off. God damned beatniks!

But due to some happy accident, instead of landing in the slammer, we were safe at home (assuming the stairs held up until we could get to the third floor, and that the six scorched steel posts supporting what was left of the building didn't buckle). Maybe there *was* a God after all!

At any rate, we made it to the upper stories and let ourselves in to the new, unlocked apartment, which was as still as an abandoned buggy whip factory. The floor was littered with nondescript lumps of fabric. At first the early morning light made it difficult to puzzle out exactly what they were. Then one of the bundles came alive. The heaps of rags were sleeping bags. And they were occupied.

The first head to pop out was that of Carol Maynard, the highly tactile female who had found me "cat-like" and had welcomed me to her interior pleasure dome. She screamed my name with a heart-toasting delight, and dashed out of her textile cocoon, totally naked, flinging her arms around me in glee. Her voice woke the others, and within seconds, over a dozen equally unclothed bodies, male and female, had piled themselves in a giant hugging mound around me. It was nice to feel wanted. Alas, it doesn't happen often.

When the human heap disbanded, I tried to introduce my follower from San Pedro to the crowd, only to discover that he had disappeared. A brisk search revealed him sitting on the creaking stairs two stories below with his head in his hands, the victim of traumatic shock. He'd never seen a naked female before without a staple in her navel, and the sight of a whole tribe of pink-skinned humans with pubic hair had thrown him into panic. In those days, *Playboy* pretended that pubic hair did not exist. So the smallest hint of hair in the private regions of the body was shattering. And the unclothed pudenda of my friends did a lot more than hint. "I don't think I can take this," groaned my hollow-lifed escapee. Within an hour, he was on the highway trying to thumb his way back to San Pedro, his parents, and his job at the post-office. His spiritual quest, had been, how should we say this…brief.

I reentered the apartment, distressed that we'd upset the kid so profoundly. But my friends had incredible news to share. They had discovered the magic elixir that unlocks the secrets of the universe, the mystic potion that allows those in psychic pain to descend into the basement of the human mind and straighten out the plumbing, the lens through which the wonders of the cosmos can be seen in all their glory. It was a substance that the graduate Biochem students at Berkeley had learned to synthesize in their spare time. As you've seen, the test-tube twiddling alchemists had been kind enough to make their magic formula available to the world on sugar cubes wrapped in handy, reusable aluminum foil. For this act of kindly sorcery, they were charging a mere pittance—$5.00 a cube. This key to the secrets of a painfully tangled cosmos was called LSD.

◆

I RECOGNIZED THE NAME immediately. It was lysergic acid diethylamide, a drug with effects of the sort that Aldous Huxley had lectured about on the BBC when I'd been glued prostrate to my bed as a sixth grader worshipping at the shrine of the breadbox-sized antique wooden Crosley radio on my floor. And it was the drug that had been written up in *Parade* magazine, a national Sunday newspaper supplement that came with the Buffalo Evening News, roughly a year later for its use by the military in experiments to shove people into a schizophrenic state. Yes, it was the very substance that sadistic experimenters had used to upend the natural order of things and make innocent pussycats fear itsy-bitsy mice. How could a drug that terrifies felines be the purger of psychic pain and the key to Nirvana? I was about to find out.

But that's not all. My companions had managed to get their hands on the plant from which the drug that had entranced Huxley—mescaline—was derived. They'd obtained genuine buttons of peyote cactus—not the dried and shredded remains that Reed College students had baked the potency out of and placed in gelatin capsules, but the genuine article, looking like each bud had just been hand-plucked from the nearest swollen *Lophophora williamsii* plant. And, miracle of miracles, this stuff had the same kind of mind-unpeeling effect as LSD.

So the next morning, the time arrived to embark on my first Fantastic Voyage and to follow Huxley into the brave new world of the cosmic interior.

First, my companions gave me culinary tips. Peyote cactus tastes about as yummy as fresh-stewed salmonella. Some advised covering it with ketchup. Others recommended blending it in a death-by-chocolate milk shake. But everyone agreed, no human could eat it raw and survive the mutinous violence of raped and ravaged taste buds. So I decided to be brave and munch the stuff without condiments or secret sauce. Indeed, it did taste as if the luckless plant had died of gangrene, and now my mouth was on the verge of following its example. But I brushed my teeth and lived.

A half an hour later, as I lay on the floor in my sleeping bag, the window facing the street turned into the sweeping panoramic windscreen of a space ship cruising the galaxies. Strange since there is no wind in space. Below this windshield was an equally sweeping dashboard replete with knobs and dials to manipulate speed and direction. And the apartment soared between the stars, looking for fresh planets to conquer. But outer space wasn't the dark place it'd been cracked up to be. It was filled with California sunshine.

Then I noticed the way the sunlight hit the walls. The colors didn't seem as permanent as usual. They shifted from pink to green to purple, depending on a slight tweak of the control knobs in your mind. I removed the housing from the dashboard of consciousness, and tried to watch the machinery of its innards at work. Sure enough, color wasn't some external absolute. It was filled in artificially by a network of neuronal machinery between the pinhole opening of your eye and the dark meshwork of your brain, as if the busy sensory cells were children crayoning between the empty outlines in a coloring book. And which color crayon they used was something you could fiddle with.

I poked around a little further in the tangled circuitry beneath the control panel of consciousness. Sure enough, just like all the mystics and Zen masters had said, way down at the bottom of my brain was a small source of spontaneity spitting out instant reactions to everything in sight. But each naked response was strapped onto a gurney and whisked through a massive surgical ward staffed with spin doctors before it was spilled, after some delay, into my carefully tailored consciousness. Every virginal impulse was checked for social acceptability and botoxed and face-lifted to fit my notions of the self that I wanted to be. Then it was given a haircut to appeal to the folks around me, sartorially inspected, and handed an official script to make sure it wouldn't make me look like a fool. Only after a careful reworking in the makeup department and a final quality check, was the no-longer-spontaneous impulse allowed to step out onto the stage of consciousness to recite its radically reshaped tidings to whoever was unlucky enough to be within listening range. And all of this took place in a sliver of a second.

So *that's* how the whole thing worked?!

Then I stared at the ceiling and saw masterworks that Botticelli and Van Gogh had never had time to paint, creations that were mine, all mine. I wanted to grab a brush and palette and get them down on canvas. But, in fact, I hadn't been capable of moving a muscle for over an hour. And I'm an incompetent at artwork. Next, I opened my mouth, let out a soft "ooooh," and noticed the sound of my voice. What an intriguing noise! I varied the pitch. The fresh resonance was fantastic. It was rough like corduroy. If I altered it a bit, it became as fine as silk. Modulate the noise a bit more, and it became soft as cotton. For half an hour, I lay there "ooohing," oblivious to the fact that other folks in the room might find this lengthy series of variations on a whale call slightly disconcerting.

Eventually, the fascination with the finer nuances of the external senses and the interior mind wore off, and I tried to move. I put on some shorts and a t-shirt and went outdoors. But I had fallen drastically down the evolutionary ladder and was bent over like an *Australopithecus*. If I'd had my druthers, I'd have knuckle-walked. However, your average hominid throwback was taken perfectly for granted on the sidewalks of San Francisco.

Those are the good parts. My mind has been kind enough to erase the bad ones, but they were legion. Every conceivable demon came crawling out of my internal depths to sculpt its personal hell from the stucco of my conscious mind. Every psychic pain ever imagined by man sloshed boiling oil on the tender walls of my skull's interior. Twenty-four hours later, I realized that I had been given the greatest tour of the human brain in my life. Assuming my brain is human. I had taken the very trip through the extremes of human suffering that Edna St. Vincent Millay had insisted on. I'd been given the kind of grand excursion through the borderlands of pain that she felt opened the infinite. For twelve hours, I'd glimpsed William Blake's:

> World in a grain of sand,
> And a Heaven in a wild flower,
> ...Infinity in the palm of your hand,
> And Eternity in an hour.

And for half a diurnal cycle, I'd stepped into the realm of madness where the truths of William James's *Varieties of the Religious Experience* lay.

What's more, I had learned things about my inner workings that would forever alter my outlook. But I also knew that I'd been dragged through circles of hell that even Dante had been unable to imagine, and I never wanted to take the stuff again. I never did.

That may have been a mistake. Some years later, Solomon Snyder, discoverer of endorphins and opiate receptors, would confess that he'd briefly plunged in where I'd left off, emerging with the "American Nobel Prize."

◆

ON SUBSEQUENT NIGHTS, I would see Carol take these prettily putrid nubbins of cactus and lay on the floor at what were allegedly parties, going through alternate cycles of death and resurrection. One moment she'd be in heaven, wide-eyed at its wonders. The next she'd be in hell's incinerator, writhing with pain. A pain that I could do nothing to soothe. Little did any of us suspect it at the time, but she was taking her first steps into a desperate world.

◆

PEYOTE WAS JUST THE overture. The opera would come with LSD. We stocked up for a grand expedition to Big Sur to try the stuff out. Big Sur, the place that the poet Robinson Jeffers had praised for its muscular, massive outcrops of rocks stretching from the cliffs far into the sea "with foam flying at their flanks." All dozen of us were slated for the trip. Some semi-stranger I never met had said we could use his lean-to on the cliffs overlooking the ocean. We'd stay there for two days.

Which meant that we needed all the steaks and Fig Newtons we could get our hands on. I took the responsibility for raiding the local supermarkets.

To understand how I fed this brood, let's take a brief flashback. Remember how the three murderers lost their appetite when I told them that the smoked oysters and cream cheese in my sandwiches had been transported past supermarket security by jock strap? My career as one of the premier shoplifters on the West Coast began when we were still living in Seattle. I'd dropped out of Reed with roughly $1.35 in my pocket. In the beginning there were just three of us. Later, there would be a dozen. And we needed to eat. Food costs money. We had none. What's worse, I liked to cook. Dick Hoff explained shoplifting to me. I was horrified. Remember the first rule of science, the truth at any price including the price of your life? I loathed dishonesty. I abhorred crime. But Dick took me to a local supermarket and showed me how easy it is to pick up one of the seven basic food groups and slip it into your pants, securing it in the safety net of your athletic supporter. How I overcame my scruples, I shudder to think. But I did.

By the time the Big Sur expedition was inserted into our calendar of upcoming events, I'd gotten truly brazen. I could carry three oversized sirloins in my pants. Plus, all the trimmings, from A1 sauce on down. And I'd learned a lesson. Defy the scripts of the normal. When you're being hunted, turn the tables. Hunt the hunters. Very much like Galileo and van Leeuwenhoek turning their instruments in an anti-conventional direction. It worked like this.

A security guard in a big, airy, modern supermarket begins to suspect you. How do you know? When you walk from aisle one to aisle two, so does he. Though he's trying to look unobtrusive by staying at the aisle's other end and blending in with the Campbell's Soup cans. Once you know he's on to you, do not get furtive. Do not look abashed and ashamed. Don't shrink as if you would like to be invisible. Do the opposite. Walk right up to the security guard. Watch him shrivel as he realizes that it's he who is in your sights, not the other way around. When you reach him and he's fidgeting pathetically, ask him how to find the Worcestershire sauce. Ask him politely. He will stop giving you trouble. And remember something. This worked in the days before ubiquitous security cams. God knows how it works today.

But the psychological lesson is still alive and kicking. Sometimes you need to turn the tables. Sometimes you need to break the frame. Sometimes you need to toss the conventional scripts away. Let's skip forward ten years. I was living in New York City. I'd helped found what would become one of the leading avant-garde commercial art studios on the East Coast—Cloud Studio. Since my wild-eyed illustrators and I all began as starving artists, our studio was in the below-low-rent district, the slum, a neighborhood where drug dealers shot each other with a regularity that subway scheduling executives would have envied. It was the Lower East Side. I was walking toward the subway station on Bowery, a decrepit avenue known for its high-density population of homeless alcoholics begging on the sidewalks. The ones known in the twentieth century as Bowery bums. I was passing Third Street. A hundred yards down the sidewalk to my right, I could see two very big men kicking a formless object three feet into the air, waiting until it landed, then kicking it into the air again. Each time it fell, it made a sickening, breaking sound. At first I assumed the object being launched repeatedly into a very low earth orbit was a sack of potatoes. Then some sixth sense pinpointed the sound. It was not the widely-distributed crunch of smashing Idaho spuds. It was the sharp, concentrated crunch of breaking bones. The object being catapulted by kicks was a human being.

I'd learned in my childhood that if you see a monstrous deed unfolding and you don't stop it, you become an accomplice to the crime. I had two choices. Use a conventional script and run up to the perpetrators of this bone destruction shouting at them to stop it. No. If I came up to them with dominance gestures and a language that opens a normal showdown, they would know how to respond to it. They would take me up on it. Showdowns were their normal fare. But not mine. I'm small and was floored with one punch within the first fifteen seconds of the only boxing match I'd ever entered. At least the only one I'd ever entered voluntarily. So showdowns were out.

What was the alternative? Run up to the thugs shrieking insanely as if I were a lunatic. Even thugs withdraw from the unpredictable. They are confused by things that don't fit any script in their repertoire. And, in fact, at the sight of a raving, undersized madman heading toward them like the meteor that eradicated the dinosaurs, the enforcers stopped what they were doing and ran. Under some conditions, it pays to abandon the scripts of social convention. Or to reverse them.

But back to feeding a dozen hungry drug experimenters. I supplied the provisions for the trip to Big Sur. Then, through some means of transportation I've long since forgotten—some variation on an automobile—we ended up on the wild and nearly untouched shores of the Pacific.

Our lean-to was just that. It had a roof and one measly wall for the overhang to lean on. But the three empty spaces where the walls of a more complete building would have been had a terrific view. If you swung your gaze to the right, you looked two miles north along the narrow cliff ridge that hung out over the beach 300 feet below. If you swung your head left, you looked south to a ridge that swept in a gentle curve and posted a stone parapet far out into the ocean a mere hundred feet away. If you looked straight out, you stared west over the corrugated, gray waves that eventually led—if you happened to be a purposeful and persistent porpoise—to Hawaii. Behind your head and on the other side of the lean-to's single wall were mountains covered with evergreens. But thanks to the screen of that single wall, you couldn't see them. Your gaze was focused on the flat that led to the cliff and past the drop to the endlessness of the sea.

Despite Robinson Jeffers' Big Sur poems hinting that he'd visited the place, it was hard to believe that any human except for the Tarzan who had built our lean-to had ever been here. It seemed to look exactly as it must have appeared before the evolution of the earliest upright creature with an oversized brain, an ocean away.

We opened our first morning with a breakfast featuring fruit, cereal, milk, and fortified sugar cubes…all your basic nutritional categories. The sugar cube's supplement was a tad of extra nutrient for the brain: LSD. Then we took off our clothes to hike down the cliff and visit the beach, despite the fact that your most intrepid mountain goat wouldn't have dared navigate that particular precipice without a parachute.

But we had all the confidence in the world. I mean, the sugar cubes hadn't discombobulated our cerebella yet, and we were in pretty good shape. Granted, none of us had ever climbed anything more complicated than an escalator, but what's the big deal about some measly overhang the height of the Sears Tower with nothing but rocks—mostly sharp ones—at the bottom? So down we scrambled, one after the other, unprotected.

Miracle of miracles, we were all doing pretty well, finding tree roots to dangle from and rock ledges three inches wide on which to rest our naked toes. Then, about half way down, a strange thing happened. Somebody kicked open those old doors of perception and invited us in. The Mad Hatter poured tea, the dormouse complained about being locked in the wrong pot (he would have preferred cannabis).

But I didn't have time for Lewis Carroll. My mind was too busy with Robert Louis Stevenson. I had been transformed into Ben Gunn, the hermit of the mountain, the miraculous old *Treasure Island* goat-man who could climb any vertical surface on the planet, then turn around and spit so accurately that he could hit a pirate in the eye from nearly a mile high. Which is no mean feat when you consider that pirates only have one eye, that the other is covered with a black patch, and, what's more, if you're an animal lover, you have to avoid spraying fugitive droplets on the parrot seated on the blaggard's shoulder.

Unfortunately, Mr. Gunn, despite his years of experience, had gotten himself into a bit of trouble. Just as he'd come to life, his host, the genial and ever-generous Howard Bloom, had done something dumb. He'd stepped carefully from one tiny outcrop to another until he'd found himself on a six-foot-long by two-inch-wide ledge. A perfect place to stop and rest, except for one minor flaw. There were no footholds below for a good twenty feet. It was a clean, sheer drop. And the niches that had provided the path down to this wonderful launch site had mysteriously disappeared, leaving no way to go back up and try again. Yes, I seemed to have two alternatives. Stay there until I turned ninety, hoping that Saint Francis's birds would feed me. Or entertain myself with a three-second drop to my doom.

Who the hell knows how I got out of this? I certainly don't. Old Ben Gunn must have taken over, because somehow I ended up sidling to the far left end of the ledge and by a miracle beyond the powers of all the virgins of Lourdes, found another crack into which I could wedge my toe and start the descent down again.

When I finally reached the bottom, I and my companions were too stoned to realize how astonishing it was that we were still alive. Embracing us was the strangest beach we had ever seen. It was solid black. There was no sand, just round, ebony pebbles. The entire expanse was a mere 200 feet across. The reason? The beach was shaped like a slivery crescent moon— medium deep in the center, but narrowing to tiny points toward the ends. Sealing the crescent off at the sharp end of each horn was a thin stone wall a hundred feet high, jutting like the flying buttress of a cathedral into the sea. One of these walls sliced far into the water on our right and another cut its way far into the waves on our left. The ocean, not content to be outdone by this architectural bravura, was tossing waves the height of bungalows at each buttress' far end, smashing like Poseidon's fists on a morning when he couldn't find his favorite swim fins.

Meanwhile, the chemical potion had pulled one of its specialties: reworking the fabric of time. Enough fantasies to program 500 cable channels for a month flashed through our brains in roughly three seconds. Then we'd shift our eyes in a new direction, and another month of scripts fast-forwarded through our interior picture tubes. There was only one problem. We were the starring characters in every teleplay, which meant we were switching identities at the rate of about one per nanosecond.

I had reverted to my prehistoric condition again, and was walking the beach on all fours, testing the ground with my front paw while my remaining limbs formed a sturdy tripod holding me hunchedly horizontal and waiting for the test results from the probing forward paw to come in. This proved very handy when climbing through the narrow twenty-foot long by three-foot wide cave-slits in the towering outcrops of rock that separated the crescent-shaped beaches from each other, since any piece of shale you put your foot on could carry you like a toboggan into the sea. That faithful antenna of the fourth limb up ahead kept you from accompanying some slate super-sled into the waves. And these waves were not the kind you'd want to mess with. They'd have whisked you to a farewell vacation in the mixing bowl at Club Cuisinart.

Then we discovered limpets. And, oh, how the limpets wished we hadn't. Limpets are dainty half-clams that cling to the rocks. Pry one off, and you can watch the naked creature at work inside, an orange and gray bit of flesh puckering up its lips in the hope of sucking solid surface, gluing itself to a stone, and feeding on algae. I'm afraid we were not very humane about these innocent beasts. We pried them out of their shells, still lip-synching to instrumental tracks only they could hear, and ate them. Meanwhile, the entire evolution of the universe flashed through our minds in an animation drawn by Disney, directed by Spielberg, garnished with special effects by the team that would someday make *Star Wars*, and animated by Pixar. Except *Star Wars* and Pixar did not yet exist. And Spielberg was only sixteen years old.

Perched on the base of one of the stone buttresses that stretched far out into the sea, with waves thundering around as they ground rocks into sand and reached their spray-tipped fingers up to grab us if they could, I had my big insight for the day. I was with Alice, a rosy-cheeked, ravishing brunette who had been lured into our group by Dick Hoff's charms. I was still very, very shy about sex, and felt that there was something essentially evil about being male, something deeply malevolent about wanting women in a physical way. Images of masculine figures flashed through my mind, villains with curling mustaches whose unspeakable sin had been their lust for the body of an innocent heroine. Simon Legrees who demanded to have sex with your teenage daughter or they would collect on your unpaid mortgage and throw your family out on the snow-drift-covered streets. *The Perils of Pauline* with me as the bad guys. All twenty of them. Including every villain who had ever tied a heroine to a railroad track. The self-hatred was on a par with being coated in salt, wrapped in razor wire, then dropped off the back of a speeding truck.

Then I remembered a little Pakistani businessman who had picked up Hoff, Carol, and me one day when we'd been hitchhiking in San Francisco. We were still living in the big, pink, condemned house in Berkeley, but wanted to move to the City on the Bay, so we were apartment hunting. With no money to pay the rent. We'd been knocking on doors in San Francisco's black ghetto all day, asking the inhabitants if they knew of any vacancies. And we'd made a discovery. There were two different subcultures of blacks in the city forced to live cheek by jowl with each other against their will by ghettoization. First, there were the folks of the street culture. The Porgy and Bess culture. People who sat on stoops from 11:00 a.m. onward with bottles of alcohol in brown paper bags and shouted their conversations to each other from one side of the road to the other with enormous energy. On the rare occasion when a pink Cadillac convertible would cruise the street, it would drive at five miles an hour so the folks on the stoops could shout exchanges with the people in the car.

But hidden in their apartments were the folks of a radically different subculture, an incipient middle class. These people shielded their children from the street culture. They didn't allow their kids out of the house after they came home from school. The fathers had jobs. And the mothers wanted their kids to get a good education. How did we discover this? From the fathers who answered our knocks dressed in the green uniforms of garage workers or the blues of janitors. So it had been a rich day of subcultural discovery. But not of finding apartments, alas.

Now we needed to get back to Berkeley for the night. It was dusk, the loneliest time of day, and we were trying to catch a ride across the Bay Bridge. A Pakistani stopped his car for us, heard our plight while he was driving, and invited us to spend the night in his home in the city. We accepted his generous offer. Staying in town would allow us to get back to apartment hunting first thing in the morning.

Our host fed us a very nice dinner, which he cooked himself, since his wife seemed to be out of town. Then he began to drink. When he got sufficiently potted, he asked Carol to sleep with him. He was little and round and the sort of person who, when he's clothed, wears a suit and tie, and Carol did not find him the least bit appealing. Plus, believe it or not, she did not sleep with men on the first date. In fact, she didn't date at all. She had reserved her body for Hoff, with a little bit of me thrown in when things looked desperate.

Carol was terrified. Dick, who was the epitome of kindness, protected her, but did it while trying not to hurt the Pakistani's feelings. But the little Paki was oozing the pain of sexual frustration from every pore. When he had a few more drinks, he started to shed his clothes. First the tie, then the shirt, then the pants, and finally the underwear. His paunch was astonishingly round. His body hair was like the decoration on the Taj Mahal. It curled in elegant spirals around his navel and his nipples.

He began to walk in circles, holding his penis, bleating pathetically, "Why won't she sleep with me? Why won't she sleep with me?" Horniness is much too flippant a word for sexual deprivation. It does nothing to capture the state's agonies. I identified with this man. His was the plight of 95 percent of the males on the planet, but it had been removed from beneath the floorboards where it is normally hidden and allowed to parade its misery for a moment in plain sight.

Dick protected Carol all night. I wished I could make this man feel better, but I simply couldn't short of sexual contact, something I, like Carol, preferred to avoid. Our Pakistani host continued to amble in his circular path. Then he finally gave up, whimpering, and went off to his bedroom to practice the skill of passing out. And perhaps another skill as well. One he shared with Anton van Leeuwenhoek.

The next morning we left, with an image of something terribly basic tattooed on my frontal lobes. Naked, painful, unfulfillable sexual need. Unwanted, unwelcome, overwhelming sexual desire. The very thing that had driven my room mates at Reed to gather like a pack of wolves in the dorm room across the hall and howl, "I'm so horny I could die."

Hunched on the outcrop of rock with Alice, while the sea tried to snatch us into oblivion, I *became* the little Pakistani. I was pathetic and frustrated and I wanted sex. Not that Alice was unwilling. But I'd never dared ask. Then I realized that the nightmare of being cast in the body of an Asian inmate from a sexual purgatory was telling me something. I had sexual needs just like everybody else. But I had been frightened to admit them to myself, much less do anything about them. My image of male sexuality as villainous, something that would get you kicked out of the solar system and frozen in the nothingness beyond the planets, might just be wrong. When I was attracted to a woman, I needed to face up to the fact and attempt to win her over, preferably charming her sufficiently so that I could enjoy a conversation unencumbered by the obstacle of her clothes.

Sometimes I learn lessons with the speed of a decorticated snail, but this time I got the message. I asked Alice to sleep with me. Surprisingly, Alice was pleased with the notion. She said yes. Much as my mind was still in the torture chambers beneath the House of Horrors dressed up as a naked Pakistani, I had enough wits about me to make a date with her for the day after next, when she'd be back in Berkeley, the rest of us would be in San Francisco, and our brains would be tucked back into our skulls.

◆

THE SUN SOON FLASHED a warning that the night show was about to go on. Old Sol dipped toward the water to take a bath, turning the sky a bright crimson. And glazing the undulating, mirror-like surfaces of the waves the red of the horizon, the white of the clouds, and the blue of the darkening sky above. On the waves' sharp crenellations were, guess what? Glistening pinpricks. Stars of light. The ocean was showing its patriotism in a sunset salute to the U-S-of-A.

So back up the cliff we went, finding toe-holds, grabbing on to roots, and hoping that the bit of bush we'd wrapped a fist around was well enough anchored in the crumbling cliff-face to hold our weight, since none of us particularly wanted to attempt manned flight without the aerodynamic aid of underwear. The sun dove beneath the surface to snorkel until morning. The last light ebbed, leaving us to the disapproving eyes of cold, indifferent stars. And we were only half way up the cliff.

With my naked body pressed against a wall of stone and soil, I felt that I was climbing mother nature's breast, and that she loved and would protect me (boy, were her nipples hard). Then I reached for the next root, and with a shower of dirt it jerked out of the cliff's surface. I quickly let it go, and didn't hear it hit the beach for three or four seconds. Suddenly I realized that

Mother Nature, for all her maternal instincts, was apparently busy just then with another of her children, and I was on my own. With visions of the sucking lips of limpets wall-papering my now darkened eyes, I somehow made it to the top. So did we all. Lord knows how.

Rather than spending the night in the lean-to, we took our sleeping bags across the highway and up the mountainside into the piney forest of fir. Then we laid our cocoons of slumber over the pine needles and huddled together. By now, I felt like the puppy dog in the group, a faithful follower of someone, probably Dick Hoff, anxious to be cuddled, willing to be warm and friendly to anyone. Though many of these people had followed me into the group, I never felt like a leader. But puppy dogs apparently have their appeal. When we arranged our sleeping bags so that we'd all be touching as many of each other as possible, everybody wanted to have his or her bag touching mine. I was very surprised. But it felt nice.

We hallucinated the fluorescent sea anemones we'd seen that afternoon in tidal pools, and they pulsated us to sleep.

◆

Two days later, I was sober again, and sitting on a front lawn in Berkeley with Alice. Once again, I felt out step-by-step her interest in me. It was there. It was real. And a pleasant portion of it was carnal. I had learned the lesson of the LSD and would carry it with me for years. It was a lesson of the kind that would help the sexual revolution hit its peak five years later in the summer of 1967, the Summer of Love. And I would be part of that summer, the Summer of Love, too. But we are still in 1962, before the Sexual Revolution had a name.

In point of fact, the vast majority of the fantasies that had elbowed their way through my brain two days earlier in Big Sur were nightmares. Most of them had carried barbs of pain and poison. I never took LSD again. But I never forgot what it had shown me. And, like peyote, it had done what Edna St. Vincent Millay had demanded. It had been an excursion through alien emotions. Emotions that are hidden deep within, guess who? You and me.

◆

THERE WAS ONE MORE emotion to explore, an emotion on the dark side of the soon-to-be-named Sexual Revolution—intimacy panic. It would arrive as I followed through on the Big Sur conversation with Alice.

◆

YOU MAY HAVE NOTICED that Hoff's copulatory dance card was always full. Mine was comparatively empty. But that's compared to Hoff, mind you. Because once every three or four months—or was it once every three or four years—some highly attractive woman, for reasons utterly inexplicable to anyone, would decide that I'd go perfectly with her sheets. In other words, I was a sexual revolutionary who was having very little sex. Alice would be an exception to that rule.

After we determined that Alice was interested in me, she snuck me into the second-floor bedroom she was renting in the three-story house of a woman who would have had us snatched by the vice squad if she'd found out that I'd even managed to pass her portals, not to mention Alice's. I'd go hitch-hiking during the day, accumulating adventures. Then at night, I'd go to Alice's, climb the tree outside her bedroom window, do the last few yards to the second floor by trellis, and crawl in through her bedroom window. Romeo would have been envious.

In hushed tones, so the landlady wouldn't hear, I'd enrapture Alice with the piping hot episodes of my day's escapades. Having adventures is often painful. But telling about them is sheer joy. Then we'd crawl into bed and she'd show me a good time.

But about day number three or four, some form of utter mania overtook me. I felt trapped, as if Alice, the woman I'd been enjoying with such total glee, was about to amputate a vital part of my highly expendable-looking body—probably my head. Anxiety hung me by my thumbs. My mind went blank. I became incapable of a word of conversation. And in my panic, all I wanted was escape. This was sick, sick, sick. But I couldn't seem to help it.

This is when I made a horrible discovery. I was terrified of commitment.

And this would not be the only time. I'd enjoy the first night or three like crazy. Often, those initial evenings of dalliance and lust would be terribly romantic. Then would come the nightmare.

Several years later, I'd discover that it was a Standard Male Syndrome. But that tale is yet to come.

◆

ALICE MADE THINGS EASY. Just as I was plunging into a paralyzed panic, she left a note on her pillow saying that she'd gone to Mexico with some tall black man she'd met that afternoon. "Love—Alice." So I was saved, and left to ache for the lost dear one I'd been trying to figure out how to flee.

Sexual revolutions, it seems, are not as simple as they are made out to be.

◆

NEXT CAME THE GREAT methedrine experiment. A waltz with that stuff was also an eye-opener of the sort that Edna St. Vincent Millay had prescribed. But it would prove to be a good reminder of the reasons to avoid asking for too many dances with pharmaceutical partners.

THE NIGHT MY BRAIN WAS ISSUED
A SPEEDING TICKET

When you're seeking the yellow brick road to satori, you can't afford to overlook any byway. And some of those side trails led through poppy fields (not that I ever touched heroin, mind you) and the farmlands where a profusion of America's pills are grown. Ah, how well I remember methedrine and amphetamine from those golden years. For six or seven hours, you talked non-stop. Not even a tablecloth stuffed in your mouth could slow you down. Suddenly, all the mysteries of the universe became clear. Those random scraps of garbage scientists and philosophers had been tossing in the trash bin of books for millennia came together in a stately minuet and demonstrated their blissful unity. Yes, you, and you alone had the key to the universe. And you were determined to let everyone else on the planet know what it was— preferably by jabbering all ten billion of their ears off.

With a little boost from these beneficent chemicals of speed, how generous you became with your wisdom. How rapidly the syllables exploded from your lips. You were a 33 RPM disk playing at 78 turns a minute and enjoying every second of it. Then, a funny thing happened. The energy ebbed. The well-lit universe that a minute ago was beaming warm rays of comprehension into your soul turned dark and bitter. It spewed meaninglessness and isolation. It flash-froze your emotions as if they were Birdseye peas. It liquid-nitrogened your very core. Assuming you had any core at all.

You felt tortured, tossed out on the barren, icy landscape of a distant, empty planet. Very, very alone. About two weeks later, you snapped out of the depression and decided you were better off never taking the stuff again. Yet you were enriched by the wisdom it had left behind.

The first time I took methedrine was the week it was introduced as a prescribable drug to the medical profession, back in 1962. A friend and I had hitchhiked from the San Francisco apartment that wobbled in the wind to San Diego so my friend could see his family. And what a family they were!

The friend was William, the lad with the Dickensian, ruddy-cheeked handsomeness who had taken us into his apartment on Telegraph Avenue. The apartment so small that a housefly standing on all six legs would have had a hard time turning around in the place. We all knew of William's brilliance on the cello. But he never mentioned his parents. There was a reason. His father and mother were Ozark mountain people who had picked up their hound dogs and fleas and moved to the land of endless orange groves to become Mormons and learn to beat the fear of God into their children using whips. (I kid you not. As a cursory inspection of the Bible will demonstrate, God is on particularly good terms with parents who master the lash.)

The fond childhood memory of whippings had apparently turned my friend into a sucker for devices with anything that resembled ropes, like catgut strings stretched beyond the point of endurance, especially if such gadgets would howl the way he had when he was a kid. That's why he had turned to the cello, in spite of his parents' resistance. Back in the Ozarks there was a pithy folk commandment—"don't get above your raisin." When I first heard the expression, I thought it odd that you should never attempt to climb higher than the dried fruit in your breakfast cereal. But apparently I had misinterpreted. It actually meant that you should not inch, quiver, or sniggle above your appointed social status, a location just below the dung beetle. Should you accidentally stray, clamber, or climb, you were doomed to be turned into a cinder block by the all-forgiving Lord.

Despite this warm family environment, William and I decided to travel on the thumb-express down to his old ancestral home in San Diego and see the folks. Our first stop in the town of William's birth was a visit to his best friend from high school, the son of the city's most celebrated surgeon. As we turned a corner on the way to the surgeon's house, we spotted a newsstand with *Life Magazine* on prominent display. It carried the spirit of Henry Luce, the inescapable culture-shaper of the 20th century, the Wizard of America's mid-century Oz. And what did the master of *Time*, space, and

Life, the Great Perceptual Necromancer, have in mind this week? Splayed across the oversized picture magazine's cover was a photo of a big, black pill, a new wonder drug, or so the folks at the Luce Empire said, a stuff called methedrine. When we got over to the house of the dissection-specialist's offspring, the kid announced that his dad had just gotten in free samples of something we might want to try. He marched into the back of his studio-apartment-sized bedroom closet and hauled out a five-gallon pickle jar filled with pills guaranteed to boggle, tangle and twist the mind. Right on top were these little black ones—the selfsame wonder pellets that had just made the cover of *Life*. The generous son of Asclepius handed us four of these black wonder-capsules, and off we went into the Southern California sunshine curious about what these molecular amusement rides could do.

By that afternoon, my friend had still not worked up the nerve to see his parents, so we dropped in on another buddy of his, Andrea Seroff, a gorgeously elegant concert pianist in her late thirties who saw that we were at loose ends and invited us to stay for dinner and bunk down overnight on her living room floor. About two hours before mealtime, we took the little black pills. Thirty minutes later, we wandered into the kitchen, where the pianist was carefully piecing together an epicurean feast in our honor, and began to rattle out sentence fragments like bullets from a machine gun. Within minutes, we decided to pull our hostess' life apart, put the pieces back together, and figure out her problems, providing handy solutions for each one. After all, who could solve life's dilemmas better than we could? We had reached the age of ultimate wisdom—nineteen.

Andrea's mother had died in childbirth. Her father, savaged by the loss, had felt that his brand-new infant was the murderer. Andrea became a hateful appendage to his existence, an encumbrance he raised while fiercely rejecting her attachment. When Andrea's musical brilliance had flowered, other men had entered her life. She'd been married three times since. After half a dozen years, each romantic pairing had detonated like a time bomb.

Why? Her latest union had been with a man she still adored: a brilliant, sensitive, and extraordinarily good-looking Brazilian who'd begun as her manager, had become her lover, and had taken her to the altar. After six concert seasons, he still accompanied her on her world tours, standing worshipfully in the wings during each performance and overseeing her career. But in the seventh year a restlessness had seized her—a growing panic about her husband's love. Her answer: to attempt its destruction. With only the most peripheral awareness of what she was doing, she invented a swarm of ways to convert her mate's adoration into agony. Her initial incitements were subtle, like striking the wrong keys at a climactic moment of a vital public exhibition. Her later provocations were more dramatic—attacks, tantrums, frigidity, and pinpoint manipulations of his weaknesses. Her husband had shown nothing but concern and an effort to calm her growing frenzy for over a year. Then his patience had shattered. The marriage was over. She breathed a sigh of relief.

Love was only acceptable if it ended in rejection. Her father had inadvertently taught her that. He had rejected her. And she knew in her bones that another rejection was coming. She could feel it. The suspense, waiting for its detonation, was more than she could endure. So she took charge and made it happen. All by herself. Or so our sizzling analytic senses decreed.

For an encore, we untangled the evolution of the universe and figured out how each strand tied into the magisterial fabric of human history. As we were braiding together several mysteries about Egyptian and European civilization that had puzzled the pros for centuries, our hostess remembered that she still needed to buy dessert, and asked if we'd drive her car down to the local store and pick up a cake. That turned out to be a mistake. A big one. Remember, we were on a drug.

We piled into her precious, expensive vehicle and piloted it to the grocery, our tongues picking up velocity as we rolled along. By the time we parked in front of the fly-specked corner food shop, we were splicing broken filaments of world history at such a phenomenal rate of speed that we totally forgot where we were and what we were there for. We never even got out of the car. We madly rushed to come up with the definitive answers to all of those messy conundrums that Isaac Newton and Arnold Toynbee had carelessly left unsolved. We were unbeatable, invincible, unstoppable, and certainly unshuttupable.

The next thing we knew, it was dawn and we were still sitting in front of the grocery. But our tongues, after twelve solid hours of flapping like hummingbird wings, had transmuted to lead in our mouths. The universe, which earlier in the evening had been beaming proudly at us as it spewed out its secrets, had now turned its back and was spraying diarrhetically from its infinite sphincter. I looked over at William. In the pre-sunlight, his eyes seemed to have sunken so far toward the back of his head that they had totally disappeared, leaving nothing but black, cavernous craters. The answers to the problems of life flickered away as the streetlights went out.

Outdoors, it was the murky, greenish cream of pre-daylight. But in our heads, we had entered the dark night of the soul.

We suddenly realized that we were late for dinner. The grocery store was closed, so there was no way to buy a cake. At 7:00 a.m., we revved up the ignition and headed back to the concert pianist's house.

She was in her bathrobe when we rang the bell. But that wasn't the worst of it. She was also in hysterics. We had disappeared. So had her car. She hadn't heard a thing from us. We could have been dead. And in those dim and distant days of the early sixties, there were no cell phones with which she could contact us. So she had been going crazy with worry all night. And dinner had been ruined. We had violated her trust. We had trashed her friendship. She never wanted to see us again.

We spent the next three days in our sleeping bags camped out in the eucalyptus groves outside the fences that wall off the more secluded regions of the San Diego Zoo. As peacocks modeled their latest fashions a hundred feet away, we were sunken in a state of meaninglessness so profound that Jean Paul Sartre would have been proud to call it his own.

Then we finally went to see my traveling companion's Ozark/Mormon parents, who fed us a wonderful meal, the highlight of which was Williams' sister, a sixteen-year-old knockout—temptingly breasted, small waisted, and firmly hipped, with high color in her cheeks and dark hair that spilled to her shoulder blades. At first, she seemed like a joyful, rambunctious tomboy. But after dinner, when the three of us went for a walk, she begged us to take her with us back to San Francisco. Her normally vigorous voice was strained with desperation.

We wanted to know what was wrong. The pleasant parents who had accepted my oddness and fed us to the gills turned out to have a darker side. The motto about not attempting to top your raisin was a clue. Their world was frozen in the cast-iron regulations of a furious God who punished every deviation from his intended course. The least misstep could trigger His wrath. So Williams' parents lived in perpetual fear.

Their daughter's sloppiness imperiled the divine order and threatened to bury them in brimstone. Her latest sin: she had been washing the dishes the previous night. A teacup had slipped from her soapy hands and shattered on the floor. Knowing the Almighty's sense of propriety, her parents had panicked. To prevent divine retribution, they had thrown their daughter on a bed, strapped her wrists and ankles to its posts, and flogged her with a leather belt until she'd bled.

The next day, we noticed a peppy pugnaciousness in the girl. She playfully did everything in her power to lure William into a fist fight. Apparently, she could only trust in love if it was accompanied by violence. Violence like the furies that her parents had unleashed when they feared she might upset their God. Very similar to the conundrum of our concert pianist who could only accept love bundled with the rejection of her father. So the deeds of the fathers do, indeed, implant themselves in the sexual and love patterns of their daughters. And their sons. Food for thought. But thought was not the most urgent thing on our agenda. Something else was.

We wanted to help William's sister escape. But kidnap laws have secular penalties as severe as those of the Mormon Elohim. We came up with an alternative. We would visit the Mormon Bishop of San Diego and ask for his intervention. Later that afternoon, we were seated in the Sears-suited gentleman's study. His holiness did not criticize my bare feet and primitive appearance. In fact, he asked for a sample of my handwriting, analyzed it, and declared that I was one of the most spiritual people he'd ever met. Apparently, flattery was one of the skills that had put him in charge of San Diego's Mormon community.

We explained the nightmare on Elm Street. The bishop made sympathetic sounds and promised to remedy the situation.

Still worried, two days later we headed for the road back to San Francisco, with my friend carrying his cello (and its case) over his shoulder. This meant we could only accept rides from very large cars. In those days, as I mentioned earlier, the Japanese hadn't yet introduced automobiles the size of running shoes, and every internal combustion vehicle was the size of the Kennedy yacht. Plus, even though I was barefoot and looked utterly disreputable, the cello helped us attract drivers who aspired to be patrons of the arts.

We hit Palo Alto, where William wanted to make a stopover, at about four in the afternoon, when the orange California sunshine makes everything look mouth-watering. Apollo's paint-crew had splashed their gilt with particular liberality on the house we were about to invade—a big, white, Spanish-style, three-story edifice surrounded by gardens with more exotic blooms than the entire Dutch wholesale floral exchange.

Turns out an old buddy of William's lived there. She was the sixteen-year-old daughter of a high-ranking physicist from Stanford University. Her papa was no ordinary atom smasher. He had a major international rep, and political connections to match. As a consequence, he spent most of his time in Geneva negotiating nuclear treaties. Big ones. History changers. That is not an exaggeration.

His wife answered the door, and barely escaped a coronary thrombosis. We could have been poster children for disreputability. But she feigned charm with remarkable skill, and invited us in. Frankly, she should have been accustomed to the odd by now. It was long, long before anyone but alcoholics scraped from the bottom of society's shoes would live together out of wedlock, but her daughter had begun cohabiting with her boyfriend at the age of fifteen. That incipient embryo of the Sexual Revolution again. What's worse, the teenager saved money on rent in some distant location by sinning nightly in the bedroom where she'd spent her infant years—the one in her parents' home.

We were allowed to stay overnight and we were treated as if we were normal human beings (which we definitely were not). But we could hear a powerful wind rushing through the foliage as we departed the next morning. It was the mother breathing a sigh of relief.

Relief, however, was not to be our fate. It wasn't until we'd returned to San Francisco that we realized we'd been conned. A surreptitious telephone conversation with William's sister made it obvious that nothing had changed. The Mormon official's "handwriting analysis" had been a trick to win our trust…and to lull us into submission.

We made a few more long-distance calls to the Bishop, and never accomplished a thing. As deliverers, we had failed. But I, at least, had learned a lesson. Sylvia of the red hair fell in love only when a man ruthlessly mastered her. Williams' sister could accept affection only if it was accompanied by fisticuffs. And the concert pianist had been comfortable in a relationship only if she were rejected. Sigmund Freud was right. In some of us, the patterns of childhood dig the canals through which love flows. And those conduits are sometimes self-defeating.

But would any of this newfound knowledge help me thread my way through the labyrinth of my own intimacy panic? We shall have to see.

OUR ADVENTURES IN THE chemical maddening of the brain would become the roots of more deliberate insanities yet to arrive on the scene. Public insanities. Mass mood swings. Shifts in the undercurrents of history. Why? Our chemical journeys were the embryonic pulse and twist of deliriums that would later splotch the world with psychedelic frenzy. Remember, we were marinating our brains in strange substances two years before Ken Kesey would make headlines with his invention of the Electric Kool Aid Acid Test, two years before the Merry Pranksters would alert the world to the drug culture, and two years before the popularization of the phrase that would capture the drug culture's goal: . In my case, where did the call for mind expansion come from? Not from Kesey and his Merry Pranksters. As yet, the Pranksters did not exist. But from Edna St. Vincent Millay, William Blake, T. S. Eliot, and William James. Three poets and a scientist; four inadvertent prophets. Prophets of the gods inside.

THE TWO DAYS OF depression that kick in after you take methedrine are hell. But in exchange for that hell, you learn lessons. For me, it was time to toss the hell away, keep the lessons, and tangle with...the law. As in "I fought the law and the law won." But the fate indicated by the lyrics of this song would not be mine. Far from it. (Maybe that's because the song would not be written for another three years.)

YOUR POLICE FORCE—KEEPING THE WORLD SAFE FOR INSANITY

You'll recall that a few chapters ago we covered the story of Ed, the ex-vaquero who refused to break a bottle of water over the head of a stallion that was turning his rump into chopped meat, and the American Indian anthropologist who had discovered his roots, then hadn't known where to put them in his already overcrowded cottage. Ed's luck with the police wasn't so good. As you know, he decided to take a cross-country vacation via freight train and got as far as New York State before the boys in blue got him and decided to show him the accommodations in Attica Prison.

However, due to circumstances utterly beyond my control, in my hitch-hiking and riding the rails days, my relationships with the gendarmerie were outlandishly pleasant. You'll recall that the police picked me up in San Pedro, California, when they saw me running down the street barefoot at night, questioned me for a while, discovered that I hadn't seen my mother in a year, became distressed, and, despite my exceedingly peculiar appearance, offered to take me for a cup of coffee. (If they'd still been desperate for information, they'd probably have threatened to dunk me in it.) I didn't drink coffee, so I politely declined.

Then there was the policeman who hauled me into his office at the Salt Lake City Airport after I'd grown tired of riding in an open-topped coal car for 700 miles. How in the world did I meet an officer of the law 736 miles east of our San Francisco apartment in the sky?

◆

As you know, I hadn't visited my parents in over a year and they were getting a little edgy. What's more, the pressure from total strangers for a family reunion was carving a crease the size of a small canyon in my cranium. So I'd promised my folks that I'd return to Buffalo for a brief hello in the fall of 1962, and you're never supposed to break a promise. I was tired of the unpredictability of Right Thumb Express, so I decided to switch to scheduled vehicles. Which meant sneaking onto freight trains and riding the rails.

I canvassed the Fillmore District laundromats for another sturdy Clorox jug (the one I'd carried when I'd met the murderers had long since disappeared), went back to the kitchen of our San Francisco apartment that wobbled in the sky, filled the jug with tap water, packets of cherry Kool Aid, and sugar, packed my sleeping bag with staples—a giant pepperoni, a wedge of jack cheese, and a loaf of sourdough bread—left my friends, then headed for the local railroad tracks. If I followed these iron rust-generators far enough, I was sure they'd eventually lead to some sort of freight yard.

At five-ish in the afternoon, I arrived at a grimy, industrial part of San Francisco whose acres were covered with box cars and shuttling locomotives. So I searched for someone who might guide me and found a man in railroad overalls and cap banging giant pins into the couplings between cars. "Which train," I asked, "goes to Buffalo, New York?" The fellow looked at me as if I'd asked what galaxy this was. Finally, he decided to be civil, no matter how ignorant my question might be. And he explained America's freight system.

"There's no such thing," he said, "as a train to Buffalo." In fact, he explained, there's no such thing as a train to any city you've ever heard of. This great land of ours is dotted with tiny burgs whose names only the experts know. But to railroad boys, they are the hubs of the universe. They're the places freight trains go, carrying cars headed in the approximate direction of every metropolis on the continent. At one end of the town's freight yard, diligent laborers in peaked caps take the train apart. In the middle of the freight yard, they shuffle the cars around. And at the far end, these masters of the coupling pin put them back together so all the cars going in the same direction are attached to the same locomotive. Then the whole string of beads heads for another railroad yard 500 miles away and gets reshuffled all over again. "That," my instructor said proudly, "is how folks like me make our living."

This did not make getting to Buffalo sound easy. So how, I asked, could I do it? "Well, first off," he said, "you're on the wrong side of the Bay. Nothing going East leaves from here. You've got to get yourself to Berkeley." Berkeley? But that would mean hitch-hiking across the Bay Bridge, and by now my thumb was plumb wore out. "Look," said my guide and instructor, "you just hop on this train here, and you'll be in Berkeley in no time."

So I found myself a flat car carrying lumber on the train recommended by my railway educator. At its front was just enough room to sit. And when we rumbled away from the big city, I got my first lesson in hoboism. Flat cars are a no-no. Seems the folks who designed these devices never heard of shock absorbers. So after about ten seconds in a sitting posture, it became obvious that my butt was being pounded to a pudding. I did the only logical thing under the circumstances. I stood. Now I don't know if you're old enough to remember this, but back when I was a little kid, we had these electric hockey games. The players were jacked up on postage-stamp-sized vertical rectangles of celluloid. And the board vibrated when you turned it on. The result: your "men" went skittling from one end of the surface to the other, allegedly in pursuit of a puck. But actually at random.

Turns out the same principle applied when the object on a vibrating platform was about 5'8". As the car jounced jauntily down the rails, so did I. Or I would have, if I hadn't held on to the lumber for all I was worth. Fortunately, my arms had more stamina than anyone looking at their pathetic stringiness would have suspected. Because the trip to Berkeley, which would have taken twenty minutes by car, was three-and-a-half hours by rail. Why? The good folks who built this particular transportation enterprise had never bothered to construct a bridge. Instead of crossing the San Francisco Bay, we crawled over every inch of its perimeter—a total distance, it turns out, of about seventy miles. Fortunately, our speed never went above twenty miles an hour, or I'd have been bounced off the car no matter how frantically I clung to the knotty slabs of pine. My first cross-country freight trip would have ended in ground round.

It was night by the time we got to the Berkeley freight yards. Fortunately, I was still alive. Again, I sought out a friendly railroad employee and asked the way to Buffalo. "Buffalo," he said, scratching his head, "well, to get to Buffalo you've got to go to Rosedale. From there, you head for Stockton.

Then you catch a train to Starkey. That's in Nevada. Next you head for" and he proceeded to rattle off a litany of obscure geographic names longer than the Hail Mary's you say for penance if you've just killed your local priest then raped whatever's left of him.

But one thing you've got to say for the service on the freight trains of the Union Pacific Railroad: it was A+. "There's the train for Rosedale," said my steward. "But it doesn't leave until morning. Let me find you a comfortable box car where you can bed down for the night. And I'll have someone wake you up before your train leaves." If only you got service of this sort from Airbnb! The lodging my newfound guide picked was superb. There was straw on the floor. And sure enough, the next morning another friendly looking fellow in a plaid shirt and a railroad cap gave me my wake-up call, then guided me to the Rosedale train.

I looked around for some place to put myself. Things didn't appear too promising. There were no sleeping cars with empty berths anywhere in sight. So, still not having entirely learned my lesson, I climbed to the top of a locked boxcar and settled myself on the ladder-like walkway running like a skunk's stripe along the contraption's roof.

There I stayed for five hours, while the sun did its daily chin-up in the east, slowly hefted itself above the horizon, headed for the top of the sky, then proceeded to transform the tin surface beneath me to a frying pan. I was just turning from sunny side up to solid, when I heard a voice down below. Another workman. "Son, what's your interest up there, suicide or travel?" And the man explained that once the car began to move, I'd have about ten seconds to live. The old vibrating hockey player principle again.

So the gentleman in overalls escorted me to an empty car that had somehow eluded my gaze and introduced me to a fellow passenger, a half Native American/half Mexican migrant worker who, despite his alcohol-reddened face and his ninety-proof breath, promised to take good care of me. Take good care of me he did. Like my friends the murderers, he quizzed me about my morals. And when he heard that I hadn't seen my mother in a year, he groaned. Then he delivered a stirring sermon on the centrality to life of the maternal connection, took a pint of muscatel out of his pocket, drained it in a gulp, and went to sleep. Little did he realize that reconnecting with my mother would be my undoing.

◆

AT ROSEDALE, MY BLEARY-EYED companion woke up and walked me to the center of the railroad yard. By now, I was a seasoned traveler. I poked my head into the tiny shack where the scheduling of the trains and their reassembly was supervised and asked, not for the train to Buffalo, but for the train to Stockton. With polite efficiency, another man in overalls gave me the departing choo-choo's number and pointed out the track it squatted on.

Who knows how I found a box car and went from Rosedale to Stockton. But I suspect that I traveled alone. What's the clue? When I got out at my destination, I spotted another traveler at least a half a mile behind me exiting from the same train. And I was so desperate for company that I waited next to the sliding doors of my cargo car until he could walk the 2,640 feet between us. Then we set out on the long walk toward the center of the yard together. We'd been turned into brothers by the fact that we'd shared a train, no matter how great the distance that had separated us.

My newfound train mate was black. And he was cursing African Americans. That seemed strange. Why would he complain about his own kind? Because, he explained, they were not his kind at all. He was from the Caribbean. And island blacks despised American blacks. Apparently the contempt was mutual. He was traveling, my newfound railroad relative explained, to escape Los Angeles. Why escape the City of Angels? In theory, the place should have been heaven. If you didn't count the fact that you could have cut the smog in LA in 1962 with a butter knife and parcel-posted it to China, where they were seriously lacking in modern industrial air pollution under Chairman Mao.

Well, it wasn't the angels he was hoping to escape. It was those pesky American blacks. "If they're not robbing from you, stealing from you, or killing you," he said, "they're lying to you." A harsh verdict. Why he felt another destination would be any better escaped me. After all, no matter what black community you head for in America, it is likely to be inhabited by American blacks. But this was my second introduction to the fact that there are subcultural divisions even in minority cultures. Big ones. One small clue to, guess what? The forces of history. The kissing cousins of the gods inside.

We parted company at the center of the yard. He went off to find a berth on the train that would take him to God knows where and I tried to find the train that would take me to Starkey, a town whose location even God has forgotten. Yes, a town so small you can't even find it on Google Maps.

This time I knew that I was going to need to ensconce myself in some sort of container out of whose sides I couldn't spill. So I reconnoitered the half-mile chain of cargo from one end to the other. But I was out of luck. Not an open box-car in sight. Finally, I heard a voice. "Over here," it said. The syllables emanated from a man a hundred feet away next to the train. "You looking for a place to ride?" this tall, rather pale, but pleasant type asked. I admitted that I was. So, praising its virtues, he invited me over to his find…an empty coal car.

Turns out my host had grown up on a small farm somewhere in Nebraska. His parents had sent him to Bible College. It was there, while studying The Epistles of Paul, that he had become aware of an abnormal amount of attention focused in his direction. He was being followed day and night. Someone had apparently installed microphones in his teeth and radio transmitters in his eardrums. It took several months of sleuthing to determine who was on his tail. But he'd finally nailed it down. A squadron of Martians determined to do him in had hooked up with the FBI. And you know those FBI types, they're relentless. So he'd taken to travel by freight in an effort to elude his pursuers. Frankly, I found the man fascinating. William James would have been fascinated, too.

The coal car, unfortunately, was not the perfect form of transportation. It was built not just to transport coal, but to do something very clever but rather necessary when it reached its destination: to dump it. But how do you dump four tons of black chunks into a waiting receptacle when you arrive? Step one: you build your tracks over the receptacle that's your target. Yes, that's a start. But how do you transfer the coal from the car to the waiting bin below? Step two: you give your car a floor that can be opened. An opening floor? Whoever heard of such a thing? And how, pray tell, do you make your floor gape like a mouth stretched open in the office of a demon dentist? You build the floor out of flaps. Six massive flaps hinged to a strip of steel that runs from the front to the back of the car like a backbone. Open the flaps, and the coal comes pouring down. Like an ebony hailstorm.

Yes, but then how do you make sure the coal will not come out until you want it to? You put handles on the outer edges of the panels, handles that you can grasp to lift the flaps, handles that, when slid, lock the flaps in place.

So my fugitive friend, the one dodging aliens and at least one law enforcement agency, guided me to the coal car, showed me how to climb in through the car's one open flap, then lifted the flap and locked it in place, giving me my own private compartment. When he was sure I was safely ensconced, he wandered off to find a coal car of his own.

There is one small inconvenience to a coal car, no matter how snugly you lock the floor in place. When they empty one of these things, they remove the lumps of potential fuel from its innards. They do it thoroughly and completely. Waste not, want not. But they don't bother to Hoover up the sand-like black dust the bitumen leaves behind.

Now a funny thing happens when one of these cars hits its top speed—somewhere in the neighborhood of sixty-five miles an hour. The dust demonstrates the finer points of aerodynamic lift. It is sucked toward the car's front. There, inspired by the Bernoulli Principle (in which an Italian named Daniel Bernoulli was sucked off the ground in 1738 every time the top of his head was hit by a strong breeze), the black grit is lifted into the air, snatched by the slipstream traveling across the car's open top, and whipped at over sixty mph toward the rear. At the car's hind end, the dark dust is suddenly stopped in its tracks by suction, settles to the floor, and begins its nomadic movement toward the vehicle's front again. What a wonderful demonstration of convection! And of thrift. The same coal dust is recycled over and over again.

Why is this restless, high speed motion of grit a problem for the casual traveler? It's called sand blasting. But what, pray tell, is there to sandblast? How about you. Or, more specifically, me. Recall a lesson from the lumber car. There are no shock absorbers on rolling stock designed to carry cargo. So if you try to sit while your lovely coal car is traveling at top speed, a strange thing happens every 1.5 seconds. A bounce. A jolt. A big one. The jouncing of the car tosses you roughly three feet into the air. Then you fall to the steel floor, hitting it at what Galileo determined was a speed of over 32.2 feet per second. If your pelvic bones survive the crash—and even if they do not—the next jounce will catapult you back into the air, perfectly positioned for another smashing descent. And here, the word smash is uniquely appropriate. You can hear the bones of your buttocks being hammered every time they hit the floor. Like the sound of the kickball victim hitting the pavement on Manhattan's Third Street. Despite the noise of the car.

So sitting can be hazardous to your osteal integrity. It can shatter your pelvic girdle like William's sister's teacup. The one that infuriated God and her parents.

What to do? Stand. For 700 miles. However this poses another problem. It puts your face in the slipstream. In the laminar flow of the sixty-five-mile-per-hour coal dust. But do not despair, there is a hidden reward. You get to experience firsthand—or should that be first-faced—the phenomena known as ablation, abrasion, and erosion. You have a one-of-a-kind, full-immersion opportunity to experience the physics of grinding, rasping, and scouring. Lucky you.

My friend left the train at a water stop somewhere in cattle country. The Martians, it seems, had figured out where he was. But I soldiered on, altering my color scheme dramatically as I went. Thanks to the fine spray of high-speed coal dust bulleting above the front bulwark, my face took on a solid ebony hue. A color driven an inch deep into every pore. This Nubian darkness was colorfully highlighted by a decorative red strip across each eye where the coal dust had crashed at the pace of a speeding auto into the white sclera around each iris.

Just to soothe any distress I may have felt over my dramatic change of skin color and the requirement that I remain upright for eleven hours straight, the car was designed to provide additional entertainment. As you recall, a coal-carrier's floor consists of six large, hinged panels, made to drop down and let several tons of black nuggets slide out. About 300 miles into my ride I got unexplainably restless and moved my sleeping bag, my Clorox jug, and myself from the front left panel to the front right. Ten seconds later, there was an enormous clang. The panel I'd been standing on for six hours slammed open. If I hadn't moved, I'd have slid out the side of the speeding box of tin and been chopped to Bloom Tartare. Could it be that precognition—the supernatural ability to sense the future—is sometimes for real?

◆

WHEN WE REACHED THE large switching yard with four buildings on a stretch of two-lane highway nearby called Starkey, Nevada, 124 miles outside of Salt Lake City, the transport company's police finally noted my presence and threw me off the train. It seems that out in California, railroad folk are friendly. They provide a major form of transportation for the migrant workers who pick the state's bountiful harvests of fruit. And the lucre from carting this trove of pre-packaged fructose provides the company's cash flow. But as you head east, the sense of economic symbiosis disappears. And once you cross the Mississippi, something I had yet to do, it turns into a surly sadism.

The railroad dicks (sorry, not the name I would have chosen for these gentlemen, even if they were upright) issued a warning. If they caught me on their train again it would be jail.

I'd had it with the rails. What's more, after standing up for 39,600 seconds and having my features chiseled away, I was too exhausted to hitch-hike another 2,000 miles.

To make matters worse, when I stopped at the bathroom of the only gas-station in Starkey and spent an hour attempting to wash the coal dust off my face, I made a discovery. The carbonaceous material in which I was sheathed was no longer a superficial coating removable by soap. It was now a permanent part of my epidermis. Under the influence of diligent scrubbing I went from Ethiopian black to creole gray. But I still retained a skin color that was distinctly African-American. What I didn't realize was that I was about to go through more than the accidental adoption of a minority skin color. I was about to undergo a switch from the animal kingdom to the kingdom of plants. I was about to become a vegetable. But let us not sprint ahead of ourselves. Or sprout ahead of ourselves, as the case may be.

◆

LET'S DO A QUICK reprise. My color-correcting coal car had carried me to the railroad mecca called Starkey, Nevada. Less than 130 miles away was a settlement of far less significance to railroad cognoscenti. It was called Salt Lake City. And it had a special grace: airline terminals. So I hitch-hiked into the town of the Mormon Tabernacle Choir, found my way to the airport, and wired my parents for enough money to purchase an airline ticket home. To them, any way of luring me back was fine. The cash arrived via Western Union in an hour.

I straggled back from the Western Union office to the airport and homed in on the American Airlines counter to buy myself accommodations east, only to discover that the next plane for Buffalo wouldn't depart for another eight hours. Eight hours in an airport with nothing to do but count the holes in the acoustical ceiling tile. Surely, I reasoned, there must be some way to keep my neural tissue from dying of stimulus deprivation. And, indeed, there was. The card and souvenir shop had a rack of paperbacks. Not that I could afford to buy one, mind you. I was carrying a grand total of $1.35 and a non-negotiable airline ticket. But I *could* browse.

So I picked up *To Kill A Mockingbird* and carted it over to my nearby molded plastic seat, figuring that eight hours of browsing should allow me to finish the book.

Unfortunately, my perusal of the merchandise was misinterpreted. I'd gotten less than fifteen pages into the plot, when a rather tall, moderately paunchy, middle-aged policeman loomed over me. His glance was menacing. "Put back the book," he ordered, "and follow me." He hustled me to his office and began a harsh interrogation. Harsh, that is, until I explained that I was a poor college student on my way back to Buffalo to visit my parents after having not seen my mother for a year. The officer's stern look liquified like margarine in a frying pan. The cross-examination turned into a chat. When it was over, the man in blue invited me to have a cup of coffee. Hopefully without hurting his feelings, I turned him down.

So he escorted me back to my seat and said that if I needed anything, I should just ask him. I went back to counting the holes in the acoustical tiles. A few minutes later, the policeman reappeared looking extremely apologetic. At his side was a man in a business suit. "This," said the policeman, "is the Vice President of American Airlines for Salt Lake City.

He says that because of your appearance, you can't fly on his plane."
Apparently, the man didn't approve of my luggage—the sleeping bag
accessorized with the aforementioned Clorox jug. Nor did he care for my
skin tone (my face had brightened to charcoal gray; but my ears, despite
over thirty minutes of scrubbing, were still pitch black). And he felt quite
strongly that American Airlines passengers should wear shoes—an article
of clothing I had voluntarily ceased to possess some eight months earlier.

I didn't know what to do. Walking to Buffalo seemed impractical.
Even if the soles of my feet were sufficiently hardened to step painlessly
on the gravel at the shoulders of the roads. What's more, my ticket was
already paid for. The distress must have somehow leaked from my facial
muscles. So the policeman turned to the pin-striped executive and pleaded
my case. I was a poor college student, he explained, on my way back to
Buffalo, New York, to see my mother after a year of separation. The
executive's glare softened. "Well," he said, "I guess you can fly American."
Then he invited me out for a cup of coffee. I did my best to turn him down
without seeming rude.

Finally, I decided to buy lunch. After all, I had my pride...and my $1.35.
So I went to the coffee shop, sat down at the counter, and ordered Lord-
knows-what kind of cut-rate sandwich—probably imitation American
cheese on artificial bread crusts. The boy waiter—a full year younger
than I—was extraordinarily curious about my appearance: my long hair,
my baggy white sweater, and my bare feet. "Are you," he asked hesitantly,
"Jewish?" I confessed that I was.

His face fell in astonishment. After he picked it up, rubbed it clean on
his apron, and woggled it back in place, he explained that he was a Mormon
and had never seen a Jew before. Obviously, I was exactly what he'd been
led to expect. I looked like a Sunday-School-book illustration of Isaiah after
a six-month desert conference with God. Even the soot fit the image. After
all, didn't the Almighty speak in tongues of flame?

The counter-lad dropped his restaurateurial duties and spent the entire
time I was ingesting my sandwich in dialog. He asked me a bunch of awed
questions, then attempted to explain Mormonism to me. I didn't get it.
Joseph Smith, it seems, had lived on a farm in Manchester, New York. One
day an angel with a name that sounded suspiciously like an Italian pasta,

Moroni, pointed him to a hill on which he found a batch of golden plates. In a three-ring binder, no less. I am not kidding. Though the plates were in a strange tongue, Smith was able to read them through the lenses of two stones, the Urim and Thummim. Just like the book that mysteriously appeared in my lap when I was ten and taught me the first two rules of science. Did this mean that Smith and I were both prophets? That seemed unlikely. Finally, when I paid the bill, gave the generous serving lad a tip, and turned to leave he said, "Wait. I want to give you this," and handed me a bible-sized *Book of Mormon*. I was grateful.

The rest of the trip home was a quiet affair. The airlines had just begun to replace their prop planes with jets. And I was lucky enough to be seated in one of these new air-munching, flame-powered machines. My only previous plane trip had happened when I was five and my parents had flown with me to New York for a family wedding. In those days you could look out the window, watch the propeller blades go from slow motion to a blur, then glue your eyes to the people, cars, and trees below as you flew at a height only slightly above the telephone poles. But in a jet flying at 35,000 feet, nothing interesting at ground level was visible. A whole new experience, but not one rich in stimulation. The stewardess was also apparently suffering from stimulus deprivation. She decided that I was the most entertaining feature of her flight, and spent all her spare time plonked down next to me engaged in conversation. Shades of the days when I got hickeys but no sex.

Thus, I returned to the East Coast, where I would wilt like last week's lettuce, elude a posse on the Swarthmore College Campus, and end up being shipped overseas. And where I would learn that returning to see your mother is not all it's cracked up to be. In fact, sometimes it's downright dangerous. But more about that in a minute.

◆

First, in the noble tradition of Hollywood's better movies, I think we'd better let you know what happened to our cast of characters after I left the Pacific Rim.

Carol Maynard, the woman of the tactile body and the highly trained internal parts, reveled in her discovery of drugs. Wallowed may be a better verb. Whereas folks like yours truly used each chemical once or twice, sucked vast pools of knowledge out of the experience, then abandoned it, Carol decided that the best way to straighten your head out (you'll recall hers was on the pleasantly round side) was to take illicit pharmaceuticals morning, noon and night. When I ran into someone several years later who had bumped into Carol, she had, much to my @@#!%%* sorrow, become a vegetable—probably a once-round and shiny eggplant, now grown soft and misshapen—and was pioneering the path that would be followed in the 1980s and 1990s by the brave hordes of America's homeless…either sleeping with desperately horny men to gain the use of the roof over their heads, or finding a nice soft spot on the sidewalk. She was a victim of The Sixties Drug Culture before that Culture even got its name.

Dick Hoff, who had never experienced an emotional pain in his life, was thoroughly intrigued by depression and self-doubt, since they were things he'd never tasted. Remember, he wanted to try everything on the menu of life at least once. While I was still in San Francisco, we had run into a former industrialist from Czechoslovakia who had fled the Communists, gone to Chicago, become a crafter of humble hand-made toys (each toy bowed obsequiously and mumbled words of self-deprecation when its betters walked into the room), and married a farm girl young enough to be his daughter just to give his fingers something to do after a busy day in the workshop. One evening, he had been lying on his bed in his dingy little room next to the overhead railway tracks when the ceiling had been suffused with light, and he had been invaded by the Universal Spirit and attained Enlightenment. The fact that the splat of light may have been a spark from the railroad wheels was irrelevant.

After I disappeared Eastward, Hoff hung around this guru hoping to experience the Dark Night of the Soul. Finally, Dick's dreams came true. He learned how to become depressed just like everyone else. Boy, was he sorry. The last I heard, he was wandering the beaches of Hawaii with porpoises offshore sniggering at his forlorn appearance. He was trying to figure out how to get back his old sense of joy.

As for me, I'd accomplished five things.

- I'd lived the sort of adventures hinted at by Jack Kerouac.

- I'd experienced just enough sex to titillate a horny adolescent or a married man in middle-aged crisis. Thus satisfying the demands of Henry Luce.

- I'd lived up to T. S. Eliot's commandment—if you have something heroic to do, begin it now.

- I'd followed Edna St. Vincent Millay's imperative—experience every form of human suffering and of extreme emotion if you want to see the infinite in the tiniest of things. Adventure!

- And I'd discovered that I couldn't sustain a relationship.

So by the time another year or two of bizarre episodes had passed, all I wanted to do was settle down.

◆

Now, IF YOU EAT all your broccoli, in just another three chapters Howard Bloom will finally meet the girl of his dreams. But first, my departure from the kingdom of animals to the realm whose citizens stay in one place and kidnap photons with a felonious chemical called chlorophyll. The kingdom of plants.

WAS SISYPHUS A SISSY?

In September, 1962, I arrived in the city of my birth only to discover that my father and mother, who had nearly lost their minds over my year of absence, had a new reason to nearly lose their sanity: my presence. Yes, they were somewhat unhinged by the fact that I ran around the house naked and that I marched into other people's expensively carpeted homes clothed but barefoot (don't worry, I still took a shower every morning). Then I was hit by that peculiar infantilization that disables even the mighty when they return to their nursemaids after conquering a continent or two. In short, I became nearly catatonic. Like Carol Maynard, I turned into a vegetable...an overcooked turnip.

You may know the state. You wake up in the morning with no goal in sight, only a murky fog where your sense of purpose should be. You remind yourself that you are back home, where your folks would prefer a modicum of clothing. But picking up your underwear seems an impossible chore. Much less putting it on. You have to muster more willpower than it took Odysseus to put out the eye of the Cyclops, to avoid the charms of Circe, to survive the Sirens, and to outwit Scylla and Charybdis. But in this case, what you are straining to achieve is to sit up, stretch your arm to the floor, and winch your thumb and forefinger around the elastic band of your Fruit of the Looms. Fortunately in my case, salvation was in the wings. Salvation... and one bright speck of wisdom.

◆

SEEING MY VEGETATIVE CONDITION, my former French teacher, Madame P. F. Hennin (whose name I haven't changed because, unlike most of the guilty—or simply hapless—parties in this book, she's innocent), took me into her home for a few weeks and let me sleep there. Despite the fact that there is no room for turnips in French cuisine. Instead of schooling me in the art of sautéing and making sauces, Madame Hennin taught me her version of the secret of life (which we will reveal to you upon request; just send a self-addressed, stamped envelope crammed with all the money you can get your hands on). OK, you wormed it out of me. The pedagogue was vivacious, slender, and brilliant. I explained what I'd been after. We circle, I said, some source of ultimate satisfaction like a planet going around the sun. But orbiting at arm's length never gets us any closer to what we want. The solution: dive straight for it—that ultimate and ever-satisfying whatever-it-is.

Madame Hennin sat me down and told me Albert Camus' version of the myth of Sisyphus. You probably remember the basic story. Sisyphus is condemned to roll a rock the size of a three-car garage up a mountain. Just as he almost reaches the top, the perverse boulder slips from his fingers and bounces back to the bottom. Sisyphus is forced to clamber back down to the valley and start the task all over again the next day. Every day of the week!

At first glance, Madame Hennin explained, it looks as if Sisyphus' life is a hideous torture. It is meaningless. After all, meaning comes from achieving an end—getting that damned boulder to sit on the peak. Right? But that's, she said, a misunderstanding. Real meaning comes not from the achievement of a purpose, but from the process of pursuing it. The satisfaction of Sisyphus comes from rolling the stone toward a goal, no matter how arbitrary that goal may be, not from positioning the stone at the mountain's top, brushing the dust off of his hands, turning his back on his handiwork and wondering what to do next.

Sisyphus isn't condemned, he's blessed. Every day he wakes up with a clear target, a task to perform, an aim, a structure for his day. Without a goal of that kind, your days are a foggy fudge. A painful blur in which you wonder why in the world you should bother to take your next breath. Madame Hennin was very persuasive. Her beauty helped. So did the fact that she held me captive for a week. Just about the right amount of time for a good brainwashing, complete with soak, suds, dry, starch, and ironing.

The result? I abandoned the quest for some primal center of permanent bliss, and sought satisfaction in something that the Vancouver murderers had agreed that all of us humans need: a goal. Any goal would do. Now all I had to do was find one.

WHILE I WAS GOAL-HUNTING, I rode horses bareback (saddles have a nasty habit of pumpkin-chunking me into the nearest thorn bush) on the Canadian beach of Lake Erie, a few hundred yards from Madame Hennin's home, with her buxom sixteen-year-old daughter, trying to initiate the girl into the mysteries of sex. Not a nice way to repay my hostess. But the rules of the budding sexual revolution were strict. To demonstrate your liberation from anti-sexual taboos, you were required to make sexual advances toward every female in sight, even if she was a cocker spaniel. Technically, I should have been an equal-opportunity lecher and hit on the horse. Yes, Lord, I sinned against the rules of the Revolution. I overlooked the beast and focused on the girl. But things would soon get worse.

◆

MY FATHER WAS IN a panic over how to shape me into something vaguely human. Shades of the summer camp kidnap, the nose job, and the dance class. So he decided to ship me off to Israel, where I would presumably become a *mensch*…or maybe even a Messiah. Little did my dad pause to think that in the land of very little milk and hardly any honey, a bunch of Jewish kooks very much like his son had also worn tattered clothes, gone barefoot in the desert, and barged in on middle class dwellings orating their heads off. Yes, in the homeland of Ezekiel and Isaiah, there was no telling what kind of demented blatherer I might someday become.

Why did I say yes? Aside from the disappearance of the will with which to pick up the tree-ripened Fruit of the Loom that was designed to cover my private parts? First, a trip to the Holy Land was something Sisyphus would have approved of, a goal. But something more was at stake. The going theories of the day said that if you changed the social structure within which humans lived, you'd change human nature itself. Under the surface was another message: capitalism kills. Capitalism breeds greed, selfishness, competition, and exploitation. Not to mention haughtiness, contempt, and bullying. Eliminate capitalism, replace it with socialism, and, in theory, humans would turn generous and kind. Not to mention egalitarian. Which meant the end of snottiness, snootiness, and snobbery. Not to mention sarcasm, cheap shots, and bullying. But was that true? Would sharing everything in common make all of us loving and compassionate? Would it make us empty our pockets according to our abilities and only sparingly bag the free stuff, each according to his need? Israel had one of the few genuinely egalitarian, let's-share-everything societies on earth, the Kibbutz. The ideal collectivist, socialist community. Had kibbutzim wrought miracles?

Finding out would take one more tiny tangle with outlaw behavior. Specifically, it would take a trip to Philadelphia. Yes, I would study up for my trip across the seas by hitch-hiking to Swarthmore College and researching the Middle East in the institution's library for a month. Without paying tuition, room, or board. And just how would I arrange this involuntary scholarship, this inadvertent largesse from Swarthmore? A friend in the student body—the next-door neighbor I'd been madly in love with at sixteen—had invited me down to visit the campus, but, alas, she'd never asked permission from the authorities. So I lived as a fugitive in the men's dorm and illegally snuck into the line at the cafeteria for my three meals a day. For a month.

The women kind enough to host me were remarkably good students. Which gave them a lofty privilege. In those days, a hi fi system was a rare and expensive luxury. Instead of earbuds smaller then acorns and amplifiers on a chip the size of your toenail, we had speakers the size of refrigerators and amplifiers that demanded the total output of power from the Hoover Dam. The bigger your speakers and amp, the higher your status and the greater your manliness. Yes, fifteen-inch woofers hinted that your testosterone level was off the charts. So the Swarthmore authorities had built a dedicated hi fi room with elite speakers the size of armchairs. They'd stocked the room with a collection of the delicate and aristocratic items known as LPs—long playing records, vinyl platters of classical music that could be damaged by a single thumbprint on their fragile grooves.

These dishes of symphonic brilliance demanded a special ritual. If you were among the cognoscenti, you put your thumb through the hole at the center of the record and used your fingertips to hold the outer edge. Under no circumstances did you touch the surface. Your skill in this art indicated whether you were a true music lover or a member of the great unwashed, the ignorant masses who listened to "singles," tiny platters of popular sewage with just two songs per record. Fail in the LP handling ritual, and you were bounced from the priesthood. You were revealed for what you'd been all along—a boor, a Philistine, a member of the ignorant illiterati who allowed their plebian disks to acquire scratches, pops, fizzles, and fingerprints. Just to show how lowly singles were, they didn't even use the going turntable speed—78 revolutions per minute. Like IQs at half mast, they played at a lowly 45 rpm.

So being given a key to the hi fi room was considered the ultimate campus privilege. Only truly superior juniors and seniors won the honor. Truly superior juniors and seniors in a school whose admissions policy insured that even the poorest achievers in the place were on a par with your above-average string theorist. Yes, keys to the hi fi room were reserved for Swarthmore's best and brightest. Oh, and for me. How in the world did that happen?

Despite the low-level criminality of my presence on campus, three of the most successful female juniors and seniors in the place had taken a liking to me. They were the crème de la crème. The marshmallow and whipped cream on the cocoa. The meringue on the baked Alaska. The caviar on the cracker. So through hard work and natural brilliance, all three had earned keys to the hi fi room. But their homework was so demanding that they didn't spend any time there. They may have had a different reason for avoiding the place. Big speakers and amps that could burn out the wiring of an entire city were marks of virility. And none of these women were into male posturing. So one of them loaned her key to me. For a month. Lord knows what that says about my maleness. Which means that I went to the hi fi room daily to listen to Vivaldi's Four Seasons with its growling, angry, storm-inspired, androgen-charged musical portrait of winter. Apparently I needed an outer manifestation of something that never appeared in my visible behavior, my inner growl.

But my real job on campus was to study up on the Middle East. What did I find out? First off, there had been a people called the Nabateans, a folk who had worked wonders. Israel was the most unpromising promised land that a geographically confused God 3,200 years ago had ever bequeathed to a people, especially a people that He claimed to have chosen. It was a hell, not a heaven. Which makes you wonder whether the Lord had chosen us Jews for elevation or damnation.

Aside from an occasional rain of manna from heaven, the Holy Land was punishingly barren. Unless you had the good fortune to be an insect. In the north, the valleys between the hunched backs of the self-apologetic, low-level mountains were swamps. Swamps in which the plasmodium protozoa and the mosquitoes played, celebrating their good fortune on a daily basis. Which means that if you spent a few hours in this insect amusement park, you became the favorite ride of the day. Lines formed for tickets. You were a walking feast. You were injected with a plague by the proboscises of eager mosquitos taking their turns slurping up your blood. And you soon came down with the plasmodium's gifts: muscle aches and fevers. Malaria. Which hints that the real chosen people of Northern Israel had six legs and possessed an epicurean appetite for human hemoglobin.

Then there was the south of the land that Jehovah had handed to us, his tome-toting, stoop-shouldered People of the Book. It was desert. Dry hills. Dry valleys. With rainfall that arrived perhaps twice a year, rushed down the slopes of the hills, gathered in the valleys, formed festive flash floods, and raucously rushed off to the Mediterranean Sea, leaving the land as waterless as a kiln-dried brick. Which is where the Nabateans came in. As I discovered by methodically pawing through Swarthmore's library shelves, in roughly 37 AD, only four years after the Romans had tortured a nice, Jewish kid named Joshua of Nazareth to death on a cross, the Nabateans had made a discovery. The dusty desert sands of the southern deserts were not just any old mineral grains. They were loess soil. If they were moistened, they became rich earth in which to raise crops. The problem was this: loess soil doesn't like to be moistened. When it's hit with water, loess soil develops a waterproof crust, a tortoise shell that shuns the rains and sends the torrents of heavenly droplets rushing to the valleys and through the valleys to the sea. But if you can hold the water long enough, the puddles will soak through the water-repellant surface, and that surface will become your friend, not your enemy. Why? Like a plastic bag protecting a fresh croissant, the waterproof crust will hold the H_2O and won't let it evaporate.

The same slick surface that sends water running will also imprison water. It will turn a caked and drought-scoured hillside into a plumbing supply. But how in the world do you sucker the rainproof surface of the loess soil into working for you, not against you? How about terracing the hills with horizontal surfaces so the water is forced to stay in place long enough to soak in? And how about putting knee-high dams at the end of each terrace so the flash flood *du jour*'s surplus can slosh over the top to the terrace below?

The folks who'd researched this Nabatean trick with vigor were the Israelis, who were determined to make a barren territory (if you will excuse the following word) bloom. Ok, let's be less egotistical; they wanted a barren land to break out in a rash of greenery.

That was the first discovery I made in Swarthmore's involuntarily generous library. The second was more disturbing. While the Jews of Israel were trying to turn swamps and deserts into farmlands, the Arabs had a different obsession.

I'd made myself at home in libraries since I was ten. And all I'd noticed were the books. However, the Swarthmore library had something more, something I'd never registered before—squat file cabinets only two drawers high. What in the world could be in there? I dug into one and found out: pamphlets. Fliers too skinny to shelve. And among the pamphlets and fliers, I found one issued by the Arab League, the biggest military and political force in the Middle East of the 1950s and early 1960s. The Arab League included six nations: Egypt, Iraq, Jordan, Lebanon, Syria, and Saudi Arabia. It represented the official views of these countries' governments. And this pamphlet was official. It was not the product of some isolated crank.

The six nations of the Arab League had an important message to convey to you and me. We Westerners had been conned. We had been sold a false bill of goods about history. Remember World War II, with its death toll of over sixty million? Remember the Holocaust, with its six million sent to the ovens? Gassed in rooms designed to look like showers? Remember the nasty little man who started it all, Adolf Hitler? All of this was false. Baloney, phony, a delusion. A deliberate subterfuge. A plot.

Hitler was not an anti-Semite. He was a Jewish puppet. The Holocaust was a hoax. It never happened. And the war had not been a product of Nazi ambition. It had been a Jewish fabrication. All of it. Why? What were these insidious people, the Jews, after? They wanted to generate sympathy. They wanted to motivate Westerners to give them a plot of land. A plot of land on Arab territory. The plot of land now known as Israel.

This was a bit of a shock. I had had the impression that World War II, Adolf Hitler, and the Holocaust had been real. One of my aunts had lost her parents and her six sisters and brothers in the Holocaust. That was in Germany. One of my cousins had lost her father and mother and her two sisters and brothers to the ovens. That was in Poland. My mother's entire family, the Shebshelovitzes, had disappeared. That was in Latvia. And my father's entire clan, the Wechelefskys, had been wiped off the face of the earth. That was in Belarus. The Holocaust seemed very real to me. Were the nations of the Arab League accusing Jews like me of hiding vast hordes of relatives in our closets so we could concoct a collective sob story? Perhaps disguising these mobs of uncles, aunts, and cousins as shoes? Really want to know the answer? Yes.

What's more, I was under the impression that us Jews had had a continuous presence in Israel for 3,200 years. And that an imperialist, colonialist invasion of Muslims occupiers had arrived in 637 AD and wiped out forty Jewish cities, but had not managed to end the Jewish habitation of the land.

This pamphlet delivered a lesson: doing an Edna St. Vincent Millay means more than feeling the sufferings of every sort of person on planet earth. It means more than just a total immersion in the extremes of psychic pain. Different people have more than just different agonies. They have different worldviews. Different perceptual frames. Different lenses through which they see the world. Radically different ways of seeing reality. What's good in one of these cultural frames is evil in another. So if you want to do a good job of Edna-ing, you have to do more than experience agonies. You have to learn to think and feel like people who see everything from headlines to history and from freedom to morality in a way that's radically different from the point of view you take for granted.

Your way of thinking is not universal. Far from it. Not everyone wants the things you want—freedom of thought, freedom of speech, human rights, pluralism, and democracy. Some people loathe those things. They think freedom, human rights, and democracy are evil. Vicious fabrications of the devil. And that's no exaggeration. It's an understatement.

Yes, the Arab League pamphlet demanded an expansion of the Edna St. Vincent Millay Imperative. A big one. One that would expand my way of thinking for the next fifty years. Its bottom line? If you want to understand the world, if you want to see the infinite in the tiniest of things, learn to think and feel like those in alien cultures. Even learn to think and feel like your enemies.

◆

AND, IN FACT, I would soon have enemies to worry about. But, fortunately, they were not fixated on genocide.

It all started when Swarthmore's dean of men got wind of my presence on campus. He was apparently disturbed. How could you tell? He organized a search party to ferret me out. A posse. One afternoon, dozens of confused sophomores were told to smell my thumbprints on the library's books and sniff my tracks like bloodhounds. There was apparently no room for a genuine canine in the school's disciplinary budget. The plan was to hit the men's dormitories (co-ed dorms did not exist in those days) and comb them thoroughly, room by room, looking under every bed, checking what was dangling from every hanger, rifling through the contents of every laundry bag, and pawing through the drawers of every desk. But my high-achieving female student friends got wind of the plot and warned me. So I cleared all traces of my existence from the men's sleeping quarters. That wasn't hard. My traces consisted of one sleeping bag, a white sweater, and a solitary Clorox jug. But where could I hide? That was easy.

The dean of women had gone into the city overnight to see the tryout of a new play featuring an unknown comedienne in the leading role. It was a variation on the old tale of the Princess and the Pea—*Once Upon a Mattress*. And the unknown female in the role of the prissily perfectionist princess was named Carol Burnett. Who did the dean of women recruit to house sit? Her most trusted acolytes, the most spectacularly diligent students in the school. The ones whose work had achieved such a stratospheric level that they had been given permanent keys to the hi fi room. And who did these students of extraordinary accomplishment treat like a dachshund, a Weimaraner, a schnauzer, a pet?

So when the dean of men's search party penetrated every corridor, coat rack, and inner spring of the male dorms, I was helping out the dean of women, who had no clue to the contribution I was making to her life. I was keeping her kitchen in practice. Making sure it would still remember how to cook by the time the theater-hopping college authority returned from evaluating the humor that a playwright could pull from the plight of an ouchy, grouchy daughter of royalty and her encounter with a spherical green seed and an inadequately cushioned sleeping slab. I was baking a cake. A chocolate cake. In the dean of women's oven.

No matter how many college boys the dean of men had drafted to catch my scent, it did them no good. The chocolate I used to create my culinary masterpiece totally masked the faint odor of my unshod feet. I may have been a failure in other departments, but I was working hard to show promise in at least one field—defiance of authority.

◆

My father splurged. To send me to Israel, he chose a luxury cruise liner. But remember, this was the early winter of 1962. Carnival had not yet invented cruise ships the size of five high-rise apartment buildings strapped together with gaffers tape and laid sideways on the waves. The deluxe ship my dad chose was about the size of a single banquet table at a bar mitzvah. But it had three different passenger classes. Hoity-toity, which bought you a stateroom twenty feet above sea-level with two portholes and a view. Not so hoity-toity, which bought you a bedroom with a single porthole. And beneath contempt. Which secured you a bed the width of a garden hose and just long enough for a small porpoise (though you could use it for any porpoise you had in mind). Your bunk was in a room the size of a highly exclusive broom closet, a broom closet designed exclusively for very slender brooms. You shared this sliver of space with five other gentlemen (or scoundrels, if the passenger had failed to check the box on the cruise application that asked if he had morals). When all of you were positioned for sleep, you looked like sardines packed in parallel in a pocket-sized tin can. Your spacious accommodation had no porthole. Sorry, you were below the waterline and an opening at your level could have seriously interfered with the vessel's buoyancy. In other words, my dad had gone all out. Blown his bank account.

Funny thing about a 5,635-mile trip across the Atlantic and through the entire horizontal length of the Mediterranean Sea. Once you've waved good bye, exited the harbor, and gone out of viewing distance of land, once you've sufficiently rounded the earth's paunch to see nothing but the sloshing of the sea, that is precisely all you see—sea. Grayish water. Yes, rippled. But still gray. Water. Nothing but. Miles of it. And sky. Suddenly you understand why Coleridge's Ancient Mariner complained, "Water, water, everywhere, And all the boards did shrink; Water, water, everywhere, Nor any drop to drink." But your problem is not a lack of beverages. It's the very opposite.

Your eyes rapidly grow tired of the view. And your mind has a curious way of demanding something new to chew on. Preferably something to ogle, to scan, to visually scour. Like girls. But that's out of the question. Once you've checked the faces and figures of all of your 200 fellow passengers, most of whom are retired and long past the expiration date of their looks, how do you amuse yourself? If you are one of the 199 relatively normal passengers, you head for the dining hall and eat your way across the Atlantic. You are like a polar bear prepping for winter. You work diligently to acquire enough spare body fat to carry you through a two-year stay on a an ice floe in the Arctic without a bite to eat.

If you are the oddest person on board, however, you take a slightly different approach. You learn how to go down the eight stairs between floors by reaching way, way down the railing, holding tight, and swinging from the top of the staircase to the bottom in one jump. Since everyone else on board is overeating and since the only-slightly-bigger-than-a-message-in-a-bottle vessel is bobbing and dancing along to the merry rhythm of the waves, this turns the faces of all the over-forty passengers in view a color that runs like a long blade of grass through this entire book: green. Which finally lends a bit of color to the scene.

Near the ship's rear on the aft deck, there is a tall mast with footholds. Passengers are strictly forbidden to scale it. So you climb to its top roughly every other day. The prow of the boat is off limits, too. So when a storm comes along with waves over sixty feet high, that's where you go. You've dared death on freight trains. And you've mocked the helplessness of murderous waves trying to snatch and rasp you into paste at Big Sur. Now you hold onto a steel cable with all your might while waves rear a story or two above the bow, threaten to toss the ship on its side, then smash with malice across the deck, making it clear that, if you were not helped by your handhold, you would be swept away never to be seen by humans again. "I have heard the mermaids singing each to each, I do not think that they will sing to me," indeed.

But you begin to notice something when the ship first sets out across the Atlantic, something that teaches you a lesson. A flock of seagulls (not the 1980s musical group) hangs out on the docks where the ship is berthed in New York harbor. On land, these big birds strut with cocky confidence and search for scraps of whatever they consider delectable. Half eaten hot dogs in the trash or discarded sushi rolls from pre-packaged lunches that were just a bit *de trop*. Then the ship slips out of its berth, and heads down the Hudson toward the open ocean. The seagulls come along. You get a mile or two out to sea, and guess who is still with you, having a merry time in the sky, landing on the waves from time to time and bobbing up and down in the water, or standing on the ship's rear railings when that's what makes them happy, and feasting on the ship's garbage when it's dumped into the vessel's wake? Two hundred miles later, guess who is still hanging in there, regarding your swill as a movable feast? And guess who makes it through the storms with a tenacity even greater than yours?

How in the world do these twenty or thirty seagulls pull this off? In the harbor, they have permanent fixtures on which to stand by day and bed down by night—guard rails, posts, rooves, and gutters. But two hundred miles out at sea, there is nothing permanent except the ship, and these birds spend almost no time resting their tail feathers on your vessel. The water is constantly changing. The waves are moving past on their long trips from mid-ocean to the East Coast. And the air, which is where the seagulls spend most of their time, is a permanent turbulence. Every molecule of slosh and windy whuffle will be six hundred miles away by the next day, replaced by molecules from far away. Yet the seagulls carve some mysterious sort of solidity from this non-stop slip and flow.

So you write a poem in an effort to figure it out. It's a piece about the seagull versus the spider. The spider finds a cluster of permanent landmarks, makes sure of those monuments' solidity, epoxies the ends of silk cables to them, then builds a grid of strands. The spider parses its territory with its web as methodically as a cartographer spinning lines of latitude and longitude to make sense of a map. The spider starts with the permanent and makes it even more comprehensible, even more manageable, even more reliable. But how in the world does the seagull manage in a sea with no permanent footholds, no grids, nothing set in place, and nothing that stays the same?

By finding the permanence that underlies non-stop change. By finding something utterly invisible—pattern—and learning to master it. By finding the secret of things that repeat. By sensing the cycles and swirls hidden within the churn. By discovering the habitual tricks in the twists of the winds and the waters, tricks that wind and water use over and over again. The seagull lives by mastering those iterations in the flow, by taming and harnessing those permanences in the most seemingly impermanent of things. It rides the tics and the stutterings, the churns and the obsessive shudderings, the predictable repetitions with which nature fashions even the most turbulent of floods, currents, courses, and streams. To survive in a maelstrom, the seagull learns to harness the whorls, the hidden structure, the invisible syntax of change.

The secret of the seagull was something you would have to master if you were ever to find a solid footing of your own. But that would take a bit more wandering.

◆

AFTER A LONG VOYAGE as ballast in the bowels of a pleasure boat, you landed in the Israeli port city of Haifa. You could tell that Israel was a vigorous democracy even when you were still a hundred yards from shore. There was graffiti on the thirty-foot-high vertical walls of concrete separating the land from the water. It said, "abolish the military government" in Hebrew. The Jewish protest industry was calling for full citizenship for the country's rural Arabs. In no Arab nation would you ever find graffiti saying "abolish hatred of the Jews."

My mother had given me the Haifa address of some distant friends who would put me up for a week. And who would teach me one of the secrets of permanent flow in humans. They were the Levis, and they were wonderful—a father and mother and two kids my age living in a Haifa suburb of small, white stucco homes surrounded by greenery. The father and mother had come from Germany, but German-Jewish culture has two manifestations: cold, icy, and cerebral; and warm, huggy, and, well, yes, ummm, cerebral. The Levis were on the warm and huggy side. One day Michael Levi, the son my age, took me to a party. Remember, I had been frozen out of every party in Buffalo, New York, including the bowling party for my own bar mitzvah. So I did not know party rituals. Not a single one of them. But Michael taught me one key rite. Walk up to someone who looks all alone. Stick out your hand and announce your name. The other person will do, guess what? He'll stick out his hand and announce his name. What Michael didn't teach me was how to remember the name. One of the hardest parts of partying.

The seagulls would have been proud. The handshake ceremony was a tiny bit of regularity in the flow.

Twenty years later I would use Michael Levi's lesson in sticking my hand out and announcing my name to Michael Jackson. And Michael would stick out his hand and say, "Hi, I'm Michael," with a warmth and normalcy that would have stunned you. But that's another story for another book.

The Levi family took siestas in the early afternoon, a common practice in the countries crowded around the Mediterranean. I wasn't interested in sleeping. So one day I borrowed a bicycle and went exploring. I rode down block after block of small, white, stucco homes with red-tiled roofs until I found a woodsy spot, parked my borrowed bike, spotted a barbed wire barrier between the trees, found a place where the wire's integrity had been compromised, and stepped over the stomped-down string of metal barbs. Often when something says "don't enter," entering is the most interesting thing you can do.

Remember T. S. Eliot's message: if you have something heroic to do, do it now. And Edna St Vincent Millay's imperative: if you want to see the infinite in the tiniest of things, adventure, explore.

I walked a hundred yards and discovered that I was in a huge compound with roughly ten single-story, aircraft-hanger-sized open work sheds laid out along the sides of a massively-wide, pounded-down earthen avenue. Coming toward me from a quarter mile away, down this barren central boulevard, was a man with a German shepherd. And he was aiming his steps directly at me. When he reached me, he said something incomprehensible in Hebrew. I didn't understand a word. So he tried again. He said something incomprehensible in Yiddish. At least my mom had taught me how to say "I don't know a damned word of Yiddish" in Yiddish. So he motioned me to follow him. We walked a half a mile through the compound and found a building totally unlike the huge sheds. It was a small, white, stucco house with vines growing on its walls and roses in the tiny strips of garden that surrounded it.

When my guide with the German shepherd stepped up the single-porch-step and rang the bell, one of the most fetching sixteen year olds you've ever seen came to the door. Miracle of miracles, she spoke English. And she explained what this strange place was. Many of modern Israel's founders had been socialists. And the socialist party—the Labor Party—ruled the country when I arrived. The socialists built housing for incoming Jews, mostly fugitives from the fierce anti-Semitism of Russia and Yemen. This was the complex in which laborers made windows, doors, wallboard, and all the other components of a well-built house. It was a socialist business run by the Labor Party, the party in power. The comely girl explained that this was the house of the foreman who ran the place. He was her dad. He'd be along in fifteen minutes. And she was proud of what he was doing. Instead of bathing in luxury at home, he was cleaning himself up in the communal shower, the shower the workingmen and women used. He was demonstrating his solidarity with his laborers. Just as the socialist ideals of his political party said he should.

Dad appeared a few minutes later, still toweling himself behind the ears. And he was a wonderful host. So, apparently, you can run a building industry on a socialist model. And even if you can't, you can offer a total stranger tea.

◆

MY SINGLE SEXUAL ENCOUNTER during this period of romantic drought occurred one night when I took the bus to Tel Aviv for a classical concert. As the crowd gathered around the auditorium, it was clear that there was not a single soul in the throng with whom I could identify. Then, suddenly, there was one person whose sloppy style of dress flashed a message: "kindred soul." She saw me. I saw her. And our eyes did that thing that almost never happened to me with a woman—they met. Yes, we had eye contact. She and I were ushered to assigned seats far apart from each other, but we were aware of each other during the entire performance. When the musical event let out, I saw her up ahead of me walking away from the concert hall with another man. A taller man. Not a hopeful sign. I rushed to catch up. She sensed me behind her, turned around, introduced me to the other guy, then abandoned him. She spoke no English. It was before I could speak any Hebrew. I don't know how, but we made a date. Sign language? When we got together again at the assigned time a day or two later, we walked through Tel Aviv at dusk and when darkness fell ended up on a jetty jutting out into the Mediterranean Sea. Horizontal. My hands probed for the personal parts beneath her blouse and her jeans. She welcomed the penetration. But, remember, I have the hand-eye coordination of a millipede wearing boxing gloves. I couldn't remove any of her garments. Which meant, that for all practical purposes, she was clothed in cotton armor. We never saw each other again. Alas.

After a month of sponging off of the Levis in Haifa and living with a college professor friend of my mother's and his wife in Jerusalem, I found my way to a Revolutionary Marxist kibbutz in the Valley of Jezreel, where Jehovah himself had once walked like the Jolly Green Giant, thundering angrily to himself about everyone's transgressions. Like The Lord, I was relatively friendless. Unlike the Almighty, I was also stripped of the only device I'd ever had for controlling my world—language. When I'd arrived in the land of the prophets, I couldn't speak a word of Hebrew. And that would be my undoing.

The kibbutz had a solution. It was called an ulpan—a six-month crash language learning program. Every day twenty foreigners on the kibbutz got together for four hours to learn the local lingo—Hebrew. We paid our tuition by doing four hours a day of farm work. Usually it was the work that none of the kibbutzniks wanted. For example, we were given the privilege of getting up at 4 am, arriving in the fields before dawn, lifting seventy pound bales of straw, tossing them thirty or forty feet to the next poor foreign ulpan student in line, then heaving them up to the flatbed of a wagon whose height grew as we sandwiched each new layer of bales in place. If Myron's discobolus thrower had tried even an hour of this, it would have reduced him to a twitching pile of charley horses. But the job had a reward. At noon, when we finished, we went over to the giant building housing the community's chickens, took fresh milk, broke a newly laid egg or two into it, added fresh honey, and had a farm-fresh organic milkshake.

Somehow, shot-putting hay bales and picking more Israeli oranges than the average Floridian family consumes in a lifetime didn't improve my utter ignorance of the language. Nor did trudging through the three-foot deep muck of the former malarial swamp in which my new habitation was located. Said muck proved so devoted that it followed me into my tiny, one-room foreign-student shack and formed an undrainable morass on the floor deep enough to drown a colony of otters.

Libidinous encounters were not something I was doing particularly well with on the collective farm either. For example, the only Swede I'd ever run into in my life was this girl on a kibbutz across the valley who made Greta Garbo look like moldy cream cheese. She had blue eyes, jet-black hair, a complexion that could make you faint, and was passionately interested in sex. Unfortunately, she wasn't interested in having it with me.

Then there was the French temptress who showed up as a two-month visitor on my kibbutz. One night, there was a dance in one of the narrow shacks with mud-covered floors that passed for shelter. Someone put a lot of old, slow records on the phonograph—things by groups with names like the Ink Spots, the Blotters, and the Smeared Parentheses. I asked the shy Gallic beauty to dance. I danced with all the suavity of an epileptic earthworm, but I did have an edge with this woman. I was the only one in the room fluent in French. The two of us shuffled rhythmically around the room in the dim light, our bodies micro-millimetering closer and closer. Finally, every one of her convex protuberances was squashed delectably against some corresponding concavity in my form and vice versa. With a certain aura of mutual consent, we lost our footing and found ourselves glued together on the bed. Then, as my hands began to seek the treasures beneath her undergarments, she went stiff and asked (in French), "Why are we doing this? Do you love me?" I guess the still-nameless sexual revolution hadn't reached Paris yet. The relationship pretty much ended with that question. I was not the type to feed a girl a line. And confessing that I was sex starved didn't seem appropriate.

Things were becoming desperate, and the survival instinct seized me by the larynx. So I tried to make up for the amputation of my only skill—the ability to irrigate unwashed eardrums with words—by doubling down on my study of the native tongue. I arose daily at 4:30 a.m. so I could find time to memorize the Hebrew dictionary (no kidding), including every definition (in Hebrew) of every noun, verb and adjective. Despair not, I only managed to creep through the good book at the rate of four memorized definitions a day. When our six months of language instruction was over, the other ulpan students left. But I stayed on, took correspondence courses at night, carried a small transistor radio so I could listen to Hebrew talk-radio programs in the wagon on the way down to the orchards, and eavesdropped on conversations in the apple groves about which cabinet minister was sleeping with what general's wife. I even listened in on shreds of Hebrew gossip rising to the tops of twelve-foot ladders high among the upper branches of the apple trees. Despite my fear of heights, I tried to convince my unwilling pores to absorb extra idioms and ablatives, and finally descended to writing some of the clumsiest Hebrew short stories since the days when King Saul went nuts.

However, I wasn't exactly swift at kibbutz labor. A charming middle-aged woman and I were given an assignment: wash 1,500 dishes and approximately 6,000 pieces of cutlery every night in the communal dining hall. This was one of the great vocational mismatches of modern times. I had such astonishing hand-eye coordination that if I *really* concentrated I could cleanse approximately one dish every ten minutes. My partner's qualifications for the job were almost as spectacular. She had gotten a doctorate in philology from the University of Heidelberg, then had taught in the kibbutz high school for fifteen years, and had finally decided she wanted to take a load off her brain and wash porcelain. It's a wonder that anyone in the communal dining hall ever ate with a clean utensil!

My fellow dish-dunker had grown up in Germany before Hitler made things uncomfortable, and she had oodles of gentile friends. Germans, when they're not gassing everyone in sight, can be the most delightful and cultured people in the world.

Then she'd slipped out of Germany to Israel in the nick of time and had realized her dream of living in a socialist paradise, which is pretty much what this particular kibbutz managed to be (thus defying the laws of nature that had turned Russia, China, Cuba and several other choice socialist paradises into Dark Holes of Calcutta). When World War II was over, she'd saved the allowance the kibbutz gave her ($1.65 a week...I'm not kidding) until she had enough money for a trip back to Europe. She went to France and Italy, but couldn't bring herself to get any closer to Germany than the border. So her old friends came to meet her. They had all the intelligence, charm, and *gemutlichkeit* for which she'd loved them. And they wanted her to come back home...permanently. She trembled at the suggestion. They couldn't understand why.

The whole Nazi nightmare, with its ideology of racial hatred and organized violence, had been foreign to the nature of her gentile German chums. To them it seemed like an otherworldly seizure, one that could never return. She didn't share their optimism.

◆

LONELY AS THINGS WERE on the kibbutz, they allowed me to get a handle on something that was ridiculously out of whack—me. You recall that at Reed College I'd pursued satori—Zen Buddhist enlightenment—with a vengeance. Merging everything I'd read on the topic with Rimbaud's command to systematically dissociate the senses, I'd come to the conclusion that habits like breakfast, lunch, dinner, and sleep were escapes, defense mechanisms, and that to get to the bottom of is-ness, to get to the tiny pilot light of spontaneity at the base of your soul, you have to peel your escape mechanisms away. I'd tossed regular mealtimes out of my life. And I'd made an unwelcome discovery. Many months later, all I could think of was food. Sleeping on the floor in the living area of a small, modern dorm at Reed at 3:00 a.m., my mind was focused like a laser on the mayonnaise and salami in the communal refrigerator. Walking down the street in Haifa or Tel Aviv, I read every menu in a restaurant window and salivated at the pastries on display in the window of every bakery. And on the kibbutz, I couldn't wait until the bread truck arrived late in the afternoon with barrels of loaves still hot from the baker's oven. When we foreign students finished our work at 4:00 p.m., we would head for the communal dining hall, take a newly-arrived loaf, carve it up, slather the thick, moist, warm slices with margarine and jam, and plump ourselves up so we could survive the next famine entirely on body fat.

The food fetish was blotting out my ability to think about nearly anything else. And it was blimping me. I'd gone from 138 pounds up to 150. OK, I was still skinny. But I didn't see it that way. I thought I was as bloated as a hot air balloon.

I'd fought this problem for a year. Then a solution occurred to me on the kibbutz. I remembered something I'd forgotten—three meals a day. Breakfast, lunch, and dinner. So I went to the kibbutz library, headed for the encyclopedia, looked up breakfast, lunch, and dinner, and studied what the essential nutrients at these meals should be. I set myself the task of reinserting those meals into my daily habits, aided by the fact that these were the precise meals that the kibbutz dining room served. To gain further control over my wildly invasive food obsession and my boundless eating, I decided to measure everything I ate. How? At the center of each table in the communal dining hall were stacked plastic coffee cups for beverages— coffee, tea, and juice. All the cups were precisely the same. I put a cup above the food on my plate, and measured out precise amounts of meat, vegetables, and potatoes. I outlawed desert.

The number of cups of food I'd picked was arbitrary. The trick was to eat only what this new, strictly-measured diet allowed. And to keep myself from going crazy, I allowed myself to eat whatever I wanted in whatever amounts I wanted on Saturday nights. Which meant oodles of extra dessert. But only one night a week. I'd have called this escape valve pigging out, but this was Israel and pigs are not kosher.

It took months of fighting my desire to snack whenever something vaguely edible floated within fingering distance. It took months of self-discipline, but when you force yourself to do something long enough, it slowly switches from a difficult imposition to habit. And once habit takes over, you're home free. Habit is automatic. Yes, you still need discipline. But habit does the heavy lifting. Within two weeks of the time that I strapped the new diet rigidly in place, something remarkable happened. I lost twenty-eight pounds. Yes, in two weeks.

Alas, that was a bit much. I was proud as hell of gaining control over my eating. I exulted in the sense of control that probably intoxicates every anorexic. But my immune system went on strike. And that was ominous.

When you walk through farm fields and orchards every day in shorts, you sustain a damage that's repaired so quickly that you never know it's there. There's a reason that blades of grass are called "blades." They cut. Specifically, they cut your skin. So why don't you notice that supposedly innocent plants are attacking you with green sushi knives? Your immune system is so swift that by the time you get home at night the nicks and slashes are gone, healed, returned to normal. But lose nearly nineteen percent of your body mass in fourteen days, and your immune system may stage a shutdown. So an invisible grass-cut in my shin turned into an infection that went up to my groin. What's worse, I looked like a walking skeleton. And every Jew has seen walking skeletons with most of their remaining body mass packed into their noses—in pictures of German concentration camp victims.

The kibbutzniks were afraid that they would lose me at any second. And not in the way they would soon prefer—by tossing me out of their midst. In fact, they might be left with a hard to explain corpse on their hands. A corpse from an American city that had unwisely named itself after a curly-haired ungulate—Buffalo. Alive I was only an irritant. Dead I'd be bad publicity. So they shot me up with Vitamin B12 every day. But inwardly, I was gloating over what I'd done.

This would be a lesson in the importance of infrastructure of habit. Despite the opinions of Rimbaud and the Zen Buddhists, your infrastructure of habit is not just an escape. It's one of the most important tools you have. Build a habit, force yourself to maintain it, and eventually it will take over and maintain you.

◆

THE VICTORY OF THE diet would later play a role in my love life. But in Israel, I had no love life. Or almost none. As you've just seen.

After eleven months, the kibbutzniks noticed that I seemed to have become a semi-permanent growth on their plantation. Something like kudzu. Or mold in a jam jar. They found me a useful device for ordering gangs of foreigners around, since it saved them from having to use their creaky English, and I could successfully swim through their floods of uvulal syllables and spit their meaning out to the auslanders in the language of Ray Bradbury and Isaac Asimov—English. They also put me in charge of crews of Israeli teenagers. While the kids spoke Hebrew fluently, I talked like a five-year-old. It was humiliating.

But I learned a lesson. Humans can escape capitalism. They can enter a social structure where everyone shares everything in common. They can eat together in a common dining hall. They can have their clothes washed in a communal laundry. In fact, if they're bored with brain work, they can take a year off and herd goats. Or they can be Israel's ambassador to Switzerland for five years, then come back and wait on tables. And they can delight in this proletarian freedom.

What's more, they can have their offspring raised on a kiddie mini-kibbutz by communal care givers. Smart ones. Deeply caring ones. They can get together with their kids every afternoon when they leave work and spend four hours playing without ever having to nag their offspring to clean up their rooms and without having to shop for food or cook dinner. They can live without pecking orders and inequality. The whole thing produces remarkably healthy, vibrant, creative, intelligent teenagers. But does it get rid of vanity, greed, competitiveness, and a tad of nastiness? Not on your life. That's why the kids raised on the kibbutz all moved to the big cities. Life in a socialist paradise was dull. In moderate amounts, vanity, competitiveness, and nastiness make life interesting.

But before we totally dismiss the kibbutz as a remaker of human nature, let me make one peculiar admission: owning everything in common does shake things up a bit. Take the annual election for key administrative positions in the kibbutz: the secretary who was the effective president of the 600-person community, the assistant secretary, and the treasurer. In America, ambitious men and women would lobby, conspire, spread nasty rumors, and recruit followers for months to achieve these power positions, these perches of prestige. Not on the kibbutz.

It was annual election time. We were all told to show up at the communal dining hall at 8:00 p.m., an hour after dinner. Why? The kibbutz was about to elect its officers. At the head of the room was a long table with the existing officers, the incumbents, and with one more person—the head of the nominating committee. He was the star of the evening. After a few opening words from the president, the head of the plucking-the-lucky committee stood to announce the fortunate kibbutzniks who had won the political lottery, the folks that he and his committee recommended as candidates for the top positions. The nominations tsar began by revealing his committee's pick for president, or as the kibbutzniks called it, the head of the secretariat. The lucky man was the former ambassador to Switzerland, the one who was exulting in his freedom to wait on tables and be out of the pressure-cooker atmosphere of international affairs. This guy, roughly five foot seven, wiry, suntanned, and in his fifties, stood to make his election speech. It was one of the longest, saddest tales of woe you've ever heard. His responsibilities in Switzerland had crushed him. He now had a list of illnesses longer than this book. So did his wife. And his seventeen-year-old daughter, after five years in the jet set, was having hellish difficulties adapting to life down on the farm. No matter how collective that farm may have been.

I knew the daughter. We'd taken a bus ride into Haifa together. She was gorgeous. But she was also deeply troubled. Part of it was the fact that we're all troubled at the age of twelve to twenty-eight. But she had it worse than most. She'd grown up for five years in an aristocracy, a worldwide elite, and an outrageously wealthy elite at that. Her parents may have loved going proletarian. But the return to Israel yanked her away from her dearest friends, from the city of her teen years, from Europe, and from nearly every handhold she'd ever known. It made finding herself and her way in life almost impossible.

What kind of sadist was the head of the nomination committee, I wondered. Of all the people to pick as mazkir—head of the secretariat, the president—this was the one man for whom the job would produce the most outrageous suffering. Then the head of the nominating committee named nominee number two—the person his committee had picked for vice president. When he let the cat out of the bag, the mouse out of the toaster, and the name out of his mouth, candidate number two was given a chance to speak. Yes, it was clear that the nominating head was, indeed, a man who would have made a truly superior torture master. Nominee number two spieled forth a long, sad, pain-riven tale of woe that wrung your heart, as if it were a supersatured swatch of terrycloth with which you'd been trying to towel down a killer whale. No way should this poor soul have been saddled with such a responsibility. He was the last man in the Middle East to burden with anything more than caring for cows. Then the election committee head announced executive position number three. Strangely, the third nominee had a tale of woe that would have stunned even Jerry Springer.

Remember the lesson of the seagull? Find the hidden pattern? Yes, a pattern seemed to be surfacing. And nominee number four clinched it. Her tale of torments would have brought tears trickling down your cheeks. Or it would have if you hadn't heard the first three stories. Something was emerging. The prestige executive positions that Americans would have scratched each other's eyebrows off to acquire were considered the worst fate that could befall you. Owning everything in common had turned the tables in local politics.

Not that ambition and the desire to climb had been extinguished. Far from it. Our kibbutz had produced a popular music group that worked extremely hard to win a national song contest and to get on the country's leading radio station. The leader of the pop group had also invented a device for spraying insecticide on apple trees without breaking the trees' branches, a gizmo that had won a national prize. And a few members of our kibbutz worked very hard to rise in the national political party that the kibbutz was part of. What's more, as you know, one had worked hard enough to become the nation's ambassador to the land of hidden bank accounts, laundered cash, starched and ironed pennies, and cuckoo clocks. So the social structure of the kibbutz had not killed ambition. But when it came to the kibbutz's internal politics, oi vey.

◆

MEANWHILE, THE POOR FOLKS who had successfully been saddled with executive positions were worried. By now I'd been on the kibbutz eleven months. They were concerned that I might become some sort of hangnail on the body politic. So the head of the secretariat called me into his office, a room I'd never seen before, and said I'd have to make up my mind: either I should apply to become a permanent kibbutznik or I should move on.

Reluctantly, I abandoned the isolation of life in a communal society of which I wasn't a part and traveled to a city in which I had no place: Haifa. Haifa was wonderful. Lonely, but wonderful. The Russian woman from whom I rented a room rapidly seemed to grow fond of me. It must have been a temporary lapse of taste. I mean, she wasn't just your normal nobody. Her son was an admiral who ran the Israeli Naval operations in the Gulf of Aqaba, which meant he commanded two rowboats and a rubber raft. And her daughter was gorgeous. Said gorgeous daughter accepted me as a brother. Frankly, I'd have preferred some more romantic mode of inclusion. But, still, I felt isolated and forlorn. Like one proton stuck in the middle of a cold and empty cosmos.

Besides, I didn't want to sponge off my father. So I went to the Technion, Israel's version of MIT, to find a job, figuring that the bulletin boards would be plastered with openings for intellectuals anxious to wield a mop in a falafel parlor. Among the maze-like corridors of the famed institution of learning, I got lost—one of my specialties. If it had been Greece, I'd probably have been mangled by a minotaur, and you wouldn't be forced to read this book. But it was Israel. So instead I wandered aimlessly like the Jews in their forty-year march across the desert. Until I spotted a disheveled-looking Jewish munchkin. The shuffling elder appeared to be a janitor, just the kind of guy who'd be able to point me to the nearest bulletin board.

I walked across the corridor and asked the linoleum-hygiene expert for instructions. The wizened soul in rumpled pants and an open-collared, rumpled shirt, gestured for me to follow. So I trudged obediently around corners and down endless hallways until we finally came to a door that was labeled "Dean of the Technion." Why a bulletin board would be located in the dean's office was beyond me, but I dutifully dogged my Virgil's footsteps, afraid that otherwise I'd get lost in the third ring of a Yiddish purgatory. The rumpled senior citizen shuffled into the anteroom, a room commanded by two massive desks, the desks of the two secretaries of the dean of the Technion. Instead of stopping respectfully and announcing himself to the secretaries, my guide walked into the forbidden zone between the desks. And the secretaries seemed unsurprised by this act of effrontery. Beyond the space between desks was yet another door, a door with a frosted glass window, a door that appeared to lead to an inner sanctum. My disheveled janitorial Sherpa grasped the knob, opened it, and ushered me in. Then he marched around an aircraft-carrier sized desk, sunk into the rather large office chair on its other side, the power side, and gestured me to plonk my hiney down on a subordinate seat. I finally guessed that my guide was not a cleaning specialist. He was the dean.

The casually rumpled Generalissimo of higher education quizzed me for fifteen minutes. What was I looking for again? I told him I wanted a job. Unfortunately, I said this in a style not normally heard on the Israeli streets. After all, I'd been memorizing dictionary definitions like a lunatic, so I spoke with the syntax of a reference book. The little man settled back in his thrift-store throne, gave me a penetrating gaze, then pronounced his verdict. "A boy like you shouldn't be working," he said, "a boy like you should be in school." So without asking my opinion, he picked up the phone and called a friend, the dean of the University of Haifa, which happened to be about four blocks away. "I have a boy here who speaks brilliant, erudite Hebrew," the head of the Technion said. "I want you to take him as a student." Then he wrote out a name and address, handed it to me, and sent me off to become a scholar.

By 2:00 p.m., I was sitting in class taking notes. My first course was the history of the Jews in Europe during the Middle Ages, in which I discovered that my progenitors on the Continent had not enjoyed a happy time. They'd been stripped of their earthly possessions and tossed out of every nation, principality, kingdom, and republic the Continent had ever invented. The greedy found them a useful target. If you wanted an extra house, a pile of gold, slightly used clothes, or even small change, you could always expel— or merely pogrom—a herd of Jews.

I continued going to school, reading every Israeli newspaper I could manage (plus a few from France and England), and spending my evenings attending performances of live theater, which were very big in Haifa at the time. Let me tell you, you have never experienced culture shock until you've seen a George Bernard Shaw play translated into Hebrew with a Jewish actress portraying a Salvation Army woman who stands on a soap box and declaims, not in the language of the King James Bible, but in the original syllables used by Moses. It brings up images of that Jolly Green Giant of a God who stomped at dawn through the Valley of Jezreel, the valley of your kibbutz. And that is the very opposite of what Shaw intended. But there was another lesson in the Israeli experience. And it would come from, of all things, pain. It would come from depression.

◆

THE MORE ISOLATED FROM people I became, the worse I felt. The worse I felt, the harder it was to behave in a way that folks would find attractive. My sense of humor, my ability to hold a casual conversation, my capacity to even *look* half-way appealing ebbed away. I remembered vividly what it had been like to walk the residential streets of Jerusalem on Friday nights, the eve of the Sabbath. I had trekked on a sidewalk of cold stone, past cold stone houses with small windows. Inside, families were gathered, singing songs and whooping it up (in a religious sort of way), emanating joy as they celebrated the arrival of the Queen of the Sabbath. They were warmly, buoyantly, loudly together, embraced by a group. Meanwhile, I ambled alone over the cobblestones, through empty side-streets, with the dusk deepening into a chilly gloom. I was friendless, isolated, and throbbing with interior pain. Within my cranium was an interior torture chamber.

One phrase from that favorite poet of Jews and Israelis everywhere, Jesus of Nazareth, kept going through my brain—"to he who hath it shall be given, from he who hath not even what he hath shall be taken away."

It was a pretty grim idea, but there I was, living proof. And the old Nazarene carpenter hadn't been the only one to notice it. Remember that old blues song "Nobody Loves You When You're Down and Out"?

Once I lived the life of a millionaire,
Spent all my money, I just did not care.
Took all my friends out for a good time,
Bought bootleg whiskey, champagne and wine.
Then I began to fall so low,
Lost all my good friends, I did not have nowhere to go.
Once I get my hands on a dollar again,
I'm gonna hang on to it till that eagle grins.
'Cause no, no, nobody knows you
When you're down and out.
In your pocket, not one penny,
And as for friends, you don't have any.
When you finally get back up on your feet again,
Everybody wants to be your old long-lost friend.
Said it's mighty strange, without a doubt,
Nobody knows you when you're down and out.

When you've got nothing everybody flees from your presence, but when you've got oodles, they all come crowding back to offer you even more. What a way to run a cosmos. Didn't God ever hear of justice? What was the sense to this anyway? In the far distant future, that would become one of the central mysteries I would solve in five books starting with *The Lucifer Principle: A Scientific Expedition Into the Forces of History*, not to mention in my *Grand Unified Theory of Everything in the Universe Including the Human Soul*. But that lunatic theory is another fifty books. Consider yourself fortunate that it's not this one.

Being he-who-hath-not 86,400 seconds a day would prove a bit more than a physically healthy twenty-year-old could bear. It would produce 86,400 points of internal agony. A day. Multiply that by thirteen months, thirteen months of isolation in a foreign land with no friends. That's a hefty, whomping quantity of agony.

One night, I went to see a movie, *David and Lisa*, about two kids more or less my age in a mental institution. Something inside of me snapped. I left the theater with the feeling that mental asylums were heaven. After all, the people in them, if you could believe the movie, spoke English...and had friends. So I commenced to have a full-scale nervous breakdown. I felt that my body was turning to water. My limbs were trickles of liquid. My head was dissolving. You could have used me to make a few gallons of Tang. Or Kool Aid.

Psychotherapy in Israel cost a mere $8 an hour, so six months earlier my father had allowed me to find a shrink and indulge in two double-sessions per week. There may have been further reductions in cost to compensate for the fact that my kindly psychotherapist could see me twice a week but could not see me at all. Why? He was blind. When I began to liquefy, I called my sightless psychological healer in a panic and gurgled my problem. The expert in mental muck could see this was trouble. Well, that's an exaggeration—remember, he was blind, and I was speaking to him on the phone. So he packed me on a two-day trip to the Negev Desert—either to keep me occupied or to dry me out like a laboratory specimen, it's hard to tell which. While I was touring the ash heaps that had once been Sodom and Gomorrah and the pillar of salt that was supposedly Lot's Wife (if Lot had looked back, would Jehovah have turned him into a pillar of pepper?), my professional cranial reducer—my blind therapist—arranged to send me back to the United States on the next available flight in the hope that someone in the land of stars, stripes, and straightjackets would put me in a loony bin. Ahhh, admission to a lunatic asylum, just what I needed, a goal. And one straight out of *David and Lisa*.

The Negev was fascinating, even to a bubbling blob of solvents like me. The desert around the Dead Sea was even more alien than the Mars of Ming the Merciless, arch-demon in the *Flash Gordon* TV serials of my youth.

Then came the airport, and the interior of a Pan Am jet. When I entered the plane, a strange transformation overtook me. I heard people speaking like Anglos and Saxons on every side. I was in an environment where my basic tools for coping with the world—my vocal chords—could work at full capacity again. (Believe me, even if a foreigner speaks "brilliant, erudite Hebrew," he sounds like a total fool.) My sense of liquidity vanished in a puff. I was solid again. This was a problem. Remember the myth of Sisyphus and the gift of goals? I'd just been stripped of mine: obtaining admission to a mental institution. But we'll get to that in a minute.

A LITTLE B. F. SKINNERING

How do you find yourself? By poking, probing, and adventuring. And what is your self? In some small part, it's a goal. A goal that engages your deepest passions. A goal that uses your strange constellation of talents. A goal that plugs what you have to offer into the lives of your fellow human beings. A goal that helps you use your strangeness to fill others' needs. And a goal that gets others to value you. A goal that gets you, if you are very lucky, admiration. And love. A goal that gets T. S. Eliot's mermaids to stop "combing the white hair of the waves blown back," to focus their eyes on you. And a goal that even gets those of the sex you prefer to desire you.

It all comes down to the veliger stage of life. What in the land of God's underarm deodorant is a veliger? It's the offspring of a clam.

Think of a clam. Visualize it hard. How mobile is it? How much walking, sprinting, shooting, or scooting does it do in an hour, a day, or a lifetime? How many marathons does it enter just for the heck of it? How many cross-seabed hikes does it undertake? The answer? None. A clam has no arms, legs, or tentacles. No dedicated propulsion appendage. Nada. Zero. The most it can do is stick an edge of its body out of its shell and push itself around pretty much the way you'd try to shove yourself around if you lost your legs and arms and were told to get from the bedroom to the bathroom three times a day using your tongue. You could stick your tongue out and make floor contact—ignoring the taste and the questionable sanitation—and move a quarter of an inch or two. Unlike you and me, who restrict our tongues to spitting syllables and moving chewing tobacco from one cheek to another, some clams are so good at this lingual propulsion that they can shoot themselves three feet in an emergency. With a flick of the tongue and a spit of water. But long marches like the twenty-five miles a day tromped by Napoleon's troops would be just a tad out of the question. So the clam is the very picture of immobility. It counts on food coming to it, not the other way around.

Meanwhile, what sort of children do clams crank out? By the tens of millions? Do they cough out kids as frozen in place as the Washington Monument? Not on your life. The clams' kids are the very opposite of their parents. They have tiny whips that work like propellers. A ring of these whips girdles each baby's body. And that girdle is designed for zipping, speeding, and racing—it's built for non-stop swimming. It's built for transport. Yes, the lucky veliger wears a propulsion girdle, a racing corset. Why? A baby clam has a problem—finding its place in life. Literally. Finding a spot in which it can settle down and feed. A spot so rich that the food will come to it, almost begging to be swallowed. A spot whose food supply will last a lifetime.

So a veliger is built to find its fortune by adventuring. And its adventures will be dangerous. On its wild scoot to find a home, it will be regarded as a tasty morsel by just about every ravenous creature of the sea. Look up pretty much any ocean animal in your thirteen-volume Grzimek's *Animal Life Encyclopedia*. I kid you not. There is such a thing. Started by German zoologist and zoo-director Bernhard Klemens Maria Grzimek in Frankfurt in 1967—yes, in The Sixties. Apparently, Grzimek studied animals instead of people because creatures with fur and fins didn't constantly mispronounce his name. Dig into Grzimek's massive reference set. Look up a water-living animal. Any water-living animal. Let's say the baleen whale. The baleen whale is named for a massive screening apparatus in its mouth, a huge sieve like the grill of a car. And in the same way that the grill of your car picks up many a splatted insect if you take a long drive—let's say to visit a tornado factory in Kansas—the mouth-screen of a baleen whale picks up plankton.

What is plankton? It's clouds of foodstuff composed of microscopic creatures. Yes, plankton is made up of creatures as individual as you and me. Creatures just as focused as you and I are on survival. And how does nature reward this microorganismic lust for life? This zest for dodging pains and tasting pleasures, for feasting, flitting, and fleeing? She turns so many septillions of her enthusiastic micro-children into sacrificial victims that she can feed a 210-ton whale. Actually, she offers up the lives of so many micro-beasts that she can feed roughly a million 210-ton baleen whales. Plus, a vast passel of other water-cruising beasts. Nature is kindly and caring, isn't she?

If you are a veliger—the young infant of a clam—you are a speck in one of these clouds of plankton. You are a pixel, a zit. So if you are going to find a place to settle down, you have to dodge an almost impossible obstacle— becoming an ingredient in a protein drink for a vast zoo of aquatic smoothie addicts out for a bite to drink.

In other words, the veliger stage of life is tough. The only way you can find where you belong is by adventuring, by doing the clam equivalent of a T. S. Eliot and an Edna St. Vincent Millay. But under it all is a purpose. To find a place where you can settle down. A place set apart from the location in which your mother and father have found their homes. A place that will fit your needs and feed you. From now until the time you die.

Clams are not alone. We humans go through the veliger stage. Alas, without the propulsion belt. We start it when we are eleven or twelve as our hormones kick in and we begin to toss ourselves out of our parents' home. What our friends think of us becomes more important than the opinion of our mom and dad. What's worse, our parents come to smell bad to us. And our armpit odors become unendurable to them. In other words, our biology is telling us it's time to go. And we don't end the veliger stage until our twenties or early thirties when we find an occupation and a mate and set up a home of our own. Which means that two goals underlie our wild meanderings: finding a mate and discovering a place where we belong.

And under my adventures, though I didn't know it, were these biological imperatives—to find a mate and a place where I fit. Two goals on which I'd make giant steps of progress just a bit further down the line. But first...

I was still in the veliger stage. Poking, probing, scooting, and shooting to find a place where I was welcome, a place where I might fit in. A place where I wouldn't be eaten alive. I would do a good deal of that hunting and adventuring in, of all places, New Jersey.

◆

WHEN I TOUCHED DOWN in the USA, I tried to arrange things so that there'd be several hundred miles separating me from my parents. You recall that when I got anywhere near them, my identity mysteriously disappeared, my backbone went limp, and I turned into an overcooked egg noodle. I'd tell you that I softened and sagged like a boiled leaf of spinach, but I've run out of vegetable metaphors.

It would take years for my feeble mind to rearrange itself in such a way as to realize that my parents were human just like I was and, in fact, they were even shorter. Meanwhile a New Jersey cousin offered to take me in. So I moved my sleeping bag into his garden apartment in Somerville, New Jersey, with his wife and infant daughter.

Which brings us back to Sisyphus. You recall that I'd gotten to America with only one goal in mind—obtaining entrance to a mental institution. This was a problem. On the plane from Israel, my liquefaction had ended and I'd become somewhat solid again. Which means I was a rough approximation of sane. Very rough. This was disconcerting. I'd get on the ferry from New Jersey to New York City day after day. I'd trudge around Manhattan, seeing shrink after shrink after shrink. And each one would conclude that there was no question about it—I was a little odd. But there wasn't a single way in hell that I was institutionalizable. My only goal was totally thwarted, and I was in danger of falling back into the existential pit of emotional poison—the void. The emptiness devoid of goals. The foggy hell of *angst* and anomie.

Then the cousin in New Jersey, let's call him Len Kuker, since that, believe it or not, is his real name, cooked up something even better than a home for the mentally deranged: Rutgers University's Graduate School of Education in New Brunswick, New Jersey.

◆

COUSIN LEN WAS TEACHING high school, taking grad-school-of-education night courses, teaching himself how to chart stocks, raising his six-month-old, and bossing around his Holocaust-surviving young wife. She'd been one of those Polish infants adopted by Catholic farmers, generous people of the soil who pretended she was a Christian haystack. Len not only had astonishing family loyalty and acted as my savior, but possessed the ability to convince an Eskimo to buy a lifetime subscription to the Ice Cube of the

Month Club. So Len persuaded the head of Rutgers Graduate School of Education to take me in as a sort of spare paper weight around the office. The department head, Dr. Merrill Harmon, one of the founders of an educational approach called "values clarification," took me into his office, gave me space to work, said I could do anything I wanted, and tossed a few books by Piaget and B. F. Skinner at me. He clearly didn't realize that I can't catch. Then Dr. Harmon let me loose in the domain of advanced academia. So I found myself quite by accident doing research at Rutgers University's Graduate School of Education.

I soon discovered that I had stumbled into a termite nest where the foundations of the American educational system were being eaten away. I read the books my professorial mentor and the mentor's friends were using as texts. None of them taught facts. This wasn't surprising. All proclaimed that facts were insidious obstacles to learning. Students didn't need information, they needed to learn how to *think*. Little did it occur to the featherheads who wrote these enlightened tomes that without facts you *can't* think.

Look, for example, at the guys who wrote the Constitution and the *Federalist Papers*. Great thinkers, every one of them. How did they do it? They knew their history—especially the history of ancient Greece and Rome. They reasoned their principles—from the balance of powers on up—by deducing lessons from a vast store of historical data. Facts, ma'am, nothing but the facts.

But the folks who'd written the revolutionary new bibles of education had never read the *Federalist Papers*. In fact, I got the distinct impression they'd never read much beyond Dick and Jane. Oh, and a few tomes on psychotherapy. Which means that I was afraid that Rutgers' Graduate School of Education's gullible professors, who were exceptionally kind to me, were not exactly towering literati.

What did values clarification suggest that you insert where the facts should have been? A positive self-image. Thus was a new breed of teacher brought into being.

I was a little shocked by all this. I was even more shocked when my department head benefactor took me to one of his classes. Remember, I was a college dropout who hadn't even finished my freshman year. I was seated in a room with grad students many years my elder. Yet most of them had heads filled with feathers. If you wanted a pool of good-natured, well-intentioned humans too ill-informed to succeed even in a career as hotel pillows, all you had to do was draft the entire graduate student body from Rutgers' Graduate School of Education.

However, the notion that facts were the enemy of education was perfect for these poor souls. After all, they didn't KNOW any. Except maybe how to drive a car from their home to the shopping center to buy a suit from Robert Hall—the McDonald's of early 1960s tailoring.

Thirty years later, in the 1990s, a series of articles would appear in journals in cross-cultural psychology. What would they show? American kids had miserable test scores in science and mathematics. Somewhere around fifteenth in the world. Japanese and Korean students, on the other hand, had fantastic scores in science and math. They led the kids of all other nations. What was the difference between us and them? Japanese and Korean kids had lowly, miserable, appalling self-images. A tiny number even committed suicide when they got mere B's on exams. So they kicked themselves mercilessly to achieve. American kids, on the other hand, had high-flying, weather-ballooning, soaring self-images. They didn't have to tackle the impossible. They were already perfect.

Any good thing in excess can be a poison. And Dr. Harmon's positive self-image was poisoning American students.

Apparently, the quality of teachers and what they're taught hasn't changed much since those dim and distant days of 1963 and 1964 at Rutgers. No wonder we've had half a century of youngsters with heads so empty you could fill them with helium and send them into the stratosphere. Their teachers were trained to use bilge pumps on their brains!

◆

ONE BIOLOGICALLY IMPLANTED GOAL of the veliger stage of life in us humans is the imperative to find a mate. Veligers do not have this problem. When they grow up, become clams, and settle down, they send out sperm or eggs. Then they let their sperm and eggs take care of mixing, dating, and mating. Yes, clams outsource romance to a generation that's too young to know better. Cruel, right? But we humans wait until we hit puberty and it hits back. That's when the dark force of biology sends us out to find either a companion who can last a reasonable facsimile of a lifetime, or sex, whichever comes first. In fact, we become so obsessed with this hunt that we listen to songs about it, watch movies about it, read novels about it, soak in ads about it, dream about it, cream about it, and use 90 percent of our waking and sleeping brainpower on it. Clams let their sperm and eggs do this legwork. Human sperm and eggs turn the legwork over to you and me. Not to mention turning over the agony. And the brief seconds of ecstasy, if you are lucky enough to have any.

The result was simple. I entertained myself at Rutgers in a variety of ways designed to help me meet girls. Unfortunately, none of my clever ploys worked.

It all began with the books Merrill Harmon had tossed at me. Piaget was fashionable and mildly interesting, but didn't kindle a fire. B. F. Skinner did. Which is strange. You'd think it would have been the other way around. As an Edna St. Vincent Millay acolyte, I was on a quest for the extremes of passion and soul. Not to mention the gods inside. Surely Piaget, with his focus on humans, should have lit a fire in my heart. But it was Skinner who grabbed me. Skinner and his pigeons. Why?

What was Jean Piaget all about? The Swiss psychologist was looking for the stages that our reasoning ability goes through as our brain goes from baby to toddler to teenager. For example, take two identical pints of water. Show them to a child. Ask if each of your measuring cups contains the same amount of water. The child will generally say yes. Now pour one of your pints of water into a tall, skinny laboratory beaker. Pour another into a flat, pizza-sized petri dish. Suddenly the two pools of water look very different. One is flat, shallow, and close to the ground. It's short and humble. The other is tall, slim, and imposing. At what point in a child's life does it realize that the two pools of water may look very different, but that the amount of water in each piece of glassware is still precisely the same? Piaget tried to answer questions like this by observing such things in real, live, tripping, smiling, crying, and cookie-loving children. What's more, Piaget was all the rage. And, for whatever reason, wildly popular things were not attractive to me. They still are not. I liked to dive off the beaten track and head for the strange.

B. F. Skinner, on the other hand, was doing things that seemed inhuman. Which should have had less appeal. I mean, he was teaching pigeons to do circus tricks by rewarding them with appallingly dull-looking food pellets. In fact, he managed to teach pigeons to play ping pong. He even taught them how to read. No kidding. Check it out on the Smithsonian's B. F. Skinner website. Skinner was accomplishing this bit of bird-showmanship with what he called "successive approximation." Let's say he wanted you, a pigeon, to climb a pigeon-sized ladder. Every time you moved in the direction of the ladder, Skinner rewarded you with a food pellet. Soon you were moving in the direction of the ladder on a regular basis. Once you'd learned to walk all the way to the ladder, Skinner waited. He waited until you flapped and fluttered by random on to the ladder's first rung. Then, finally, he rewarded you. Step by step, he very carefully paid you off until you'd gotten the hang of the whole maneuver that Skinner wanted from you—walking over to the ladder and climbing to its top. Then waiting for applause. Applause and another food pellet.

But there was something far more interesting in B. F. Skinner's bag of pigeon tricks. The Harvard psychology professor had motivated pigeons to create strange rituals by varying the ways in which he rewarded them with food. Yes, Skinner was getting feathered bread-crumb-and-pellet lovers to create rituals, to develop the avian equivalent of superstitions. Maybe even to generate the bird-brained equivalent of religion.

Let's put you in the position once again of the pigeon. Skinner would reward you at random. So you tried to find a pattern in the arbitrary deliveries of food. Yes, pigeons, like humans and seagulls, are pattern finders. If you hopped on your left foot then food arrived, you'd continue to hop on your left foot to bring the next bit of food raining down from the sky—or from the feeding-chute. You hopped and hopped and hopped. That's faith. Finally, food arrived. Proof positive that hopping on your left foot worked. What's more, if you lifted your right wing for a second, then another bit of tasty treat came tumbling down the chute, you added the right wing maneuver to your left-foot hopping routine. And so on. You were so persistent in your ritual that eventually, while you were performing it the twentieth or the two hundredth time, food arrived. Absolute proof that your dance controlled the food supply.

Yes, you, a mere pigeon, a creature with a bird brain, invented a ritual to bring the food pellets your way. You invented a tool with which to control your fate. What you failed to see was that the pellets arrived at random. There was no pattern.

Skinner implied that religions are similar dances. Dances we humans do to control uncontrollable events. Dances we become devoted to because every great once in a while after we finish the dance, the reward we desire arrives. Which convinces us that our dances coax the reward to appear. Even though the dances—or the prayers, the church services, the gerbil sacrifices, the poisonous snakes coiling around your neck, the all-night ceremonies with sacred masks, or the readings from the good book—have nothing to do with it. And even though church buses on their way to prayer conferences with fifty of the faithful all busy practicing their supplications to the Almighty have a nasty habit of going over cliffs.

One more thing. B.F. Skinner had created an educational invention he called "programmed learning." And it was brilliant. Programmed learning was very simple. You take a topic, any topic. You break it up into a series of simple facts explained in short paragraphs. Paragraphs so simple and vivid that anyone with a brain moderately above that of your average pigeon can grasp them. You put one paragraph with one simple idea on a page. At the end of the page, you put a one-question quiz to test whether the reader understands the concept. If she does, you let her go on to the next page. But here's the real trick.

You test what you've written on some poor, innocent, passing person who knows nothing about the topic you are trying to teach. If that unwitting civilian fails on any page of what you've written, if she gets the answer wrong, you do not consider it the failure of the person plowing through your programmed learning booklet. You considered it the failure of the page. You consider it *your* failure. So you go back and rewrite the offending paragraph. You simplify, break it into two pages, give a more vivid example, whatever it takes. After twenty or more tests and twenty or more revisions, you finally refine your material to the point where just about anyone with the brainpower to walk from one college building to another in search of a Reese's Peanut Butter Cup can whiz through it.

Where do pigeons come into this?

Remember the quick quiz at the bottom of each page? You refine your booklet until everyone who goes through it gets every answer right. Getting the answer right after each paragraph is the food pellet. It's the reward. Getting the answer right engages the mind of your reader. And it makes her feel good about herself. Who can resist demonstrating omniscience and being patted on the head for it forty times in a forty page pamphlet?

One more thing. Programmed learning demanded that the writer of a programmed learning pamphlet do exactly what Albert Einstein had called for—writing even the most complex concept so clearly that anyone with a high school education and a reasonable degree of intelligence could understand it. And could get a kick out of it.

So I took an existing book on the most boring topic I could find—the various forms of electrical circuits and their official names—and rewrote it as a series of simple pages with quizzes at the end of each, then tested it on as many kindly subjects as I could ensnare. I perfected it to the point where everyone who went through it got every quiz question right. Then I went off to meet girls.

In those days, Rutgers had a girls' college—Douglass College—whose campus was right down the street. That's where I did my testing. Every girl who went through the short programmed learning booklet ended up an expert. She became adept at naming the various forms of copper wire connections that shuttle electrons. Programmed learning, it turned out, was a dynamite tool for hammering impossible-to-remember facts into Teflon-coated gray matter. Like mine. And possibly yours. Thus did the young women of Douglass College allow me to discombobulate their brains. But, alas, not a single research subject invited me to discombobulate her body.

Programmed learning may have been working brilliantly, but my girl hunt was getting desperate. So desperate that I actually played *four* parts in a Douglass College production of George Bernard Shaw's play *Caesar and Cleopatra*. Surely this would allow me to meet a girl or two. Right? Well, not exactly. The costume lady couldn't find a tunic long enough for me in the act where I played a Roman guard. All I was wearing was a jock strap under my microscopic toga, and, since I had to perform most of the part with my back to the audience and the wind of the outdoor stage lifted my skirt at least fifteen times, I provided one of the first bottomless male exhibitions seen onstage in the Garden State. Unfortunately, that was before women realized they were supposed to reward such spectacles by rushing the semi-disrobed male and stuffing money and as many fingers as they could fit into his G-string.

My veliger wandering was not working out. I was not coming up with a mate. And I was not discovering my place. Or was I?

◆

PERSISTENCE IS THE KEY to everything in life. I finally got so desperate that I edited official reports on psychological symposia for the head of the Middlesex County Mental Health Clinic in New Brunswick, New Jersey, Dr. Sol Gordon. Those of us who have never known a moment of mental health have a unique perspective that gives these documents a special *je ne sais quoi*. Just shows you how low you go when you lose your sense of purpose, your sense of a goal. From this editing I learned a lesson. Dr. Gordon would hand me his original manuscript. I would find it incomprehensible. So I'd use a scissors and cut it up sentence by sentence and sometimes clause by clause. Then I'd look for a sentence with an overarching idea, with one of Dr. Gordon's points. I'd make that a topic sentence, the lead sentence of an as-yet-non-existent paragraph. Then I'd gather together all the sentences that supported the idea proposed in the lead. Ahhh, an entire paragraph that made a point! Then I'd do the same with all the other random sentences and phrases of the original work. My job was to read Dr. Gordon's mind and to help him express himself. Clearly and convincingly. In a manner that Albert Einstein would have approved of. So when I presented the finished result to Dr. Gordon, every word was his. And he was impressed by his brilliance.

The lesson? Work hard enough and you may be able to find the message in even the most confusing patchwork of verbiage. But remember the ego of the person you are writing for. You want him or her to see the new thing you have put together as a manifestation of his own brilliance. Which it really is. Sort of. With the aid of this lesson, I would eventually lose a very strange job and get straight A's. But that's yet to come.

◆

WAS I GETTING ANYTHING out of this failed wandering. You bet. Knowledge. Insights into peculiar corners of the culture. Edna St. Vincent Millay-style insights. And these were the pointillist dots, the pixels, that would someday help flesh out a big picture. But at the time, those future payoffs were hard to see.

Another thing that I failed to see: I was ever so slowly approaching true love. And true love would be far stranger than it's generally made out to be.

◆

OK, THERE I WAS flapping around like one of Skinner's pigeons trying to find a pattern in random deliveries of food. But a strange thing happens when you pursue your mission in life with a passion. When you follow the commandments of Edna St. Vincent Millay, T. S. Eliot, and Jack Kerouac. You sometimes leave a trail behind you. You sometimes leave a path on which others build a highway.

In my case, the nameless movement that I had helped kick into motion on the West Coast a year and a half earlier was about to be discovered by, of all people, Henry Luce. And it was about to get a name. The Time/Life Wizard of Id was about to spot the next hot property with which to entertain prisoners of corporate employment. Yes, Luce was about to pinpoint the next band of rebels whose escapades would provide a weekly excuse to shovel sex into the open caverns of perpetually sex-deprived American minds. Sex delivered with a tone of outraged disapproval that would make its perpetual appearance appear prudish. Luce was about to give his newly discovered handful of seekers after Lord-knows-what a label—the "Hippies." And in 1967, he would even put a story called "The Hippies: Philosophy of a Subculture" on one of the most-coveted media locations in America: the cover of *Life Magazine*. Yes, thanks to Henry Luce, the movement I'd accidentally helped start was about to become the next big bohemianism. But that's not all.

The sugar cubes that had helped me learn the art of nude cliff-dangling were about to migrate to the East Coast, where two Harvard professors—

Richard Alpert and Timothy Leary—would use them to make headlines. Thanks in part to Alpert and Leary, LSD would be the subject of nine articles in Luce's *Time* magazine in just one year, 1966. The professorial pair would claim that the active ingredient of the sweetener could be used to redecorate even the drabbest mind. In fact, if you felt the breadth of your mental acreage was inadequate, Alpert and Leary offered the solution: the form of psychological enlargement you've run into before, the brain-stretch they called "mind expansion." How very much in the spirit of Edna St. Vincent Millay's, "the world stands out on either side, no wider than the heart is wide."

Topping it all off, the sucrose cube's obscure chemical additive would be semantically restyled by the intrepid Luce journalists to make it sound more zippy. Lysergic acid was about to be dubbed LSD, or "acid." And within a year, a foursome of unlikely singers from Liverpool, England, who had stupidly named themselves after the world's most abundantly varied insect, would invade the United States and start a trend in hairstyles that was eventually destined to make my coiffure the rage. My past was preparing to haunt me. The Sixties were about to officially begin.

◆

OH, AND ONE MORE strange event would happen any month now. Barbara would appear.

THE JOYS OF LIVING IN A CLOSET

When we last left off, my French teacher, echoing my pistol-packing Vancouver wise men, had informed me that what I needed in life was a goal. My father had sent me to Israel, where I had found one…getting myself into a mental institution. Unfortunately, no mental institution would have me except for Rutgers University's Graduate School of Education.

So I spun the wheel of fate, rolled the dice, tossed the I Ching, flipped a coin, and came up with the most obvious next big goal in sight—going back to college.

In those days New York University in Manhattan was the only school interested in dropouts. Little wonder. Leaving school early hadn't yet acquired a name. Remember, the term "dropout" was not in popular use. And we humans prize words more than we prize realities. Biologists in the early 1800s had names for the cell's membrane and nucleus, so when they drew the cells that were under their microscopes, that's all they drew—membranes and nuclei. There were lots of other dots in the cell, but the anally meticulous biological sketch specialists thought the flecks and smidgens were dirt and ignored them. Then someone came up with names for some of that dirt— chromosomes, mitochondria, and organelles. Now that the specks had names, the formerly invisible dots showed up in every sketch of a cell in sight.

What's worse, we run from phenomena so far off the beaten path that no one has yet dignified them with a terminology. People flee from a friend with a crippling illness that has no name. Or they insist that "it's all in your head." Which is a back-handed way of naming the unnamable while claiming that the unnamable illness does not exist.

College admission officers are human. Yes, I know that comes as a surprise. So, they, too, flee from nameless things. Nameless things like, well, errr, me.

But beyond the fact that NYU was the only school that would have a dropout like me, the school in the land of skyscrapers had another advantage. It was in one of the most cosmopolitan, global cities of the 20th century, a cesspool of strange people where a strange person like me could feel at home. At Reed I never felt I belonged. The school was small. And the students buddied together in tight little cliques. No clique I'd ever encountered had wanted me. And that included the brainy, bohemian cliques at Reed. In New York, you could dodge between the cliques and pick friends like wildflowers. If you wanted, you could put together a clique of your own. Your own private, personal, human bouquet.

I got so excited about this fact that I would write an ode to it thirty-seven years later, shortly after the jolt of 9/11. Here's how it went.

New York is not just a city of concrete. It is not just a city of glass. It is not just a city with ribs of steel. It is not a city of mourning. It is a city aborning. New York is a spirit, a flicker, a flame. New York is a city whose brilliance is born in the strange. It's a mega-nest for those who were too bright, too adventurous, too pregnant with imaginings. It's a giant hive for those who did not fit back in Wilmington or Waterbury or Waxahachie. New York is a place for those who cannot squeeze themselves into the America of the everyday. It is a gathering place for those who cannot just be normal, joke around, party, and play, those who cannot be content with a life of nothing but beer and football games. New York is a city of those who find that something out of kilter with the ordinary, something odd, unnamable, teases and tickles their brains.

Those who had no one to understand them come here and find they suddenly have a home. We New Yorkers are the oddballs, the misfits, the outcasts, the brilliant, the vision-ridden, the eerie, the nerdy, the incomprehensible, the bizarrely gifted, the ghosts of futures searching for a home, the restless souls who elsewhere have no grounding, who, without New York, are forced to roam. Here we strange ones, we too-swift-ones, we who open strange emotions, feelings haunting others but which today's words won't yet let them say, we who see new passions, new astonishments, new forms of theater, new ways to dance, new cinematic visions, new prose, new jokes, new poetry, new fashions, new ways to work and play, we gather here and find each other. Here we come together in strange packs, new kinds of tribes. Here those who had no place in the heartlands help give each other friendship, energy, brainstorming sessions, lives.

New York cannot be shattered, it is a bonfire of the spirit, it's a flickering twist of connectivity. I, the strange, find you, the strange, and together we set others free. I feed you when your soul's on fire, support you when you drown in mire. And you, you do the same for me. What got you beaten up at home becomes a revelation when you say it not to them but to me. There's brightness in your eyes as I spell out my visions, and in the brightness of your pupils, your attention sets me free. You power me with what you sense that no one ever saw in me.

Yes, NYU's biggest gift was New York City. But there was an arthropod in the academic ointment. NYU wouldn't accept my previous French courses and was determined to stick me in some elementary class, a humiliation I couldn't tolerate. A humiliation that would lead to love. But let's not get ahead of ourselves.

Miffed by NYU's witless insult to my mastery of French, I went back from Rutgers to Buffalo for the summer and my dad used his political connections to land me a job. As a legislative assistant, a gofer for the mayor, a researcher on policy positions, or as the city's monarch and budding commander-in-chief? Not on your life. My father secured me a sinecure as a garbage man.

Since sanitation specialists work from six in the morning until noon, that left my afternoons free. When my work was over, I showered off the odor of deteriorating table scraps and spent the rest of my time writing position papers for a Congressional candidate who would later win against enormous odds...and perfecting my French.

My major linguistic problem involved a serious gender mix-up. I perpetrated millions of tiny surgical operations in which I castrated male nouns and added testicles to feminine ones via a totally mangled sense of *las* and *les*. Fortunately, none of the words I crippled for life ever sued me for malpractice.

Meanwhile, I had haughtily challenged NYU to give me the toughest French test it could muster. To pull off an improvement in my mastery of the Gallic tongue, I came up with a sneaky trick. A very B. F. Skinnerish trick. I bought one of those volumes of Voltaire with the French version on one side of the page and the English on the other. Every day, I covered up a French page, then set about translating the English on the facing page back into my best approximation of Francais. At day's end, I'd compare my version with Voltaire's. His was usually better. But after a full summer and 84 pages of this, I'd pretty well gotten the kinks out of writing like a genuine Frank, and could knock off a 3,000-word essay with nary a sexually-abused noun. What's more, I was inspired to write a little book called *Candide*, for which I understand Voltaire has been hogging the credit. OK, this time I'm kidding.

Meanwhile, the idea of plowing through eight academic semesters and getting a degree didn't entirely soothe my troubled spirit. I needed to add more meat to my goal. Yes, I was about to return to school. But what in the world for? What did I want to become? Soaring over the landscape like an eagle would have to be a major component. Soaring over the landscape of the sciences. But talons, test tubes, and lab rats were not enough.

The answer lay with this kid who lived a half mile away from me on a Buffalonian avenue with huge houses, wonderfully full lawns, and an arch of elm trees that was astonishing. He could afford it. His parents were doctors.

Late every afternoon I'd bicycle over to the lake in the middle of the 220-acre Frederick Law Olmsted marvel called Delaware Park, wander through the scrub to a huge construction pile, climb on top of it and watch the sunset. Henry Rubin, the guy from the street with the gothic arch of elms, had heard of my ritual, I don't know how. So he contacted me and said he wanted to come along. While we were standing on the pinnacle of this hill, with vast spreads of greenery and a huge horizon stretched out before us and the sun turning everything in sight a Maxfield Parrish gold, Henry explained a twist that providence had recently thrown in his path.

He'd gone to Oberlin to major in pre-med and to follow his parents' example suturing intestines. They were both doctors and they insisted that to make a good living, he must be a doctor, too. But ever since he'd been small, Henry had played the violin. One day, Isaac Stern, one of the most legendary violinists of the 20th century, came to Oberlin and heard Henry scratching some Mozart out of his poor, tortured strings. Stern took the kid aside and quizzed him about his future plans. Then the maestro made a pronouncement. Henry, he said, would have to drop medicine. His musical talent was simply too great to waste. If Henry would agree to fiddle full time, Stern would make him a deal—he'd let Henry have a semi-permanent loan of his spare Stradivarius. Stern's deal convinced Henry's parents to let their son leave the lucrative world of the scalpel.

So Henry switched from pre-med to Oberlin's conservatory of music. And he made a discovery. When you concentrate intensely on one thing that you love, at first it seems as if you've imprisoned yourself in a very tiny corner of the universe. But a strange thing happens. The nano-discipline into which you've squeezed yourself becomes a lens. Details of the world that seemed half dead come alive with whole new meanings. The finite becomes a telescope to the infinite—or something like that. Something very Edna St. Vincent Millay.

Remember William Blake's seeing the universe in a grain of sand? Apparently the poor man had just come from the beach and had gotten something in his eye.

But by the time Henry finished his story, I'd decided to pick one skill at random—writing (the choices weren't too great—if you've seen me play pool, it's not a pretty sight). Then I remembered that Einstein had tried to put me on the path to literature and I'd somehow fallen off. Obviously the universe was trying to tell me something. And despite the fact that I never listen, the message was getting through. To be a scientific thinker, you have to be a writer. Or, as Einstein put it, to be a genius it is not enough to come up with a theory that only seven men in the world can understand. To be a genius you have to be able to express that theory so clearly that anyone with a high school education and a reasonable degree of intelligence can understand it.

Thanks to Henry Rubin, I went back to college invigorated by the hope that an army of English literature professors would stand over me with a whip and make me learn to write like de Maupassant, Faulkner, Tolstoy, and Woody Allen. That would not quite happen. But quite a bit else would.

◆

IN SEPTEMBER, MY PARENTS drove me to the Big Apple, where I got a case of permanent neck strain from looking up at tall buildings. My dad and mom helped me find a place to live. There was this lovely brownstone on Bleeker Street near Eighth Avenue in the heart of the West Village, the former capital of the East Coast beatniks. It was the home of a family who had two rooms for rent on their top floor. One was a luxurious bedchamber with a wood-burning fireplace and windows looking out on the triangular micro-park across the street. This room went for $15 a week. Then there was the room next door. It used to be a walk-in closet, but it had been converted into a cute little sleeping cell, *so* cute that even a person my size (5'8" and 140 pounds), had to walk sideways to fit between the dresser and the six-inch wide bed. Even then, it was impossible to pull off a trip from one end of the room to the other without snagging your navel on the dresser's knobs.

This furnished coffin rented for $10 a week. My parents did a little arithmetic, and lo and behold, the closet was mine, all mine.

Then my generous father and mother (don't worry, if you knew the fortune they were spending on my psychotherapy, you'd be glad they were saving their pennies) waved goodbye and headed back to Buffalo.

Now back to French. I passed NYU's test with flying colors, and was allowed to take the most advanced Gallic courses they could throw at me. Meanwhile, I figured that the folks in the English literature department would get out their cat-o-nine-tails and put me through all the basic torments of wordsmanship—forcing me to bang together tales of flatulence in the style of Chaucer, plays about murdering your step-parents in the manner of Shakespeare, war stories complete with nurses who couldn't keep their hands (and assorted other body parts) off you in the mode of Hemingway, and nonsense in the vein of Edward Lear (here the task would be to come up with a couple even more genitally incompatible than an owl and a pussycat).

But I was horrified to discover that NYU's literary dons had no intention of lashing me into shape as the next Dostoyevsky. In fact, they weren't even prepared to make me an honorary Karamazov. Their idea of a good education consisted of learning to count the adjectives in a deservedly forgotten fifteenthth-century story and write a paper so dry that even cockroaches wouldn't eat it. The major issue in English Literature at the time was the significance of verbal modifiers for western civilization.

So to learn anything about writing, I had to turn to my French lessons. There, in addition to absorbing great gobs of Racine, Corneille, Anonyme, and just about everyone else who had ever purchased a pen somewhere in the vicinity of Paris, I was given the flogging I'd come to expect. Only they called it *"Exercises Du Style."* They picked one august author every week, stripped the covering off of his primary tricks in front of your eyes, then forced you to write in his style. When you finished imitating Montesquieu or Pascal, it was time to spit out sentences that aped Flaubert and Stendhal. You even had to learn to walk like Jerry Lewis (they were convinced he, too, was French).

Actually, my creative mind worked better in the dusky atmosphere of French literature, since I was filled with college-age delights—alienation, despair, and the desire to dramatize even the most minuscule hint of gloom. So I wrote reams of fiction in the language of Jacques Cousteau. Yes, I dove into a veritable sea of Gallic saliva (a necessity for sailing r's around your uvula), not to mention Gallic *angst* (so how come the Germans have a better word for it?).

On the side, I minored in psychology, just so I could keep paddling around in the old scientific swimming hole with such amiable creatures as hippocampi, limbic systems, adrenocorticotropic hormones, and stimulus-response models.

If you are wise, and I suspect you are, you will be virtually certain that I am now rambling far, far from the subject at hand. But guess again. For my fling with French would eventually lead to love, a misshapen semblance of lust, and one of the world's most bizarre mutations of romance. Not to mention more adventures in the nascent quirks and shudders of The Sixties.

NIGHTS IN A TRANSVESTITE DRESSING ROOM

My progress in the absorption of new eccentricities was remarkable. Let's rephrase that. My accidental dive into the sort of extremes that Edna St. Vincent Millay had demanded was far from at an end. Very far.

One night I was walking through the club and restaurant district of Bleeker Street in the West Village, where hovels for entertainment clot the side of the road, and a voice from the other side of the street called my name. I sauntered across to the opposite sidewalk and discovered this ebullient little fellow who had recognized me from an NYU history class and wanted to make friends. Why was he standing outside in the cold? Because he was the barker for the Crazy Horse. And what was the Crazy Horse? The city's leading transvestite nightclub. A club where grown men dressed up as grown women and performed onstage. My new friend told me that if I ever needed a place to hang out, I could use the club's dressing room. Yes, he said I could drop in any time.

So I spent my Saturday post-midnight hours writing letters home from the dressing room of this tiny emporium where female impersonators were busy changing sex. I sat half-swallowed by the gums of an ancient couch—yellow pad in hand—chatting with imitation Diana Rosses, Bessy Smiths, and Marilyn Monroes while they sidled out of their female attire, shucked their phony hips and breasts, and zipped themselves into their all-leather, one-piece, skin-tight, supposedly-male jumpsuits to swish back over to Christopher Street, the capital of the gay community.

These gentlemen were walking paradoxes. They were more feminine in their male clothing than they'd been when they were dressed as women. In dresses they had a vigorous mastery, a total command. In their male outfits, they were walking apologies. Their limp wrists and body swish were submission gestures incarnate.

My message to my parents generally ran something like this:

Hi,

Nothing is happening in New York. Absolutely nothing. This place is so normal you could die.

Your son,

Howard

Admitting that I was writing from a diminutive Disneyland of sexual extremes and doing it on their dime didn't seem advisable at the time. But surely Jack Kerouac would have approved. And there were more Kerouacian adventures to come.

Stewart, the barker, soon introduced me to his friends. One was a guy named Tom Reichman. And Tom's story would turn to tragedy.

Reichman was a tall, red-headed film-maker who'd already won awards for a documentary on bass-playing jazz giant Charles Mingus despite the fact that Tom was only twenty years old. Plus, he was a source of unmitigated delight, and knew how to woo a woman. When I introduced him to one of my female NYU acquaintances, Lark Clark, an ultra-Bohemian whose buddies included folks like then-embryonic playwright/actor Sam Shepherd and the members of the quintessentially Sixties rock band The Fugs, Reichman asked her out on a date.

The russet-headed cinematographer arrived at Lark's apartment on Eighth Street, in the core of the Village, in the middle of winter with a picnic basket and a blanket. Lark was a little perplexed. Then Tom took her by the hand, led her to a subway station, walked her to the end of the platform where metal stairs descended to the mysteries of the tunnel beyond, guided her down those stairs into the tunnel's darkness, and forward a quarter of a mile along the forbidden territory on the margins of the tracks. Then he swept her through the entrance of a comfortable and commodious cavern carved into the stone wall. Tom spread his blanket, removed candles from his picnic basket, lit them, opened a bottle of champagne, and laid out a gourmet feast. Lark and Tom became an item. I took total credit for making the match.

That provided one lesson in romance. But another was coming up. And it would prove crucial.

◆

You could barely squeeze a prefabricated sandwich into the room I inhabited over on Bleeker Street, much less find enough room to make one, eat one, and brush away the crumbs. So I rented the kitchen of a fellow Buffalonian and NYU student named Andy Kulberg, whose West Village apartment at Bleeker Street and Sixth Avenue was less than a ten minute walk away from my walk-in closet. Kulberg was not your average kitchen-lord. When it came to music, he knew more than Richard Wagner, Richard Strauss, and Richard Nixon combined. And like them (well, two of them), he could write the stuff. He played God-knows-how-many musical instruments, had a collection of nearly every Beethoven recording ever made, and was on his way to a degree as a composer. Yes, his stuff was actually being performed in public. By a genuine string quartet.

But every three weeks or so, Andy would enter the kitchen in the first phases of a romantic seizure. While I chopped carrots, celery, and onions, he would rave that he had just met the girl of his dreams, the universal male fantasy come true. All he wanted was to woo and win her, and he'd be happy for the rest of his life. You could look into his rapturous face and see that, inwardly, he was projecting every mushy fantasy he'd ever had onto this female person he scarcely knew, as if she were a blank movie screen. His exhilaration was positively giddy.

His next two weeks were spent in a state of ecstasy as he plowed through the uncertain phases of pursuit and conquest, finally discovering that she liked him, too. Then a sudden transformation would set in. Once Andy and the ideal maid were going out like clockwork, the big screen on which he'd been flashing his own *Gone with the Wind* was taken down, and there, standing onstage in place of Scarlett O'Hara, was an uncomfortably normal human female. Andy's erstwhile eruptions of enthusiasm were replaced by complaints about where she put the toothpaste cap and how she hung her panties in the bathroom to dry. He never discussed his sentiments about warts, moles, or hairs in unexpected places, but you can guess. The hidden motivation was obvious: the man was searching frantically for excuses to escape.

Usually, it was all over in a month. Then a strange thing would happen. Andy would meet another girl.

So I wasn't the only one who panicked when the whale-like jaws of a genuine relationship closed down around me. Based on a sample of two, it looked like the terror was universal. Since names mean everything, as the tale of the organelle indicates, let's give it one: "intimacy panic."

From this, I began to suspect that romance is a temporary seizure of the hormones designed to suck us into attachment, procreation, and the torments of a baby's midnight wails. The glandular fever rapidly retreats, leaving the average male in a cold sweat. Some primordial instinct warns him that if he continues on his enchanted path, he will end up with infants who refuse to allow a hard-working adult to sleep. And he will discover that his wife has lost all interest in sex—except, perhaps, with someone else.

Kulberg's ultimate fate would have less to do with women than with the curved beauty he kept in a corner of the kitchen—his six-foot-high bass violin. One of his chamber music compositions was about to be performed by the NYU String Quartet, which was rehearsing the thing for its big unveiling. Then Andy walked down MacDougal Street from NYU to his apartment one afternoon and dropped in—for reasons unknown—to a small club called the Gaslight. The Gaslight was dark and dingy and a tight squeeze for any more than 110 people, but it had hosted early poetry readings by beatnik legends Allen Ginsberg and Gregory Corso, then had achieved a place in Sixties music history. It was the club in which Bob Dylan had recorded a live album just two years earlier.

Turns out that a blues quartet—the Danny Kalb Quartet, to be specific—had shown up that afternoon at the Gaslight to rehearse for a performance that night and had discovered that it was afflicted with a small problem. It was down to a trio. The bassist had disappeared. Someone asked the shadowy figures hanging out in the club's gloom if anyone possessed a bass. Andy happened to have a large bass languishing next to his refrigerator. What's more, he could play it.

So, as I stood at the cutting board performing brain surgery on a cabbage one late afternoon, Andy rushed in, grabbed the instrument, gave a quick explanation of why he wouldn't be home for dinner (by now, I'd taken to cooking for him and his roommate as well as for myself), and dashed off, his pocket protector still full of pens, the sleeves of his white shirt unbuttoned and flapping in the breeze.

Not long after, Andy Kulberg, the classical composer, dropped out of school. The next time I saw him, he was swaggering down the NYU corridors in tight gray suede pants, an equally tight gray suede top, and gray suede high-heeled boots. It was merely a visit. He'd become a rock and roll star. The quartet had become famous (for about ten minutes) as The Blues Project. Andy's composition "Flute Thing" was all over the airwaves. The band had been touring the country, and Kulberg had just gotten off the plane and come back to show off on his old stomping grounds. How in the world had he managed to function without a pocket protector and half a dozen pens?

Nine years later, I was taking a long bus trip to upstate New York with the huge silver earphones and Martian antennae of a brand new 1973 Sony headphone radio clamped around my temples (sorry, no unauthorized worship allowed) when this amazing piece of music came on—a long, ostensible rock and roll instrumental with all kinds of allusions to Beethoven, Prokofiev, Aaron Copeland, and God-knows-who-all-else. Though I hadn't seen Kulberg in years, I wished he could hear it. It was his kind of music. I eventually found out there was a reason. Andy wrote it.

Andy had found his place as a musician who fused rock and classical music. And Andy had also found a mate. Actually more than one. He eventually married. Twice. The world's population of veligers would have applauded. Even the seagulls would have been proud. I guess Kulberg got over the terror-phase of his relationships' "intimacy panic." As I would, too. Very, very soon. But it wouldn't be easy.

◆

WHY ALL THESE RUN ins with musicians and creative types? Why the violinist Henry Rubin, the filmmaker Tom Reichmann, and the composer Andy

Kulberg? Not to mention the "girls" at the Crazy Horse? Was fate trying to tell me something? Something about how the mass passions pulled together by music and film would someday fit into my science? Something about how sex and the relationship with a woman fit into this puzzle, too? Something about the forces of history? Something about the gods inside? And something about a possible place for me in this world? A place that would have pleased T. S. Eliot, Edna St. Vincent Millay, William Blake, William James, Jack Kerouac, and your average veliger? Maybe even your above average veliger?

And what were these adventures revealing about the spirit of The Sixties?

THE DEAD HORSE AND THE MAGIC SMILE

You'll recall that when I was in California wondering why I weighed less than one of Charles Atlas' biceps, I compensated for this deficiency by helping kick off the Sexual Revolution of The Sixties and discovered that I couldn't sustain a relationship with a woman for more than three days straight.

As you know, I fled from this fact by returning to the East Coast, where I realized to my dismay that though I might be found physically appealing by California girls, back in the chilly states bordering the Atlantic, civilization still kept up some of its standards and I was considered on a par with an oversized wart. Yes, I could hold girls spellbound with tales of my adventures, and even get my hands into their panties, but because of my athletic disabilities, I couldn't get those panties off. And due to the sluggish manner in which the Sexual Revolution crawled from one coast to the other, the girls in question, while quite willing to have certain regions digitally massaged, were not willing to remove their garments *for* me. What's worse, on those infrequent occasions when women showed an interest in something that might last longer than a short case of the flu, I ran in terror.

So one afternoon I retired to my converted closet on Bleecker Street, perched on the bed (only a small portion of my nether end could fit at any one time, since the mattress was the width of a bannister) and evaluated my life to this point. What lessons had I learned from all of my spiritual quests and travels?

- Don't hitch rides on railroad flatcars. It takes roughly 30 seconds to bounce to the car's edge and wave good bye to the world before the churning wheels turn you into anchovy paste.

- If you're hitch-hiking and get stuck in the desert for more than eight hours straight, don't stand on the asphalt. Move a few inches to your left and plant yourself on the dirt. Black tarmac absorbs the sun's rays, reaches a temperature of 4,000 degrees Fahrenheit, fries the soles of your boots, and generates nuclear fusion in your feet.

- Something is seriously wrong with your relationships with women.

The last point seemed the most relevant under the current circumstances. So what was I going to do about it? I retraced the stages of my sexual evolution, and discovered there was a missing link. I had been a mere innocent reading about "quick encounters in the forest" and wondering whether natives of opposite sex just shook hands and claimed to be Dr. Livingston, or managed some more complex maneuver, when all of a sudden I found myself actually sleeping with girls. I'd missed a couple of vital steps: like dating, petting, necking, begging for mercy, hoping to get to third base, acting like I'd had fifteen women when in reality I'd never seen a bra on a female outside of the ads in *The New York Times Sunday Magazine*, etc. My problem was that I *had* had fifteen women (OK, less than five) back in the dim and distant days of my 19th year, but hadn't gone through the necessary preparation.

So I held my breath, steeled my nerves, and took the plunge. I decided to *date*! If I retraced all the evolutionary steps of courtship that I'd missed, I figured, I'd be normal. My terror and brain freeze would go away. Little did I realize that terror and brain freeze *are* normal.

During my first few weeks at college, I noticed something strange about human (or in my case, inhuman) nature. When you have no self-confidence, you look for every excuse to avoid the difficult. You convince yourself that each girl you see has some fatal flaw that makes her inappropriate for you. Well, maybe appropriate for a nice daydream or two. But certainly lacking the right stuff to make you force yourself, sweating, stuttering, and trembling in your socks, to actually walk up and attempt a conversation!

My sudden pickiness disguised the reflex of the skydiving novice, who takes one look out the open door of the plane, envisions what he'll look like if the chute doesn't open and he's reduced to two dimensions, then refuses to move.

So I made another resolution. If I saw a woman I found attractive, I would stop cataloging the unsightly freckles a microscope might reveal, leap out of the hatch, land by the hapless maiden (the East Coast still had a few virgins left back in 1963—sorry, but the West Coast had run out of them), and open a chat, no matter how awkward and inane it might be.

Well, believe it or not, it worked. Within a short amount of time, I was actually dating. In fact, I was dating two or three separate girls. And, true to my plan, I was going through all the frustration I'd missed out on in adolescence. I was petting, running into resistance, having trouble getting past first base, etc. The scheme was working perfectly. But was it solving my problems? This was very hard to tell. None of my relationships were sufficiently intimate to bring on panic. So I had no clue to whether my fright-and-flight devices were successfully being wiped away.

When I couldn't actually get a real date (and that, fortunately, wasn't too often), I'd go out with this good friend who had stowed away on a freighter, hitch-hiked around the world, and made it all the way through the Muslim countries to India, where she'd earned a modest living acting in early Bollywood films. This was not her only appeal. She possessed the kind of body that *Sports Illustrated Swimsuit Calendar* art directors search for but never find. She was also reasonably promiscuous, but reserved her physical attentions for drug addicts and outright psychotics. I was merely your run of the mill neurotic. So, though we spent a great deal of time together, I wasn't her type. (We did, however, while away a summer sleeping together platonically in a narrow single bed with no clothes on—but that belongs to a later part of the story.)

On the whole, things were not going all that well. My grade point average was seriously flawed. I was getting only four As per semester and one intolerable, embarrassing, zit-like B. Now, why I was embarrassed about this, Lord alone knows. Remember, I'd read two books a day under my desk in grammar school and never even noticed my grades. Only my teachers and my mom knew they were abysmal. But for some reason, my emotional core took college grades as a personal challenge. I wanted straight A's. Yes, I know it's crazy. But often we don't pick our obsessions, they pick us.

How did I solve the problem of the embarrassing B's? During my first two semesters at NYU, I ignored my class notes, focused on the textbooks, then wrote papers and exam essays trying to offer original ideas. Yes, my own hopefully brilliant ideas. Then I remembered the lesson of writing for Sol Gordon at the Middlesex County Mental Health Clinic in New Brunswick, New Jersey. That lesson? No matter what you do, you are surfing the waves of ego. So I reversed my priorities. What did I study the hardest? My class notes. And whose ideas did I promote in my papers and in my test essays? The professor's. From that point forward, it was all straight A's, thirty of them in a row. So much for the notion that college is there to prepare you to think independently.

Meanwhile, my social life was leaving certain glandular tissue very unfulfilled. And, what's worse, I'd had this case of serious depression that had hung in there every waking minute of the day since I was thirteen. (Before the age of thirteen I hadn't been depressed, I'd merely been miserable.)

Then, one afternoon, I ran into a totally unexpected antidote for depression.

◆

I DID ALL MY studying in the school library (large books wouldn't fit into my rent-a-closet bedroom), and was sitting at one of those long, wooden library tables trying to comprehend a diagram of the Krebs Cycle (there are actually two of these: in one, Professor Hans Adolf Krebs, a German biochemist, walks around in circles worrying about how he's going to pay the bills on his children's orthodontia until his wife breaks the cycle by calling him in to dinner; in the other, a bunch of microscopic con artists lure innocent ATP molecules onto what looks like a merry-go-round, then, when the poor ATP's have gotten very dizzy, the scoundrels pick their pockets of a phosphorus atom, thus providing you with the energy you use to walk, talk and breathe, and making us all accomplices to trillions of sleazy criminal acts per second).

Suddenly I looked up and way, way across the room, seated at yet another long wooden table, was the most angelic smile I had ever seen in my life. Attached to the face of a girl. Needless to say, I had been depressed while my head was still buried in my book. Lack of oxygen may have had something to do with it. What's more, I was worried about how poor Hans Adolf Krebs' children were going to end up with straight teeth. However, one sight of this exquisite woman's facial expression did very strange things to my brain. It lightened my mood and made the somber freight of cares and woes lift from my weary and staggering dendrites. It was a miracle.

You'll recall that I'd started going to shrinks when I was in Israel. By now, I was on my third therapist or so. I'd eventually get up to seven. And none of them would be able to accomplish in years what a single glance at this woman's face could do in seconds.

It was obvious even from a distance of forty feet that this gorgeous creature was my mirror opposite—the all-American girl, a slender 5'6 1/2", 115 pounds, with auburn hair and the kind of natural facial coloring the average *Cosmo* cover model employs an army of makeup artists to simulate. She could have posed for Breck Shampoo ads, led cheerleading squads, and dated the Arrow Shirt man. But it was the smile that really did the trick. No one on this earth possessed anything quite like it.

So I established a new routine. When I got out of class and retired to the library for a few hours of bashing my brains with books, I cased the joint carefully to see where this woman with the healing visage was parked, then found myself a table located a discreet fifty or sixty feet away in a spot from which I had a clear view. Her smile never went away. And whenever my gloom descended, I'd simply look up from my verse of Chaucer, sneak a quick glance, feel infinitely better, and get back to mispronouncing the English language the way they did 600 years ago.

Now as you'll recall, I had made a resolution to start a conversation with any female I found even vaguely interesting and secure a date. But my dating card was quite full, and for some reason it took me weeks to realize that I'd been so enraptured by this lovely being's face that I had utterly forgotten to live up to my self-imposed dictum. When it finally hit me that I'd been derelict in my duties, I hoisted myself out of my wooden seat, ambled over, stood behind the otherworldly girl, tapped her on the shoulder, explained that I'd noticed her smile for the last few weeks, and asked what she might be reading that brought on such celestial delight. I expected something riddled with comedy, like maybe Lucius Apuleius' *The Golden Ass*.

"Oh," she said, and showed me the book in her hand. It was Charles Baudelaire's *Les Fleurs Du Mal*, one of the more pathologically troubled collections of poetry produced in the last few centuries (if you didn't count the stuff *I* was writing).

And exactly what wisp of whimsy had brought a sublime expression to the lips of milady today? A little ditty about a bunch of flies throwing a feast in the entrails of a horse lying dead by the side of a road. Very cheerful…if you're an insect. Somewhat more distressing if you lack an exoskeleton and call yourself a mammal.

This should have clued me in that there was something a bit askew about the otherworldly grin that had lifted me from the bowels of the earth. But instead, I was preoccupied with prying the conversation open.

As I mentioned in what you mistakenly thought was one of my delirious rambles, I'd become a hot shot in the language of frogs' legs and goose livers, using the vintage products of France's finest lunatics, the surrealists, to drive myself slightly crazy on the West Coast. I'd even gone so far as to insult every Gaul walking upright on dry land by writing all my fiction in the language of his ancestors.

And the creature with whom I had just opened a conversation was a French major who had actually been accepted for graduate school the upcoming year at the Sorbonne, the most prestigious institute of higher learning in all of continental Europe. So, having rapidly established a point of common interest, I moved my books next to hers; and in subsequent days, we studied together on a regular basis, swapping gossip about Moliere, Racine, and other folks with a congenital hatred for Englishmen.

Sitting next to this person, who happened to be Barbara, turned out to be a deprivation, since it made it much harder to stare at her face when I needed a mood boost. But what the heck, I was enjoying the company, and was willing to endure the hardship. However, I never asked her out. Seems there were only seven nights in the week, and despite my gnomish appearance, I had all of them filled.

One day I *did* invite Barbara to a greasy spoon next door to the library for a cup of coffee, something my contacts with the police had taught me that men in uniform do as an excuse to get together—much more of an excuse in my case than most, since I not only wouldn't touch coffee with a ten-foot pole, I wouldn't even drink it if the Pole invited me to her boudoir for a demonstration of advanced sipping techniques. But the trip to the coffee shop was about as close to a date as we got.

Then one afternoon something very strange occurred. Barbara turned to me all of a sudden, forcing me to lose my place in *Madame Bovary*, and blurted out some words *apropos* of nothing. "We can't date," she said. "I'm much too old for you. I'm twenty-five, and I have a five-year old daughter." Well, I was twenty-one, and what she said made a modicum of sense (though it turned out that she was exaggerating; she was actually twenty-four, and her daughter hadn't quite turned five). So I agreed that we'd just be friends. Little did she know that there was no room for her on my social calendar.

Then one night, I'd made arrangements to see an off-Broadway production of The Trojan Women (in those days, I had no taste) with the girl with the *Sports Illustrated* body and absolutely no interest in my physique. Early in the afternoon, Ms. Swimsuit called and said she couldn't make it. So when I arrived for my daily rendezvous with my Francophilic study mate, Barbara, I made her a proposition she could easily refuse. "Look," I said, "I've got these tickets to a play that all the critics are raving about, and the girl who I was supposed to go with cancelled out on me. Now I know we can't go on dates and have to be just friends, and I'm perfectly willing to go along with that. But how would you like to come with me so this expensive extra ticket doesn't go to waste?" Sounds like a come-on, doesn't it? It wasn't. When I told her I'd abide by her boundaries, I meant every syllable of it. Or so I thought.

Well, we watched this bloody play and both managed to stay awake, don't ask me how, then I offered to walk her back to her apartment. After all, she lived in a pretty rough neighborhood, one where you had to bob and weave through a hailstorm of .38 caliber slugs if you wanted to make it safely from one street corner to the next. I wasn't very athletic, but at least I could shield her with my body if the local boys cruised by with their zip guns blazing. Then I could get a good job in a processing plant as an industrial sieve.

Barbara's place was a hefty twenty-minute trek from the theater. It was on Seventh Street between Avenues B and C on the Lower East Side, sometimes called the East Village, in a territory where civilization dared not stretch its tender fingertips for fear of being bitten and where even the police felt besieged. I kept the chatter as innocent as possible, though I must confess, I strayed from my promise a little bit. I *did* hold her hand. And she didn't pull it away and slap me with it.

But the real bombshell came when we were within a block or so of our destination. As we passed a small park where muggers held raucous nightly conventions, she said, "You know we can't sleep together until next Tuesday [this was a Thursday night]. I won't have my diaphragm until then." Clearly the girl had plans that hadn't crossed my mind. But why?

In a very confused state, I said goodbye to her outside her door. I didn't even attempt a kiss. I was in shock. It took the whole walk home (two miles—forty minutes) to sort the thing out. I had been a perfect gentleman (aside from the hand holding). I had kept our conversation on strictly neutral territory. But she had consistently taken my innocent words and turned them to the subject of sex. It had happened over and over again. Then she had gone a step further and announced that not only were we going to *talk* about sex, but we were going to HAVE it. And she had specified exactly when! Next Tuesday! To add to the mounting pile of peculiarities, I hadn't even made a pass. I finally came to a conclusion. Through no fault of my own, we weren't just friends anymore.

Frankly, I should have breathed a sigh of relief. It meant I wasn't going to have to go through all the petting and necking and other stuff that I figured had been missing from my youth, but that, in reality, was wearing me down to a frustrated frazzle. The difficulties my awkward fingers went through trying to cope with fasteners and zippers was on a par with those of an armless earthworm attempting to play Isaac Stern's spare Stradivarius. This was much more the California approach to which I'd grown accustomed. Besides, like males from Tenerife to Timbuktu, I was a slave to my hormones.

So I showed up, as ordered, on Tuesday night to have sex. The apartment, a six-story walkup in a Lower East Side tenement planted in the wilds of a solidly black and Puerto Rican neighborhood, was unlike anything I had ever seen. No item of clothing in the place had ever been introduced to a hanger, much less to a closet. The entire wardrobe was in a heap on the floor. There was no such thing as a bookcase. Not that there weren't books, mind you, there were lots of them. It's just that they were all in piles on the floor. And the dishes—an ample, though thoroughly mismatched, collection—were haphazardly jumbled in the sink. At least they were not on the floor. But frankly, it was hard to tell whether they were clean or dirty. Maybe there were some of both. My guess is that only the cockroaches knew for sure. After all, they formed a sort of wall-to-wall shag carpet in the place, thus providing its decorative motif.

This was my introduction to Barbara's idea of housekeeping.

Nonetheless, we had more important business to transact than sanitary inspections. Barbara's most elegant piece of furniture, a mattress, was spread out on the floor in one corner. On it Barbara had draped herself, using a pose she'd borrowed from the barge scene in Elizabeth Taylor's *Cleopatra*. Barbara was wearing this very open neck, gray, knit wool sweater artfully baring one shoulder. It was a pose no man whose circumcision hasn't removed an extra organ or two could resist. So we had sex. No skyrockets went off. The earth failed to move. Sure, a couple of bullets bounced off the brick walls outside. And the cockroaches all stopped to watch. But it had been a long time since I'd left the sensual pleasures of California, and, frankly, I wasn't about to rate these things on a quality index.

When we were finished, Barbara hitched herself up on one elbow again and said, "What are we going to do next September?" It was currently October of 1964, so next September was almost a year away. Continued Barbara, "I'm supposed to go to France for graduate school at the Sorbonne." I have no idea of what my answer was. I was flabbergasted.

Once again, it took the entire walk home, all forty minutes of it, to get the implications of this latest query straight in my head. First, we weren't supposed to date because of the gulf of several light years between our ages. Then we were supposed to have sex, even though I hadn't asked. Next, we were destined to be together for at least the next year. And I was just getting to *know* this girl. Barbara clearly was a long-range thinker, and she seemed to have my future well mapped out for me. She was simply revealing it to me one small step at a time.

So I went back to my place, perched on the full width of my bed, and did some more deep examining of my life. I had demonstrated that I couldn't handle a long-term relationship. I had attempted to remedy the problem by filling in the sexual steps that I'd missed out on in adolescence. Despite this regimen, nothing much seemed to have changed. So maybe what I needed was to pick a long-term relationship, *any* long term relationship at all (and in this case, one seemed to have picked *me*), and stick with it, go through the hellish parts, endure the panic, the urge to flee, the brain locked up like a Rubik's cube coated in ebonite, the whole emotional nightmare, and use raw willpower to endure until I could come out on the other side, presumably cured. Then, if I ever wanted to get into some other long-term relationship, I'd at least have gotten my emotional debris out of the way. Perhaps the answer to the perils of intimacy panic was...persistence.

So Barbara's decision that we were hooking up for an extended run sounded like just what the doctor ordered. Besides that, anti-depressants hadn't come on the market yet, but she was capable of pulling off the same effect, and she was cuter than a bug in the rug of insects that pulsated across her apartment floor. Maybe I was being sucked into the whirlpool by my heels, but it seemed like a good time for a swim.

BEWARE THE BACKSEATS OF AUTOS
WITHOUT BRAKES

To procure the sexual privileges that Barbara was planning to allot, however, I was going to have to live up to certain conditions. First of all, I'd have to remember to bring my ration coupons. Sex would be handed out on a strictly regimented schedule, since it was apparently in short supply and there was a war going on (in Viet Nam). Second, I could not show up in her apartment until after 11:00 p.m., and I'd have to leave at 6:00 a.m. She didn't want her daughter's morals corrupted by seeing a man in the house. A man without a marriage license. This meant, said Barbara, that I should continue dating other women to keep myself busy, but not stay out past curfew. If she was setting up a romance here, she was going to make sure it ran according to the rules. She'd apparently gotten said rules from Mussolini's handbook on *How to Make the Trains Run On Time, Despite the Fact that They're Driven by Italians*.

So I continued my usual dating schedule, though I stopped trying to pet and neck and get to first base. Marching around town with girls and exchanging the intimate details of our lives (minus Barbara, a detail it didn't seem appropriate to divulge) was pleasant diversion enough. And Barbara and I had our highly-disciplined dole of quick encounters on the mattress. We had sex.

Not that there wasn't any romance involved, mind you. I'd have Barbara over to my closet on Bleecker Street from time to time, we'd both perch on the railing-like bed, and I'd give her dramatic readings from Dylan Thomas' *Under Milk Wood* and—her favorite—performances of stories direct from the Old Testament. Why in Baal's name would she find readings from the King James Version of the Bible the least bit entertaining, you may ask? Because I did the thing with a Yiddish accent, turning all the *dramatis personae* into ethnic characters. Barbara frequently tumbled off the bed chuckling uncontrollably, thus becoming lodged in the six-inch crack between the mattress and the dresser. But there was more historical authenticity to this rendition than you might imagine. I mean, the bozos in the Bible were Jewish! So there's virtually no question whatsoever that King David acted like George Burns. How else could he have gotten young girls to keep him warm in bed when he was in his late seventies?

To add to the intimacy that enlivened our timetable, Barbara would tell me tales from her youth, which she delivered with a vivacity that was riveting. She had grown up, she explained, in Kingston, New York, in a family so poor that it had to borrow money from the local church mice. The ramshackle shed in which she was raised, she recalled with a beaming gusto, was surrounded by bits and pieces of rusting cars and had a barn in the back. Though she never said it explicitly, she gave the distinct impression that her Ma and Pa never wore shoes and that they covered their heads with tattered straw hats, carefully color-coordinated with the long stalks of hay they chewed when they were trying to look thoughtful. Sort of the destitute cousins of the couple in *American Gothic*.

Then, in a series of episodes that unfolded like the *One Thousand and One Arabian Nights*, Barbara spoon-fed me tales: the tale of how at the age of six she had handed out the locomotive from her brother's train set, his most cherished toy, as a gift to another six-year-old she had a crush on. The story of how, as she got older, she'd refined her talents by wrecking her brother's boat, totaling his automobile, nearly biting off his big toe, and accidentally putting a pitchfork through her sister's thigh when the two of them were having a rollicking time out in the barn with the horses. Then there was the tragicomedy of how her pet chicken, the runt of the litter, who'd been picked on by every other piece of poultry in the neighborhood and had not a single feather left on its hide, would follow her like a shaven puppy through her parents' house and into the homes of her neighbors, thus making her *persona non grata* pretty much everywhere she went, despite the fact that the chicken, believe it or not, was housebroken.

And there were the family's two horses. Horses, explained Barbara, have a sense of humor. How did she know? One of her horses liked to get hold of the family's Pekinese, squash it under his hoof until the puppy's tongue stuck out and its death seemed imminent. Then the horse would give Barbara's mom a sneaky glance. Said Barbara, the ignoble steed was trying to get a rise out of her mother.

Barbara also told me about how the captain of the football team had fallen in love with her in high school, and how all the future fraternity types had gradually succumbed to her charms. Then, when she had shattered their coronaries, they had formed a "Barbara Lover's Club" and had moped in unison.

Why had she turned down all these highly desirable young men—future leaders of Kingston's Elks Club and Chamber of Commerce? It wasn't that she didn't care for suitors who aspired to sport antlers. It's just that she had, for Lord knows what bizarre reason, fallen for this person from the nearby town of Woodstock, a burg that specialized in preserving the remains of embalmed bohemians and their offspring, and which sent said offspring to Kingston's high school in the hope of mooching small change from nice, wealthy, upper-middle-class girls.

Xavier Vautour, the teenager to whom Barbara had become attached like a limpet, was 6'3", had not been in contact with reality since long before he was born, but had an IQ that hovered somewhere above your normal communications satellite, and showed promise of becoming a nationally recognized poet. What's more, he was handsome, blond, and aside from being totally helpless (a trait that doesn't reveal its full menace in high school), was an exceedingly pleasant person. In fact, like Barbara, he had one of the most winning smiles on this wrinkled little planet of ours.

Barbara was convinced that there wasn't a brain located anywhere in her *own* head, and that her father wasn't suddenly going to surprise her on her seventeenth birthday with one he'd been hiding in the attic, so she was fascinated by this guy's knowledge of Ezra Pound, Jean Paul Sartre, Pablo Picasso, and all the other usual intellectual moldy cargo. (Her estimate of her mental powers was a tiny bit off base. She'd later graduate from NYU Phi Beta Kappa.)

What's more, Xavier's family background was totally flabbergasting to a girl who had spent her entire life suffocating in the navel lint of a small town. Xavier's father was an artist who had sailed from Aix-en-Provence to the United States around 1921 or so, had become a highly successful advertising art director in Manhattan in his (and the century's) roaring twenties, had found a huge Midtown, rent-controlled apartment, had sublet it at a high profit, and had used the proceeds to become a full-time painter.

His work was brilliant (I saw a bunch of it eventually, and it is beyond belief). But it wasn't bringing in much income, and the stipend from his rent-controlled apartment was not enough to keep him in the manner to which he felt he should be accustomed. So he took advantage of his suave, continental manner and began luring wealthy women to bed, then bleeding them of their fortunes. A financial Dracula.

One of the girls he had seduced—and eventually married—was a scion of the Zeisberger family of Philadelphia, who apparently owned Fort Knox, the State of Pennsylvania, and four hotels on Boardwalk. He whisked the heiress off to Woodstock, fathered two children, among them Xavier, then when the Zeisberger clan realized what was going on and cut off their wayward daughter's million-dollar-a-year allowance, Xavier's father decided that he needed to find a new meal ticket and moved on.

However, Xavier's brood managed to keep up its impeccably bohemian credentials. Xavier's sister married a poet whose name is far too august for me to mention without being rendered penniless by the lawyers for his estate. She became the official translator for the work of one of the greatest Yiddish writers of all time, despite the fact that she was about as Jewish as a ham sandwich with three kinds of cheese. What's more, Xavier's sister's friends included such notables as Nanette Poulenc, the woman responsible for the subtitles of classic films like Shoot The Piano Player and Jules and Jim. (Barbara's daughter, Nanette, would eventually be named after Ms. Poulenc.)

Barbara, being your normal teenage girl, was bubbling with hormones and couldn't figure out what to do with them. Xavier, however, could. So they pooled their lunch money, bought themselves an ancient, fifty-dollar automobile with no brakes, learned to stop the car by sticking their feet out the door, and made ample use of the back seat, which apparently was also brakeless. Barbara would prepare for dates by getting drunk so she could convince herself the next morning that if anything had happened the night before it was the alcohol's fault. I mean, this was the 1950s, and Barbara's mother had fainting spells at the merest hint of the word s-e-x. What's more, though her body craved penile penetration, Barbara's mind had picked up her mother's prejudices on the subject.

Eventually, Barbara graduated from high school, and just to prove to her father (who she was sure thought she had Down's Syndrome) and herself that she wasn't a mentally deficient duffle bag, got into Skidmore. Xavier plopped with ease into Dartmouth—on a full scholarship, no less. But the onslaught of college classwork did not stop the old hormones in either of this pair from flaring like a bonfire in a rocket factory.

So one holiday weekend, Barbara and Xavier agreed to rendezvous in the old automobile back seat after lubricating Barb's inhibitions with the requisite quantity of hooch. The result was a permanent amelioration of the hormonal excess and a swelling in the abdominal region.

In those days, nice girls didn't do things like this, and even when they did, they didn't have abortions. So Barbara told her mother what was about to happen in seven or eight months and her mother fainted and was put on a heavy diet of sedatives, and, despite the fact that both her parents thought Xavier was about as valuable to humanity as the Poliovirus, they clenched their jaws and planned for a wedding.

Since Xavier had inherited his idea of patrimonial obligations from his father, Barbara was forced to drop out of school, have the baby, get a job as a waitress, diaper the baby, diaper Xavier, take care of the housecleaning, and listen to Xavier's complaints that the house wasn't clean enough and the baby was making too much noise and his diaper was getting messy. Xavier's contribution was to study, to have lively intellectual conversations with his friends in which they concluded unanimously that Barbara was, at best, a "clever peasant," to ask Barbara for money, and to avoid taking out the garbage, doing the dishes, changing the baby, or in any way performing chores that could be construed as useful. After all, like his father, Xavier was an artist!

One evening, Barbara was overcoming her growing dislike for Xavier by giving him what he wanted: another opportunity to enter her interior using only body parts below the navel and above the knees. But the muscles of her sexual organs were out for revenge. They tightened like a fist around Xavier's upright organ and refused to let go. After an hour in an involuntary clinch, Barbara and Xavier came to a hideous conclusion. There were only two ways to end their epoxy-like adjoinment at the hip—cut off a tiny bit of Xavier, or go to the hospital and put themselves in the hands of experts. Not that any expert on earth had ever seen this dilemma before. How they put clothes on is something beyond my imagination and outside the range of what Barbara explained. They had well and truly made Shakespeare's beast with two backs, and now were unable to unmake it. Unfortunately, most socially acceptable wardrobes are designed for beasts with only one back at a time. But they managed to cover themselves with something (a big skirt? a sheet?) and take a cab to the emergency room, where presumably they were shot full of muscle relaxants.

That was it. Wearing the scarlet letter in the town of Kingston, becoming the talk of a town of 50,000, being slathered in shame, being forced out of college and turned into a waitress who tried not to dump bowls of broccoli bisque down the sparkling white shirtfronts of upscale restaurant patrons, and now this.

Barbara concluded that she never wanted to have sex in her life again. In fact, she began to fantasize about severely altering the shape of Xavier's skull with a cast-iron frying pan, which she hung in a prominent spot on the kitchen wall in the hope that she might lose control of herself some evening. Xavier became aware of this ambition, was afraid to fall asleep with his eyes closed, and started to have stress-induced nosebleeds. He didn't think his poetry would improve if his brain was flattened like a cutlet of Italian veal.

Finally, Barbara couldn't take dragging this 6'3" burden around anymore, and after three years left the man. To earn a living, to overcome the feeling that her father felt she was mentally retarded, to eradicate Xavier's notion that she was a peasant with the conversational skills of a parrot, and to support her daughter Nanette, Barbara figured she'd have to go back to college, where she planned to outwork John Henry on one of his more energetic days punching holes through the granite mountains of the West. So she started school in California, then migrated to NYU, where she majored in the highly lucrative field of French literature.

Living on scholarships, welfare, government surplus spam, a steady diet of books, and a heavy dosage of abuse from her four-year-old—who had discovered that Barbara felt so guilty about not being able to bring her up properly, and so traumatized by the whole unplanned-pregnancy-and-Xavier episode, that any kid over the age of two could manipulate her like

Silly Putty—was driving Barbara crazy. She was living in total isolation with only a tyrannical, tantrum-throwing tot for company. And it was beginning to warp her mind.

Barbara got the first hints of brain-rot when she was seized by sexual fantasies about her math teacher, a man she'd never spoken to outside of class. These became so obsessive that they blotted out all her other thoughts. Then things got worse: she had sexual fantasies at the sight of fire hydrants. Her sanity was going down for the third time, and she realized that only a desperate maneuver could bring about a rescue.

Just then, an apparently teenage Woody Allen look-alike (me) began hanging around her in the library, blathering about Racine and Montaigne. Gradually, a plan took shape. Her fantasies were telling her that she needed a man. Well, this creature sitting next to her at a long wooden reading table was not exactly a man. In fact, it was not even a boy. It was more like a Muppet from Mars. But at least it came closer to filling the requirements than those oversexed fire plugs.

What's more, it was willing to talk to her. It looked available. It also appeared to be Jewish—just like her father's business partner, who had become one of the most cherished adopted members of the family. And it bore a nano-resemblance to the father of Barbara's best friend when she was a kid, since her best friend was also Jewish. This meant that someday the fly bumbling Francophilically in the region of her web might make a bit of money. He also might come in handy for baby-sitting; and the pressures of parenting were killing her. So she planned a kidnap (with the emphasis, as she saw it, on the word kid). She was convinced I was sixteen. Wrong. I was twenty-one!

This is how I became the privileged co-tenant of her mattress from eleven at night until six in the morning.

But can a relationship built on desperation, calculation, an occasional angelic smile, Mussolini's railroad schedule, and Yiddish interpretations of the Book of Genesis last?

◆

How DOES ALL OF this relate to the birth of The Sixties? Sex is more important than we think. It leads to basic life decisions, decisions about how to settle down, where, and with what career. So the most important part of The Sixties Sexual Revolution was the part that no one publicized— the Revolution's aftermath. The aftermath in which life got serious and the veligers came home to roost. And you got to that aftermath earlier than most. Why? Because you got to the Sexual Revolution two years earlier than your peers.

THE DAUGHTER OF THE OMEN

Barbara had me on a schedule that involved dating another girl until 10:30 at night, coming home at 11:00, having sex (if Barbara was in the mood that night), getting up at 5:30 a.m., jogging across town to my converted closet in the West Village, and preparing to recommence the whole routine during the next twenty-four-hour rotation of the earth around its axis.

I don't know what softened her heart, but after three or four months of this surreptitious substitute for a relationship, Barbara finally broke down and decided she'd allow me to be seen by her offspring...not necessarily a great idea since small children usually give me a puzzled look, then conclude that I'm an appropriate target for stones, toys with sharp edges, and whatever else can be lofted at high velocity by a small but murderous hand.

However, Barb's subsequent suggestion that I move in with her meant that I could decamp from my elegant Bleecker Street cubicle and experience the joys of living with my inamorata in a magic kingdom where thieves visit your apartment with the regularity of unusually diligent mailmen. And we could split the $23-per-month rent. That meant $11.50 per month for each of us.

As an elderly gentleman would explain to me a few months later while I stood in the first floor hallway of Barbara's tenement gawking at the empty spot from which my fifth bicycle had just been stolen, this moldering patch of urban blight had once been a safe neighborhood where everyone knew everyone else. Alas, he said, those days would never return. He shuffled on up the stairs. I'd never seen him before. I never saw him again.

Nanette, the daughter I was now privileged to haunt, was like a picture out of a fairy tale: blond, gorgeous, charming, pixie-ish, and in every way delightful. In every way, that is, until she made a minor discovery: I was going to be spending nights with her mommy. In other words, mommy would be sleeping with me, not her (not that mommy had *ever* slept with her, but this definitely seemed like a deprivation of a precious, if seldom exercised, right). From that moment on, the smiles and hoydenish charm vanished. Small fangs emerged from Nanette's mouth. Her head swiveled 360 degrees. Hot green soup shot from her tonsils, redecorating a gray room that hadn't been painted since the Depression. I was THE ENEMY!

Getting up in the morning in a house occupied by Nanette and Barbara was an experience. No more stretching and yawning and looking out the window at the sunshine flooding the small park across the street from my old gerbil cage in a ritzy neighborhood. For one thing, the managers of Barbara's tenement had last cleaned the windows when Boss Tweed was posing for political cartoons, and even if we'd been able to see through the scum, all we'd have spotted were the roofs of the deteriorated dwellings on the other side of the street.

For another thing, the contemplative calm of morning was broken almost immediately by Nanette, whom Barbara was trying to dress for day-care center. By now Barbara had been living alone with her child for two years in dire poverty. She was convinced that her parents had disowned her on the grounds of premature pregnancy, so she didn't apply to them for financial aid. She was overwhelmed with guilt that she didn't have more time or money to spend on her daughter. As we saw a bit earlier, Nanette, a cagey toddler, had apparently spotted this chink in her mother's armor and made the most of it. She had become a total tyrant, taking a perverse pleasure in reducing her mom to a blubbering wreck. Barbara would offer a dress. Nanette would throw it aside and shout "No!" Barbara would offer another. Nanette would loudly toss this one on the reject heap as well. Within minutes, every piece of clothing Nanette's size in the apartment would lie discarded on the floor while the little queen would stand defiantly in her underwear, daring her mother to try something else.

Finally, Barbara would pick a rag at random and insist Nanette put it on. Out came the second in the bag of pint-sized tricks. The beautiful blond child would fling herself on the floor and scream at the top of her lungs. If Barbara uttered another syllable of entreaty, Nanette would elevate the decibel level and pound her fists and feet on the floorboards. The daily climax came as Barbara shriveled to a bewildered blob and cowered in a corner of the room, certain this was all her fault. How Nanette ever got to day care in anything but panties is beyond me.

But this *did* help explain why when I'd arrive home at 11:00 p.m., Barbara often was in no mood for sex. In fact, it helped explain why she would not allow me to get anywhere closer than fifteen feet away from her. She never wanted to have another one of *these*!

What is a house guest who is gradually turning into a surrogate parent to do? I hauled every book on child-rearing I could find out of the NYU library. I read them all, down to the last semicolon and period of the index. Then I tried out the books' recommended methods. I calmly reasoned with Nanette. That didn't work. I talked to her like a buddy. No soap. I had her draw pictures of Barbara and me and release her aggression by slicing and pummeling the portraits to bits. This was fun, but it didn't solve the problem of getting the child clothed.

As things proceeded, I made a horrible realization. Nanette perceived this as a form of warfare. I was using every rule of decorum in the book. Nanette was following Sun Tzu's manual of dirty tricks. And she was beating Barbara and me to bits.

So I did the unthinkable. I turned to B. F. Skinner's pigeon experiments, the ones about positive and negative reinforcement. For Skinner, positive reinforcement was food. Negative reinforcement was an electric shock. But frying Nanette with an electrical jolt was out of the question. Instead, when it came time to clothe Nanette in the morning, I used sweet reason and offered her a food pellet. If that didn't work (and it never did), I gave her a directive even a bird in a cage could understand. "If you don't have your dress on by the time I count ten, you'll get a spanking." The first two times I said it, Nanette didn't believe me. She stood there defiantly and stuck out her tongue. After the second spanking, she no longer doubted my word. By the count of eight, the child was fully dressed.

This was not an easy approach for a nice Jewish believer in nonviolence to implement. I loathed the idea of hitting a child. My father had probably only whacked me about four times in his entire life. So I went to my shrink—psychotherapist number five—to seek absolution.

Now this was one of your more unusual practitioners of applied psychology. She was a German who, if she'd only been a male, would probably have ended up in the Prussian cavalry. She was taller than I was, and when she opened the door to allow me into her office, she glowered down at the top of my head with supreme disdain. Then she walked to her high-backed office chair and swiveled it 180 degrees so she could stare out the window at the garden behind her brownstone-based office. In other words, she turned her back to me. And I spent the entire session opening my heart to the rear of her severely disciplined hairstyle.

This had astonishing therapeutic effects. I began to come down with stomachaches so severe that I could barely walk. My family doctor couldn't figure out the cause (but he was in his eighties, so he could barely figure out how to operate a roll of toilet paper). In desperation, I began a diary, keeping track of what I was eating, what I was doing, and when the stomach pains occurred. After two weeks, a pattern emerged. The attacks always punched me in the gut at 2:30 on Tuesday and Thursday afternoons. Guess what came at 3:30 on those very days? You got it—my visit to the Prussian shrink.

And it was this Teutonic tower of comfort I went to confess my sin— physically disciplining Nanette. Yes, I had transgressed. I had spanked a child. And not just once…*twice*. I desperately needed someone to tell me that this was okay, that I had solved a difficult problem in a reasonable way, and that I had not turned overnight into the Snidely Whiplash in this play. But I had come to the wrong person. My compassionate therapist immediately offered comfort. She swiveled around in her chair, stared at me with smoldering eyes (thus allowing me to see her face during a session for the first time in a year), and called me a Nazi. Then she threw me out of her office.

As I bicycled back from her high-priced neighborhood to our moldering urban boneyard, I was suicidal. I thought of steering myself in front of a high-speed truck. But all the vehicles were mired in Broadway traffic, so the best I'd be able to accomplish was a broken wrist. Since this seemed unlikely to kill me off quickly, I continued peddling miserably downtown.

Barbara, however, was grateful for my minor exhibitions of violence. Peace had descended on her household for the first time in years. She didn't consider spankings a big deal. Making mischief on a major scale had been her hobby when she was Nanette's age, and her father had pulverized her rear at least once a day. In fact, with her brother, her dad had gone farther. He'd picked the kid up by the ankles and dangled him outside the second-floor hall window. So what I was doing seemed mild by comparison. Nanette, on the other hand, already hated me for taking away her sole possession: her mother. Now she began a mental list of my monstrous qualities. Item number one: child abuse.

But there was some question of who was abusing whom. For example, one night Tom Reichman of the red hair, the Mingus movie, and the subway-tunnel romance volunteered to babysit for Nanette while Barbara and I went out for dinner at a genuine restaurant, one with metal knives and forks. Nanette had her friend Maria with her. Both Nanette and Maria were precocious, articulate kids. It would turn out that they were just a tad too precocious. Barbara and I had a steak dinner on University Place and Eleventh Street, a twenty-minute walk away from Barbara's slum apartment but a light year up in neatness. The table cloths were on the table, not on the floor. When we finished our ribeyes, our baked potatoes with sour cream and chives, and our apple pies a la mode, Barbara, unbeknownst to me, tucked a few forks and steak knives into her purse. We walked back home from the restaurant only to discover Barbara's apartment destroyed and Tom Reichman reduced to a nearly catatonic wreck.

What had happened, we wanted to know. Well, Nanette was not supposed to touch the potted plants, so she and Maria had dumped the contents of every pot on the floor, crushing the splooted greenery under pot-shaped lumps of soil, lumps with their hind ends in the air. Nanette was not supposed to scatter stuff on the floor. So she and Maria had taken every issue of the *Village Voice*—a paper that was obscenely fat in those distant days of overweight print—defoliated it page by page as if they were removing the petals from a daisy, and scattered each page randomly on the floor, pretty much as you'd do if you were preparing to paint your ceiling. But there was more. Nanette was only allowed to eat one dill pickle a day. So the five-gallon pickle jar in the refrigerator had been looted, and not a pickle was left, just enough gherkin juice to fill an aquarium. Nanette was not supposed to touch the ice cream. So that, too, had been plundered. The empty box was on the floor with the plants, the potting soil, and the newspaper.

But this was nothing compared to what Nanette and Maria had done to Tom himself. They had reduced him to a quivering porridge. His face no longer looked lively and alert. It seemed to have melted into a pudge of featureless baby fat. Why? Because Nanette and Maria—both, you will recall, a mere five years old and still in their age of innocence—had told Tom a very Jack-and-Jill-like story. A story with at least ninety verses of extraordinarily graphic misadventures. But the two starring characters in the tale were not named Jack and Jill. They were called Dicky and Pussy. Which hinted that at the tender age of five, Nanette know more about sex than you, me, Barbara, and Tom combined. The bottom line? Nanette and Maria had broken down the boundaries of Tom's self, the boundaries with which he maintained his sense of control, and had turned him into a helpless infant.

Sigmund Freud said that we become sexual at the age of five. Silly idea, right? But maybe Siggy was on to something. Six months later, gorgeous, blonde, lively Nanette would be discovered playing with an equally gorgeous blond male child up the street. The two of them were naked in a closet, carefully hidden from parental supervision.

A year after the pickle-and-newspaper trauma, Tom put a gun in his mouth and blew his brains out. I was furious at him for removing himself from my life. Yes, the suicide of someone you love can trigger very selfish reactions. But I always suspected that Tom's night with Nanette, Maria, and Dicky and Pussy had touched one of the hidden pains that would lead to his death.

However, it was Nanette who was compiling a dossier on Howard the Monster, not the other way around. Over the years, Nanette—a brilliantly imaginative child—would build the list of my sins to mythic proportions, adding many fanciful embellishments and reciting the final product to anyone who would listen. The tale of my villainy would become a permanent part of her arsenal for eliciting sympathy from adults, a skill she developed to a high degree. For example, a year later, I'd make her lunch every day and send her off to first grade. I'd give her two fat sandwiches and a piece of fruit. Then one evening I had a call from her teacher, who sounded extremely disturbed. So I went in to the school the next day to see what was the matter.

Why, the teacher asked, did I perpetually ship my child to school with only half a sandwich? My jaw fell so far down my neck that you would have thought I was wearing a necklace of teeth. One half a sandwich,

I asked? Then I explained what I actually packed in Nanette's bulging lunch bag. Two gourmet peanut butter and jelly sandwiches. Or, when the mood for health-food hit, two cream cheese and jelly sandwiches. Plus some fruit. The teacher deduced that her waif-like pupil had been throwing most of her lunch away, then pretending that she was being starved and telling everyone in sight about her evil stepfather and his techniques for destroying her life. The result: all the students her age with parents wealthy enough to provide high-class luncheon cuisine had pitied her and taken her home to be fed a proper meal. Nanette had used the myth of Howard-the-Monster to trade up from peanut butter and jelly to Lobster Newburg. And more. Much more.

One family that fed Nanette her mid-day dietary upgrades took her to Mexico. Another took her to Europe. And the film-producing dad of one of her upscale mid-day meal partners took her for a helicopter tour of Manhattan. The tale of Howard the Monster and the half a sandwich worked a magic that even the Wicked Witch of the West couldn't equal. Not even with an NIH grant and the diligent research and development work of every one her flying monkeys.

"I have a class of very disturbed kids," said the teacher. "Most of them," she said, "come from middle class, single-parent homes." White, middle-class, single-parent homes were brand new at the time, and single moms did not have a playbook of social convention to work from. The result was what were called latch-key kids. Kids who wore their house keys around their neck so they could let themselves into an empty, lonely family domicile after 3:00 p.m. when school threw them out and left them to their own devices. "But of all my kids," said the teacher, "yours is the most disturbed." That's when Nanette's teacher suggested that I get Nanette into the hands of a good therapist. Knowing how valuable these professionals can be (look how useful mine had been), I immediately complied.

The psychological expert worked wonders. The proof? Eventually Nanette would use the tale of the spankings and numerous variations on the half-a-sandwich routine to make herself the star of a small circle of co-dependency and child-abuse self-help groups. But she swears she's trying to get over it and is beginning to look at my good points. I hope they don't make her ill. They certainly don't comfort me.

◆

PART ONE OF BARBARA's plot had worked. She'd ended her sexual fixation on fire hydrants and had found herself a baby-sitter. For part two, you'll have to wait until our next exciting episode, in which you will meet Barbara's father and discover the truth behind the story that Barbara was raised in a hovel.

THE BEAR THAT HUNTED BARBARA'S DAD

A strange restlessness began to grip my bedmate. She hadn't talked to her family in years. Remember, she was sure they'd disowned her. But, apparently, someone had planted salmon genes in her chromosomes, because she wanted to swim up the Hudson and take me to see her parents. I was game for anything. After all, I hadn't been despised by families of impecunious Protestants for years. And given my bohemian look, there was little chance of any reaction from Barbara's clan other than nausea.

Nanette was too small to walk very far without demanding to be carried. She looked as dainty as Alice in Wonderland, but since she was five and tall for her age, she weighed as much as a Honda Civic. So we made it to the Port Authority Bus Terminal with me lugging Nanette like a Volga barge hauler trying to carry the boat up the footpath instead of letting it merely fight the current at his side. (You'll recall these poor Russian boatmen had to bend over so far to tug their craft that most of them scraped off their foreheads on the pathway. This explains the high intelligence of today's average Russian citizen.)

When a Greyhound bus finally let us off in Kingston, New York, Barbara's hometown, I hoisted Nanette on my back again and we trudged through a neighborhood that didn't exactly look like Barbara had described. There were no tarpaper shacks or people living in cardboard boxes with disemboweled automobiles heaped on the barren sod that passed for yards. The yards, in fact, were large and lush with manicured grass. The houses were immense wooden structures that would have done an upper-middle class Buffalonian proud.

Finally, we rounded the corner of Lounsberry Place, which, according to Barbara's version of her history, was supposed to be filled with chickens and heavily-muscled rats who handled collections for the neighborhood's money-lending church mice. The street was a Hallmark greeting card paradise. Standing in a conspicuous location, with ample lawns on all four sides and a small stream flanking its southern perimeter, was a large, immaculate white house of the sort the Disney people would have gladly used for family films. This was the "crumbling shanty" in which Barbara had been born and raised.

Yes, there was *some* truth in the tales Barbara had told. The second-story hallway window was, indeed, high enough for Barbara's father to have held her brother out by the ankles for the purpose of making a disciplinary impression. After all, the place was the biggest building on the block! And there was more than enough room for the yard once to have housed a barn. In fact, a couple of horses of the kind Barbara claimed she once possessed seemed entirely appropriate to the place. Though the handmade plows Barbara implied the beasts had been forced to drag appeared decidedly unlikely.

I began to get the impression that something was moderately askew with Barbara's self-perception.

We knocked. A cheerful little woman came to the front door and, despite its gargantuan size, managed to drag it open. She was Barbara's mother. She did not seem to be clothed in rags.

We were ushered into a large dining room. We'd arrived just in time for the evening meal. I was introduced to Barbara's brother, a fellow in a red and black checked flannel shirt. He was slightly larger than a Mack truck and obviously manufactured entirely of muscle. He crushed my hand and gave me a friendly grin. At the head of the table was an older presence who, without ever standing, dominated the room. He had the scowling face of a Puritan elder waiting for the next heretic to come along. We had arrived late and were holding up the commencement of dinner. As he ordered us to sit, he gave the distinct impression that he was the guy who had taught Jehovah how to exude an air of authority.

I was unaccustomed to gentile eating patterns. The emphasis here did not seem to be on shouting and screaming, but on food. The fifteen-foot-long table was covered with so many serving dishes there was barely room for them all. I tried to count the courses, but my arithmetic failed me. Then

Barbara's father ordered that we bow our heads in prayer. I was an atheist. But the tone of the command made it obvious that being a conscientious objector at this moment could be fatal. I listened while Jesus Christ was injected into the nutriments. I gathered the meal was not kosher.

We ate. I forget whether anyone attempted to make conversation. Apparently, witty banter is not an Episcopalian (Barbara's mother) or Quaker (her pa) specialty.

I was on a diet. After all, remaining a ninety-nine-pound weakling takes willpower. A willpower I'd worked very hard to achieve on the kibbutz. So when the four hundred dishes went around the second time, I attempted to politely decline. Barbara's father wouldn't hear of it. A voice from the whirlwind ordered in no uncertain terms that I eat. Otherwise I would probably be forced to swallow a leviathan whole. Then the dishes did their third funereal parade around the table. I could feel the mashed potatoes coming out of my ears, but I didn't dare refuse. People had been plagued with frogs, lice, and locusts for less.

Finally, the table was cleared. And out came the pies...all three of them. Followed by the ice cream. One element of my diet had become sacred. I would not, under any circumstances, eat dessert. I hadn't done it in the three years since I'd licked my compulsive eating problem in the Valley of Jezreel and had managed to lose twenty-eight pounds in two weeks. It had taken a will of steel to install my new eating habits, and I was damned if my metallic discipline would be crushed by some mashed pumpkin in a pastry shell.

The time had come for a test of wills. Armstrong Aurelius Steele, Barbara's dad, began to cut pie number one, placing slices on fine china plates, crowning them with balls of ice cream big enough to be used as the bellies of overweight snowmen, and passing them around the table. I explained meekly that I didn't eat dessert. Armstrong responded by cutting a slice twice the normal size, putting on enough Sealtest ice cream to cap Mount Everest, and shoving it in my direction. I politely demurred.

For the first time since we'd entered his palace, Armstrong Aurelius Steele rose to his feet. His head scraped the ceiling. His shoulders barely fit into the room. There wasn't a scrap of fat on him. He came over to my side of the table. A fist the size of an Easter ham descended in front of my face.

It bore the sidewalk-sized slab of pie. "Eat," he said, in that hospitable sort of voice with which the giant used to rumble his fee-fi-fo-fums. The floor shook. So did the other inhabitants of the table. I refused. The plate moved to within an inch of my nose. Once again Vesuvius erupted with a single syllable: "Eat!!!!"

I'd lost the battle. I took the pie. Then I ingested the second helping proffered by the ham-like fist. For the first time in the evening, Armstrong Aurelius Steele looked content. When dinner ended, I was rolled out of the room like a beer barrel and propped up in a living room chair for an evening of what passes in Protestant homes for conversation. That is to say, utter silence.

But I had apparently passed some arcane gentile test. The Steeles liked me. The fact is, after the first husband Barbara hauled in, they'd have liked Jack the Ripper.

Eventually Barbara's brother, the only Steele offspring who had managed to dodge college, went home to his trailer in the woods. Ten o'clock arrived, and Armstrong and Elizabeth Steele said their monosyllabic goodnights, then retreated upstairs to their separate bedrooms. They had also chastely assigned Barbara and me to separate bedrooms, somehow overlooking the fact that the two rooms they gave us were connected by an adjoining door. Maybe they were hoping that we were more than just friends.

Once her parents had trudged up the stairs to chastely slide themselves between the sheets and enter snoozeland with at least one solid wall separating them, Barbara and I were alone. Alone in the living room that had witnessed the family gatherings of her childhood. And whose every wall had probably winced at the sight.

The hint of sexual possibility provided by the adjoining bedrooms upstairs, the bedrooms with an easily-openable door between them, wasn't good enough for Barbara. She, unbeknownst to me, had come up here to her parental home to exorcise a demon. For months, the guilt left over from her out-of-wedlock-pregnancy had mixed with images of her mother frowning every time she had allowed me, a man she hadn't married, into her bed for the night...not to mention into her body. To untangle the knot of guilt, she had her own test of will in mind.

During the last six or seven weeks she'd had a headache every night, and sex had been out of the question. But now that her parents were upstairs and we were left alone in the living room, she grabbed me like an animal and wrestled me to the floor. Within minutes she had unzipped several vital items of apparel, and we had sinned on the family carpet. She grinned with far greater glee than even her father was able to exude over the Victory of the Pie. Then she dragged me upstairs to my assigned bedroom to do it all over again, this time within earshot of her mother's room. And that earshot made a difference. The mattress on which we pumped away was like Walter Mitty—it had a secret life. It imagined it was a musical instrument. And every spring shrieked as if it had been strung with pickups by Les Paul and had been blown up to Little Richard proportions by Marshall amps. So every move we made was blasted by the box springs through the entire house. Including the rooms Barbara wanted to reach the most—the separate bedrooms of her mom and dad.

Finally, after another hour of calisthenics in the missionary position, Barbara snuck through the door and into the adjoining room she had been ordered to occupy. I was exhausted and overstuffed. So, if you'll excuse the expression, was Barbara.

It was the second time that Barbara had made love with gusto. At least with me. The first had been the night when she'd draped herself across her mattress on 7th Street to hook me like a fish. Apparently, to Barbara sex was something you saved for use as a tool on critical occasions.

The next day, Barbara's mom pretended she'd never heard a thing, which seems highly unlikely given the decibel level of our a cappella mattress. And I learned the truth about the Steele family's poverty.

◆

YOUNG ARMSTRONG AURELIUS STEELE's parents died when he was an infant, and he was raised in Philadelphia by Quaker aunts who, without realizing it, were actually Calvinists in disguise. One was the first female to graduate from Swarthmore College. Later, she became head of a school where hellfire and damnation were the primary staples of the cafeteria diet. In her spinsterish bedroom, she carefully copied amusing quotes into a tiny leather-bound notebook. I know. I read it. Her favorite subject? How suffering strengthens the soul, fire tempers steel, and banging your head up against obstacles until you bleed gives you character. So Armstrong grew up a fiercely rectitudinous young man, tall, built like a football player, and apparently extremely good looking. He drove a bread truck in New York City back when a one-horsepower engine consisted of exactly one horse. But he didn't see much future for himself in the loaf-delivery business, so he moved to Central Valley, New York, and got a job selling utilities shares back in the heady 1920s, the era of Samuel Insull, who built a giant trust of electrical companies and electrical railroads, floated his trust's stock in mega-quantities, stirred Americans into a speculative frenzy, was credited with founding General Electric and creating America's electric infrastructure, then was accused of defrauding the public and starting the Great Depression, and driven out of the country.

Arm (as Armstrong was called by his friends) met a fetching upstate maid and took her off to a restaurant where a great deal of tea was served from a lovely antique china pot. It was Prohibition, and the tea was stronger than most. Those who imbibed more than one cup tended, like the liquid, to become potted.

Arm was a dapper fellow who, despite his Calvinist Quakerism, had purchased an ancient Rolls Royce. He let the subject of his affection drive it while he sat at her elbow and used the opportunity to chastely paw her elbows and shoulders. She had very little mechanical aptitude and piloted the vehicle into a creek. Armstrong, being slightly larger than your average Caterpillar demolition excavator, hauled the thing out with his pinkie.

Young Steele could not resist Liz's automotive skills, and hastily married her. She had spent her younger years sailing boats on the local lakes with her best friend, the daughter of a geology professor at Syracuse University, so she was fairly sharp. She'd also read the *Koran*, the *Bhagavad Gita* and the collected works of Emerson. But this didn't keep her from having children.

Meanwhile, some hapless Jewish immigrant had gotten off the boat at Ellis Island and been given the misimpression that there was a fortune to be made in the Catskills. He had bought himself a knapsack, a bunch of trinkets, and some household cutlery, and had set off on foot to peddle his wares to the farm wives isolated from civilization in the mountains. In those days, there were no Jewish comedians to liven up the Catskills' hills and valleys, so someone with Yiddish pronunciation trying to sell you a pot was about the only entertainment for the year.

The peddler eventually saved his money, married one of the non-Jewish farm girls (they were the only girls he'd seen for ten years now, if you don't count the occasional flirtatious cow), dragged her off to the bright lights of the big city—Kingston—and proceeded to make himself the local Croesus by going into more sedentary businesses.

Along came young Armstrong Aurelius Steele and attempted to sell the former peddler a utility share or two. The kid looked honest, earnest, hard-working, and had an awesomely flinty Old Testament morality. So the former peddler took the young man under his wing, and eventually helped him start an oil business.

Now in Texas, the oil business means that you sit around all day on the back porch shooting jack rabbits while the pumps chug up and down, pumping money into your bank account. In Kingston, New York, it isn't that easy. Up there, you work twenty hours a day during the winter, delivering oil to folks about to freeze like oversized Popsicles, or you get calls at three in the morning from citizens whose burners have just broken down and you haul yourself over to their basements to spend the rest of the pre-dawn hours talking recalcitrant machinery into behaving itself, occasionally punctuating your message with a firm twist of the wrench.

Then, during the summer, you loaf and figure out what to do with your profits. In the first years, the profits were somewhat marginal. So Armstrong Aurelius Steele spent the money on needle and thread and sewed pregnancy girdles for his young wife, who popped out one kid after another until the total reached four. Then, as the profits grew more substantial, he discovered that he liked torturing boards with nails and other sharp objects. So he built a big, white house for his growing family on the outskirts of town where the occasional chicken and goat could still be seen demonstrating the life of leisure. Yes, he built his own house. With his own hands. Hands the size of a pig's hind end. Then he slapped together a barn in the back and got a couple of horses, making sure that none of them had bread trucks grafted to their hindquarters.

Gradually, the oil operation grew until it was pulling in bundles of bucks. At that point, Armstrong's Jewish mentor came along with another scheme that would make them all a crate full of cash, if only they were willing to put off luxuries like meat, butter, milk and air for the next fifteen years or so. The Steele's Jewish financial protector wangled them an opportunity to purchase the International Diamond Building on Sixth Avenue in Manhattan. Eventually a builder decided to put up a high-rise office tower on the spot, and paid them several barge loads of greenbacks for the thing.

Armstrong got restless, spent ten years looking for the patch of property of his dreams, finally found sixty acres on Mount Mombaccus overlooking an unending vista of Catskill peaks, cleared enough trees to create a meadow that allowed you to see the view, and built a summer house made of stones the size of small refrigerators…once again, with his bare hands. He called it a camp, but the man couldn't fool anyone. This was a full-scale second home, complete with a massive stone fireplace, every rock of which he'd pried out of the fields himself. The man was never happier than when he was riding a bulldozer—or lifting it out of the muck when it had bogged down after a rain storm. The hard part was telling the difference between Armstrong and his earth-moving equipment.

Not that papa Steele didn't have his flaws. There was the day that Barbara's dad, shotgun in hand, was tracking a bear through the Catskills when he noticed that the number of footprints on the trail had doubled. Not only were there now the paw marks of *two* bears, but there were also the indentations of two pair of human boots—both, curiously enough, of identical size. This is when it dawned on Arm that he was going around in circles because the bear thought it might be fun to reverse the nature of things and start trailing *him*. Like the Steele's horses, the bear had a sense of humor. Why these upstate New York animals did not go into standup comedy, I will never know.

Armstrong Aurelius Steele apparently made it out of the woods uneaten. Sometimes bears are willing to forgo a snack if they can pull off a practical joke.

Barbara's dad's friends were also Great White Hunters. Like there was the day they all went to his stone "cabin" on Mount Mombaccus to prepare for a weekend dedicated to the manly sport of putting holes in unsuspecting deer.

The universally accepted preparatory ritual for one of these slaughters, as Hemingway would tell you if he hadn't put a hole in *himself* some time ago, is to swig down a couple of bottles of Jack Daniels early in the morning. Apparently this acts as either anti-freeze or lighter fluid, I'm not quite sure which. But with enough of the stuff on your breath, you can put a lit match in front of your face, exhale, and do a pretty good imitation of an industrial blowtorch.

Once the men had thoroughly stoked their bloodstreams with ethanol, they set off to stalk the mighty deer. Now, the deer on Mount Mombaccus are either total idiots, or have a much better sense of humor than even the bears. The men set off in two parallel lines about twenty feet apart. They'd only gone a few hundred yards up the mountain when suddenly a magnificent buck came charging out of the woods and ran like blazes straight between the two files of noble hunters. Every man, his reflexes operating like lightning, hoisted his gun to his shoulder and spat lead by the pound. The problem was, the single file of guys on the left just happened to be shooting directly at the folks in the line on the right, and vice versa.

Fortunately, no one was hit. The deer got away without a scratch, though I suspect it had to put a hoof over its mouth when it went back into the brush and told the story to the rest of the herd. After all, you don't want those pesky drunkards with guns to discover your whereabouts just because you're laughing too loud.

When the men realized just who they'd really been shooting at, they checked themselves thoroughly to make sure their heads were still on their necks and there were no six-inch holes in anyone's chest. Then they figured that they'd done the preparatory ritual all wrong and went back to get out another case of Jack Daniels. Fortunately, most of them passed out before they could venture into the woods and threaten each other with lethal weapons again.

Which leaves us with a simple moral, a lesson in geometry. Not all circular firing squads are circular.

◆

MEANWHILE BARBARA, FOR SOME reason, overlooked another simple lesson in life. If you're a girl, you're supposed to follow the role model of your MOTHER. Over the years it would become apparent that I had unwittingly met a clone of Barbara's father, carefully disguised by certain minor sexual alterations and a considerable diminution in height and overall heft. As time went on, Barbara was seized by strange attractions toward horses, barns, hammers, and nails. Fortunately, she never went in for guns.

On this initial visit, there was only one small tip-off to the fact that her father's soul was caged within this delicate female form. Barbara hauled me out onto Lounsberry Place, planted herself in the middle of the street, and ordered me to catch a football. She tossed the pigskin, and I went into my normal receiver's stance—both eyes closed, hands protectively shielding my face. After retrieving the ball from the gutter, I lobbed it back in her direction. Despite my lack of coordination, the missile was moving pretty fast. There was, however, a snag: it wasn't headed anywhere near Barbara. No problem. She took off like a banshee, leaped into the air, snatched the errant torpedo, hugged it to her midriff, and wrapped her entire body around it—arms, legs, chin, everything. That ball didn't have a chance in hell of escape. From this I learned that Barbara and I had diametrically opposite approaches to the physical world.

Yes, there were giants in those times. Most of them in Barbara's family. Thank God she's the runt of the litter.

◆

SO BARBARA HAD NOT grown up in poverty. The family chickens (yes, they at least had existed) were never forced to lend the family money. The local church mice had been unable to collect from the Steele clan, which had enough in the bank to buy the church and all its rodents several times over. And Barbara's girlhood impoverishment was all in her head. Lord knows how it got there, since she is a very brainy soul. But maybe she shared something in common with her daughter, who, as you'll recall, invented the half-a-sandwich lunch. The mystery of Barbara's delusion goes unsolved to this very day.

FLEEING FROM THE FLAMES OF HELL

When we last left off, Barbara had attempted to expel the flaming tapeworms of guilt from her conscience by dragging me up to Kingston, New York, and ravishing me on her parents' living room floor. But she'd failed. Not in ravishing me. She'd done that quite effectively. But in banishing the fire-snorting Platyhelminthes from her brain. This spelled trouble.

To understand why, you have to get to know a little bit more about my family. Let's start with my grandparents. You've already met the ones on my father's side—the great grandfather who was a courier for the tsar, and his son who worked his boot-making skills up into a pocket-sized real estate empire in Asbury Park, New Jersey.

My grandmother on my mother's side was a gorgeous redhead. Or so the lore of the family has it. She grew up in Riga, Latvia, a suave Baltic Sea port, a seaport suffering from a cultural split bigger than the Martian canyon that cracks open a fifth of the Red Planet's surface. Riga was established in roughly the second century AD by the Latvians. A thousand years later, in 1200 AD, an ambitious German bishop attacked with twenty-three German war ships and 500 German warrior-monk crusaders and took the town over. In 1282, the Germans went further— they made Riga a member of their Baltic Sea trade web, the Hanseatic League. Which meant that Riga had two cultures, a "high" German culture and a "low" Latvian culture. The very name of the Latvians— "Latvis"—implies a hayseed lower class, a people of the margins—"forest clearers." Fringe people. Uncouth folks with wood chips in their beards. Needless to say, the Germanic master race looked down upon these log-splinter-covered Latvians. Who knows what the Latvians thought of the snobby Germans.

This culture clash would later drag at least two marriages in my family down to the pits of hell. Not the mainstream pits in which normal sinners writhe in socially acceptable ways. The side chambers in which Lucifer snickers at the fact that he doesn't have to lift a pitchfork because couples handle the invention of new agonies totally on their own. And they do it with an inventiveness that would impress even Vlad the Impaler. This creative approach to agony would make me one of the most peculiar mate-seekers on a planet where peculiarity, torment, and love seem to go hand in hand.

My young, russet-haired grandmother was from the Jewish culture that had caught the fever of German aspirations. She hungered for the aristocratic distinction of advanced degrees. And she dreamed of playing the lady of the manor in a living room from whose grand-piano strings the arpeggios of Mozart and Schubert would frequently roll, battling underweight pizzicatos for attention. Preferably, these highly refined musical notes would stream from the fingers of her precocious progeny, children whose talents prestigious impresarios would beg her to make available for performances in public. Which means that her clan was proud of the fact that in the final decades of the 1800s, the family had produced ballerinas, dentists, and other high class, semi-intellectual types. Unfortunately, this would snarfle the red head's love life...and mine.

The young and pretty *madchen*, my grandmother, fell in love with the perfect, high-prestige, Germanic-Jewish catch: a doctor. She seemed about to snare him. In fact, she considered herself engaged. Then the medical graduate horrified her by finding some other woman more appealing and promptly running off to the rabbi with her. Heartbroken, my grandmother immigrated to America at the turn of the century, did needle work in a New York sweatshop, met a tailor newly arrived from the boondocks of Latvia, and married him. The pair moved to Western New York, where her freshly-caught husband eventually managed to open his own shop and provide a modest living for his two daughters and one son.

The little tailor was one of the nicest, best-humored people on the planet. What's more, he was madly in love with his wife. But this availed him nothing. He wasn't a doctor. Worse, he wasn't from Riga's Germanic culture. In fact, he wasn't even from Riga. He was from a nearby town, Golding, of less than 5,000 inhabitants. A town of primitives on a par with the Piltdown Man—an alleged half-human, half-orangutan who turned out to be a fraud. In other words, her tailor was from the culture of the locals, the hicks, the rubes, the rednecks, and the barbarians: the Latvian-ish Jews. My grandmother would never forgive him.

In fact, she would make every day of his life a walking misery. She would belittle and scold him, pecking at him like a chicken with high aspirations punishing Barbara's pet, the runt of the litter. When he was fifty, my grandfather couldn't take it anymore and moved out. Then he came down with liver cancer, and his youngest daughter was delegated to plead with him to come home and die with his children…who loved him.

What were this poor man's sins in the eyes of his wife? To repeat. He was from a culture of bumpkins. And he wasn't a doctor. This pattern of marriage would poison my mother. It would poison me. And it would erect barriers taller than the Burj Dubai for Barbara.

◆

You recall that my mother was a bright young girl with the kind of vocabulary Samuel Johnson dreamt about. She had only one goal in life: a college education. But the family was poor. So they used all the savings they had to send her brother off to college and incarcerated her in secretarial school, despite the fact that some institution of higher learning had actually awarded her a partial scholarship. Eventually, as you may remember, she became the private secretary to the head of the New York State Liquor Authority, a strange position for a girl who didn't drink, and by the age of thirty was still unmarried, don't ask me why.

Then this thirty-two-year-old bachelor came to Buffalo from Asbury Park, New Jersey, and started a children's clothing store in the middle of the Depression. In those days, parents preferred that their children wear hand-me-downs from deceased relatives who had shriveled to only twice the child's size, so the business produced just enough money to feed a very small family of fruit flies. As you recall, my dad ate a lot of beans and tried to concoct a stew from the cans, but found the results inedible. However, despite his poverty, he had one advantage. He was exactly like my mother's much-adored dad—loyal, patient, pleasant, and the bearer of a good sense of humor...but not a doctor.

So my mother married him. Then she realized that he was missing something critical—an MD. Following in her mother's footsteps, she opened a campaign of verbal harassment. She unleashed a barrage of brilliantly articulate insults. A daily campaign. And though Irving Bloom, my dad, worked fourteen hours a day, seven days a week to build the biggest liquor store in Western New York State, thus showering my mom with comfortable quantities of cash, the warfare never ceased. After all, my mom had a family obligation: to keep her mother's marital legacy alive.

Along came a child, and my mother trained him well. I became an expert in the arts of conversational sabotage and ambush—all directed at my dad, of course. My mother reserved the more subtle stratagems for herself—forms of mental flagellation so heinous that even medieval torture masters would have judged them inhumane.

Every day my dad came home from his store at 6:00 p.m. to have dinner with us, then went back to the store to work until eleven. Every evening he slid into his habitual position on one of the two red, padded banquettes of the breakfast nook, a tiny room like a restaurant booth with built-in benches set up on either side of a built-in table. Every day, he radiated smiles, eager to tell the stories of the people he had met during the day—his customers, people he loved. Like Erskine Caldwell, who wrote the novel *Tobacco Road*. And like the auto dealer who took a big chance, stepped outside the box, ignored cars from General Motors, Ford, and Chrysler, and went with the strange autos turned out by an industrialist who had helped America win World War II—Henry Kaiser, the aluminum king, the father of American shipbuilding, and the maker of the Liberty Ships. My dad loved to tell how Kaiser had turned out the huge ships that helped America win the war at a rate of three per day. Which meant that my dad's customer was selling cars with strange names like the Henry J (for Henry J. Kaiser) and the Kaiser. And we were eventually driving in them.

Every day my dad would begin one of his stories of the day's adventures. But before he could get out more than three sentences, my mom would cut him down with a withering fire of put downs. Brilliant, gifted, but undeserved insults. And she trained me and my younger brother to join in the fusillade. My dad was a man of natural good-heartedness and joy. But every day, my mom turned that joy into an agony. With, alas, my help. And my brother's.

Astonishingly, my mother recognized the destructive savagery of *her* mother's guerrilla attacks. How do I know? She spent decades trying to track down what was left of her family in Europe, taking trips to New York City to pour through the archives of The YIVO Institute for Jewish Research. Of the hundreds who had lived in the 1930s, only two were left. One was a woman who had married one of the Russian soldiers liberating Riga from the Nazis, had moved from Riga to the Russian portion of the USSR, and had become a tractor driver. The other was a dentist in South Africa. In one of my mother's letters to the South African dentist, she told the tale of her mother's marriage, complete with the tortures her mother had inflicted on her tailor spouse and why. She pinpointed the sources of her mother's venom with precision: the fact that her husband did not have the lofty stature of an advanced degree and a medical practice, and did not come from Riga's German-cultured Jewish aristocracy. What's perplexing was my mom's failure to see that even as she typed her analysis of her mother's mistakes, she was faithfully repeating them.

I, however, was much too wise to get my notions of marriage solely from bits of carnage blown across the family dinner table. I sought other, counterbalancing examples. And I found them…in my father's New Jersey sisters. There was no New York State Thruway in those dim and distant days. So in the depths of winter, we'd climb into our brand new Henry J and wend our way to a patch of ice-covered switchbacks of asphalt through mountains that I can't find on Google Maps, but that my dad aimed at with the accuracy of a sea turtle swimming a thousand miles to the patch of beach that gave it birth. The roads that snaked through these steep slopes never failed to entertain. The cliffs to our right were peppered with cars that had gone off the road and had been stopped by the trees in a vertical position, standing on their noses with their trunks in the air. Our destination: Asbury Park. There, in the former playground-on-the-sea for the super rich, I would see what true marital bliss could be.

My Aunt Beck and Uncle Al lived in an enormous, seven-bedroom, white-painted, ornate home that my grandfather had bought, a house that gave Beck and Al enough space to spend their days without seeing each other. But distance could do nothing to diminish the boom of their long-range artillery. Though they were located a dozen rooms away from each other, you could have heard their shouting above the crowd noises at Ebbets Field, sixty miles to the North.

My Aunt Golda and Uncle Nat had an equally blissful ménage. Close-quarter vituperation was their specialty. Their shrieks in their tiny breakfast room were so shrill that you could have used the sonic vibrations to dislodge kidney stones.

The household hell I'd seen in my extended family was one I never wanted to be battered and deep-fat fried in. By my teen years, I had made a simple vow. Never, ever in my life would I get married.

This would have consequences just an inch or two down the line.

◆

FAST FORWARD TO BARBARA and me taking the bus from Kingston back to the Lower East Side. The weekend's exhibitions of prurient behavior had done nothing to tranquilize the hyperactive tapeworms of Barbara's guilty conscience. In fact, her self-punishment festered and grew.

The neighbors in our tenement were all Roman Catholic Puerto Ricans. Barbara was sure that her illicit sexual relationship was all they talked about. When she walked down the block, she ignored the drug dealers and stick-up artists. All she could see were the faces of Virgin Mary worshippers frowning on her extra-marital immorality. How the Virgin Mary would have disapproved is hard to understand. She'd had an extra-marital affair with an undersized animal—an oversexed dove. But the Catholic Church nonetheless does everything in its power to chill the libido. And that chill was making Barbara shiver.

Finally, Barbara couldn't take it anymore. After four months of living together, she handed me an ultimatum. Either I married her, or in two months I'd have to move out. Marriage, I explained, was out of the question. I warned her about the booby-traps of connubial bliss—in other words, I gave her the story of my mother and my aunts. No dice. It was marriage or exile!

Two months later, I went apartment hunting. This led to a fourth story walk-up on Eleventh Street between First Avenue and Avenue A, a few blocks from Barbara's, with a splendid view of a playground and the outrageously high rent of $45 a month. There was a petite girl at NYU with red-tinged hair—the sort who wore makeup and knew how to use it to look like a model—who had set her sights on me and figured that this would be her big chance to move in for the kill. She'd spotted me slitting fetal pigs in biology class and had probably concluded I'd become a brain surgeon. A very rich brain surgeon. Little did she suspect my manual incompetence. This vision of loveliness seemed to want to share my new apartment, not to mention my bed. I somehow managed to sidestep her snares. Then there was the girl from the Andy Warhol crowd who had asked me to move in with her two days after I'd moved in with Barbara. She was kind enough to help with my housewarming by letting me stay overnight in her bed, a convenient one block away from Barbara…and three blocks south of my new apartment. For even further convenience her name was also Barbara. So I had help in making the move. And in remembering names.

But when the first weekend after my banishment came, I invited Barbara number one to take a load off by letting me baby-sit for Nanette. Barbara, who was being reminded of just how rough handling The Daughter of the Damned by yourself can be, was more than willing to toss me her bundle of Satanic fury. So I made Nanette meals and let her horse around on the playground while I kept my eye on her through my kitchen window.

The experience was an epiphany. Suddenly Barbara remembered why she'd tolerated me—because I had taken the burden of her kid off her shoulders. I kept my separate tenement apartment in the slums of East Eleventh Street. But within a week Barbara and I were living together again. The subject of marriage faded from our conversations. My function as baby-sitter was blessing enough. Ironically, the child who wanted to tear us apart had brought us back together again.

HOW TO SLEEP WITH YOUR GIRLFRIEND
UNDER HER MOTHER'S NOSE

My renewed relationship with Barbara was marred by a little glitch: her imminent departure to the Sorbonne. For the first five or six months of the relationship, the intrusion of the Eiffel Tower into our bliss seemed too distant to worry about. Then it finally occurred to me that the 3,000-mile separation might make it more difficult for me to see Barbara's smile, thus somewhat dampening the therapeutic effects of our togetherness. Even worse, it would make sex impossible.

I pondered this dilemma for a while, but being a slow thinker, it took six months before I hit on a solution: accompanying my semi–loved one to France! There was only one small, six-legged invertebrate in the unguent. It was April by the time I arrived at my momentous revelation, and the application deadlines for all the French exchange programs in America had whizzed past roughly four months earlier. By now, the professors in charge were all looking up the phone numbers of Gallic girlfriends and making lists of what brands of brie they wanted to buy once they hit the Seine.

This is where my Francophonic obsession once again came in handy. In a school with over 3,000 undergraduates, I happened to be NYU's best French student. I know, it's hard to believe, especially for me. But it's true. So I went to my *exercise du style* dominatrix, who, when she wasn't wearing her leather bra and spike-tipped boots, was one of America's top Camus scholars. I asked if she could do anything to help me. She offered me a chair, cuffed me playfully with her iron-studded gauntlet, phoned a friend at Williams College who ran the school's student exchange operation, and ordered him to accept me into his program. He whimpered with erotic pleasure, imagining the spanking he might receive if only they were together. Within half an hour, without an application, I was scheduled to head for Paris.

Then came the end of my freshman year and the beginning of the summer. I wanted a summer job in editing and writing. I was still following Einstein's commandment—to be an original scientific thinker, you have to be a writer. First, I made a list of every job I'd ever had, intent on writing a resume. The process was depressing. Most of the jobs I'd been given involved painting. And I can't paint. While others coat a few hundred feet of wooden siding with a new layer of colored sticky stuff, I manage to paint one. One foot. So I finally went to Barbara in despair, showed her my very long compendium, and wailed, "Look at this list of failures." Barbara stopped me with a simple statement: "Those are not your failures. That's your *experience*." See? I told you she had a brain.

Next, I went through *The New York Times* want-ads, took down the information on a hundred employment agencies that dealt with "editorial" jobs, then methodically began to call the agencies, one by one. And one by one they told me they had nothing for me. But, remember, the difference between an idea and a reality is persistence. Persistence and money. But money is a subject for another book. When I got to agency number ninety-eight, very close to the last agency on the list, I got a very different response: "We think we have something for you. Could you come in and see us?" Yes I could, and yes I did. Who was the employer they had in mind? The Boy Scouts of America.

This was a bit peculiar. Lieutenant General Robert Stephenson Smyth Baden-Powell's organization for turning horny young boys into horny old men, and some of those horny old men into sexually predatory leaders of scouting troops, had thrown me out when I was eleven. The troop leader told me it was for incompetence at Morse Code. But he could just as easily have tossed me out for incompetence at knot tying. Yes, the people who wanted my writing skills worked for the very entity that had spit me out like a long-haired caterpillar in a Caesar salad.

So when my freshman year of school let out, I began a daily commute to the Boy Scouts of America's headquarters in New Brunswick, New Jersey, the very town in which I'd taught nubile young women the nomenclature of electrical wiring just a year and a half earlier.

In those days, there were no word processors and no spell checkers. Just extremely expensive and totally clueless electric typewriters, typewriters so rude that they never lifted a lever to tell you when you'd spelled a word so badly that even the ceiling over your head could see that it was wrong. So the Boy Scouts gave me the chore of proofreading. God knows whether I was the least bit effective at this task. I have a strong suspicion that delinquent periods and commas snuck into what I was doing, then, when I failed to catch them, then got together and made fun of me behind my back. Like the bear and the stag who snickered at Barbara's dad.

After two days of this, the chief of the editorial department yanked me out of the proofreading pool. He had a crucial assignment. The Bible of the Boy Scouts is its Handbook. And that Handbook had a problem. Its chapter on masturbation had been written in the 1930s. Its reasons for not touching yourself down there, much less not touching yourself to the point of arousal? You'd go blind. And a three-foot-long black hair would emerge from your palm, be impossible to pluck, and would label you as a sexual weakling whenever you tried to gesticulate. I kid you not. For some reason, the head of The Boy Scout editorial department did not think that these reasons would cut the mustard with kids in 1965. Could I rewrite the chapter, he asked? But what he really wanted me to do was a bit sneakier. He wanted new reasons not to do it. So I came up with one—you'll feel guilty. My boss—the head of editorial—was delighted. And there's just a chance that my, ahem, handiwork is still a chapter in the Boy Scout Handbook today.

Then the kindly editorial head wound up for a big pitch and tossed a more challenging assignment my way. Rewriting the Boy Scout Merit Badge pamphlet on stalking and tracking. He didn't bother to ask if I knew anything about this woodsy art. I didn't. Other kids in my Boy Scout troop had trouble finding their way out of a forest. I had trouble finding my way into one.

What's worse, when I had applied for merit badges before my expulsion from the Boy Scouts, I'd filled out the paperwork for each award, then had slipped it under the bathroom door and left it on my parents' night table in the hope of getting something that the Scouts absolutely required, a parental signature. My dad and mom had always been too busy to sign. Then, when my brother had hit Cub Scout age, my mom had become his Den Mother. Go figure. So I was as well qualified to write Merit Badge manuals as a rusty lawn mower.

But the Boy Scouts had a very good research library. And I figured that if you love the kids you're writing for and want them to be able to stalk and track so successfully that they can get close enough to a bunny rabbit to rub noses with it before it sees them, you can write about anything. One day, on the way from the New Brunswick bus terminal to the office, I spotted a wild bunny in the middle of an empty lot, dropped down on all fours, and tested what I'd learned from my library research. There was no grass and there were no trees. No natural cover. This was the equivalent of crawling across a parking lot without the benefit of black paint on your back to make you look like asphalt or a white line. But the rabbit was extremely indulgent. It pretended it didn't see me and let me get within three feet. Lord knows what impelled it to be so charitable. Maybe it needed a good story to tell the bunnies in the burrow back home.

My boss was happy with the stalking and tracking pamphlet, so he gave me one on camouflage. Again, he didn't ask whether I knew anything about the subject. Does turning white as a sheet in bed and blending in with the cotton count? When that was over, he gave me the ultimate assignment: Ten Steps to Organize a Boy Scout Troop—THE book used at the most critical phase of Boy Scout expansion, the book you relied on if you wanted to establish a new Boy Scout troop from scratch. He tossed an existing manuscript for Ten Steps to Organize a Boy Scout Troop at me. It was worse than rough. It was incomprehensible. So incomprehensible that no cut and paste would work, no matter how thorough. So I went back to basics. I researched every topic covered in each chapter from scratch. I watched a ream of pre-packaged audiovisual presentations. And I read books and other scraps of verbiage. Thank God for the library. Then I wrote new chapters from the ground up.

When the process was finished, I took the new booklet to my boss. He read it, mumbled what may have been good things about it, then revealed something he had not previously told me. The big task was not to rewrite the book. The really-big job was to get what I'd written through the booby-trapped corridors of bureaucracy. Corridors blocked by the razor wire of ego. It seems that the original ball of incomprehensibility had been written by a very big cheese down the hall, the Vice President of Munster and the Chief Executive of Camembert. I had worked for weeks to turn an abused and battered slurry of screaming syllables into a stainless-steel tool. But the real labor of Hercules was getting past the man who was proud of the slurry. And my new mentor, the head of editorial, was going to give that job to me. All me. We'll tell you how that turned out in a few minutes. But first, let's get back to Barbara.

◆

IN FACT, LET'S SLIDE all the way back to early June, when I was still trying to corner fugitive misspellings during my two-day proofreading task at the Boy Scouts of America Headquarters. The chore that, unbeknownst to me, was my tryout for the big masturbation assignment. That's when Barbara had to prepare for her upcoming Sorbonnerie by trooping off to Middlebury College for a summer-long crash program in Gallicisms—you know, the sort-of-concentration-camp-style session in which you're thrown into the pastry oven if you utter a non-French syllable at any time during the summer. At first, I took our two-month separation fairly well. I lost most of my marbles, blithered a lot, and contemplated going to the local Purina factory and volunteering as a cat-food ingredient.

So to soothe my loneliness, I did two things. I had my platonic friend with the *Sports Illustrated* swimsuit physique move in with me. You'll recall that this remarkable lady was the one whose inability to show up for "The Trojan Women" had triggered my first non-date with Barbara. If I give you this lovely woman's name, you will throw spittoons at me. Why? The woman with the perfect tan everywhere (she enjoyed nude sunbathing) was named, don't hit me, Barbara. Apparently, the name Barbara was the only one that new parents could think of in the early 1940s. World War II had bludgeoned these young couples into a stupor. And they didn't want to saddle their baby girls with the only other name on their mind— Adolf. For simplicity, let's call the Barbara of the Coppertone tan Barbara number three.

Barbara III and I slept with no clothes in a single bed the width of a plank of wood. But, hey, what are friends for? We both abided by the rules. No sex!

Meanwhile, two and a half months earlier, Tom Reichman, the red-headed film-maker whose idea of a date was a trek to a cave in the subway, had bought Nanette a tiny, fluffy, yellow baby chick for Easter. Yes, yellow! And like everything sold on the Lower East Side of Manhattan in those days, this chick was a counterfeit. It had been sold to Tom as an infant chicken. But two months later it was summer and the chick had grown up, shown its true colors (white with an orange beak), and developed webbed feet that would make any self-respecting hen feel ridiculous. It was not a chicken, it was a duck. A big one. What's worse, the duck had developed the prudish instincts of a chaperone. Or a puppy. So it got into bed with Barbara III and me and slept between our heads.

Somewhat lacking in sexual fulfillment, I decided to visit Barbara I in Middlebury. A big mistake.

◆

On the long bus-ride from New York to Vermont, I managed to earn money working madly on Ten Steps to Organize a Boy Scout Troop. Yes, using a yellow pad, a pen, scissors, and Scotch Tape, I labored diligently to instruct would-be makers of men on how to put troops of innocent youngsters into ill-fitting green costumes and persuade them to hike into caves filled with hungry bears. The Scouts believed in the honor system, so they let me do my writing even in moving vehicles, then they took my word for the number of hours I'd put in. The consequent earnings would come in handy at a slightly later point in our story.

Late on a Friday afternoon, I showed up on the Middlebury campus with my Boy Scout scribblings and my sleeping bag. Being at least as capable of speaking French as your average Algerian dish of couscous, I gladly dove into the linguistic discipline of the place and put my English behind me. I mean, I fit into the all-French-all-the-time snobbishness perfectly. I was obnoxious about my ability to toss accent agues like Frisbees. If you overlook the fact that I can't actually toss Frisbees. Then, when Friday night fell, I intended to do something about my sexual deprivation. In perfect French. So, like Abelard guiding Eloise, I took Barbara by the hand, tucked my sleeping bag under my arm, and headed off for the woods. I had lascivious intentions written all over my face, apparently in jumbo magic marker! But in perfect French. As we passed the dormitories, I saw numerous female ankles disappearing into the windows of male bedrooms. But what business was that of mine?

I promptly found a nice, soft anthill between the pine trees, laid out the sleeping bag, and we made love. Yes, in French. Then, the next morning, we woke up and cursed our ant bites in the language of Rabelais.

A few days later, I was back in New Brunswick. My moment of truth had arrived. My boss, the head of editorial, sent me down the hall to the corner office with windows on two walls. Why? So I could present my total rewrite of Ten Steps to Organize a Boy Scout Troop to, gulp, the man who had written the original. I was up against a problem. Eighteen months earlier, when I'd presented radical rewrites to Sol Gordon, the head of the Middlesex County Mental Health Clinic, nearly every word was his. But with Ten Steps to Organize a Boy Scout Troop, not a word of the original remained. With the exception of "a," "the," and "scout." So I had a problem.

I was ushered into the office of the big muckety-muck, the chief honcho whose love child I'd left on a mountain to die. I took my place across from him on the peon's side of the desk. And I told him something that was only partially true—that I'd taken his magnificent ideas and clarified them. In what way was this for real? First of all, I had used the very meat and marrow of the man's masterpiece—the same twenty-four letters of the alphabet. Every one of them. Honest. Secondly, I had leaned on his original for a vital element of punctuation: starting each sentence with a capital letter and ending it with a period. Thirdly, this earnest executive had written a book that aimed to tell generous-spirited, beer-swilling Americans how to organize Boy Scout troops from scratch. Without spilling their barley-malt. I had been true to the author's intention. I'd written exactly what he'd aimed for—ten steps to organize a Boy Scout Troop. I mean, I'd even followed his game plan. I'd laid out a number of steps precisely equal to the total of your toes. I just hadn't used the man's incomprehensible prose. But I had kept his title. Surely that counts for something. Right? Wrong.

My attempt to give the guy in the power seat credit for the finished product didn't work. He had noticed a small flaw in my handiwork: there wasn't a single sentence of his in the new book. The bottom line? I had spilled raw sewage all over his ego. Two days later my boss called me in and told me that it was with great regret that he had to inform me that I no longer had a job concocting instructions on how to terminally mismanage Boy Scout affairs. But both he and I knew that he'd taught me many a valuable lesson. Including this: don't mess with people's egos. Feed their sense of self-worth. Do it honestly. Find what others offer of value then let them know that you see it. Remember that every master or mistress of human affairs is a surfer on a tsunami. A tidal wave of hungry readers, voters, or viewers in search of affirmation. A rider on a foaming crest of ego.

A rider who occasionally has to tell truths others do not want to hear.

The timing of my job loss was fortunate. A day later I got an emergency call. Barbara was hysterical. It sounded like she was calling from the bottom of a fishbowl. Tears were running down her cheeks and flooding the receiver. Why? The dean of Middlebury had ordered an assembly and delivered a lecture on sexual indiscretion. During his fiery oration, everyone in the room had stared at one person and one person only: Barbara. Or at least that's the way Barbara saw it. In her view, there was a scarlet "I" ("indiscreet") on her forehead in not-so-invisible ink.

Discretion, it turned out, meant sneaking into men's dorm rooms after dark and pretending no one noticed. Barbara had broken the code. She had brazenly marched off to the woods with a boy and a sleeping bag, and Sam the Cook (not to be mistaken for Sam Cook, the famous American soul singer) had seen her. Sure, she'd done it after dark. But it violated the rules of romance laid down by the Académie Française. Sneaking through windows is civilized. Entering the woods is not. The old nature versus man-made artifact conundrum.

There was a certain irony here. Once upon a time, my French teacher, Madame Hennin, the woman who brought the Myth of Sisyphus into my life, had convinced a dean from Middlebury College to visit my high school to address the student body. I was her star student. I had skipped from French One to French Four, then had been moved to French Five in two weeks. That's what having two gorgeous, brainy, and vivacious French teachers in a row will do for you. Especially when your hormones are brand new and you haven't ever tried them out. Madame Hennin was looking forward to introducing the dean to me. But, alas, no one informed me that he was coming. And it gets worse.

As you probably recall, I had been elected the Chairman of the Park School's Program Committee for two years in a row. We had school assemblies every morning from 8:00 to 9:00 a.m. Being Chairman of the Program Committee meant programming two of those school assemblies per week, and emceeing all five.

The school was terrific. It left me entirely to my own devices (and those of my committee members, all comely maidens). That worked most of the time. Most. But not on this occasion. Why? No one had given me any training in how to treat a surprise guest.

The august dean showed up unexpectedly on the school's stage at 8:00 a.m. and gave a talk. For half an hour, he said his bit. When he was finished, if I'd known anything about manners, I'd have come up, thanked him for his glowing coals of wisdom, shown him to a chair, and taken the day's announcements from the student body ("I lost an algebra book in the woods while I was sneaking a cigarette yesterday, so if anyone sees a book half-buried in the mud next to a three-foot pile of tobacco ash, could they please return it to me," etc.).

Unfortunately, I knew nothing about human etiquette. You'll recall that I had come from a home in which my parents made a habit of attempting to detonate each other with smart bombs. I had early in life turned my bedroom into a bunker, surrounding myself with a small army of guinea pigs, white rats, lizards, and guppies. None of my late-night conversations with these companions had covered diplomatic protocol. In fact, any social nicety not in the standard behavioral repertoire of a guinea pig was beyond me.

When the dean who my teacher had so nicely persuaded to leave Vermont finished his finely polished words, I didn't have any idea of what a guinea pig would do with him, except perhaps sniff his shoes and urinate in appreciation. So instead of praising the dean for his eloquence and gracefully shuffling him away from the podium, I stood in front of him, slouched in my unkempt winter coat, displayed my three-day growth of pubescent stubble, and asked for announcements, leaving the poor man to wonder why he was staring at the back of a student who had seized his platform and was now treating him as if he didn't exist.

Needless to say, the administration was not pleased by my display of small-mammal etiquette. As I concluded my botch of the social graces, three projectiles hurtled down three separate aisles toward me, all converging on the spot where I stood. One was the headmaster, another the assistant headmaster, and a third the football coach. Steam shot from each of their balding heads and sparks leaped from their eyeballs in a frantic attempt to escape the inferno within. I was less fortunate than the sparks. I couldn't escape. The burly trio cornered me, and each gave me a piece of his mind, thus presumably leaving his brain with one smoldering chunk permanently missing.

I was easily embarrassed in those days. (I still am.) If I'd been Japanese, I'd have covered my face with my sleeve, gone off to the biology lab, found a clean scalpel, and removed my intestines. But being a nice Jewish boy raised by small rodents and guppies, I improvised. I found a large, dark closet and hid for the rest of the day. When my patient French teacher hunted all over campus to find me and introduce her prize student to her favorite dean, I was nowhere in sight.

It seems Clotho, Lachesis, and Atropos (the three Fates, who hold the textile concession on Mt. Olympus) had decided to weave my threads together with those of the poor, innocent Middlebury dignitary once again. Six years later, he was the dean who delivered the speech that reduced Barbara to a weepy mess.

Under circumstances like these, what is a man educated on *Aucassin et Nicolette* supposed to do? Come to the rescue, of course, preferably mounted on a gorgeous steed. So my firing from the Boy Scouts turned out to be a gift. It gave me the freedom to catch the first Greyhound Bus (I couldn't find a horse) back to Middlebury, and secure us an apartment off-campus (though the Puritanical landlady was extremely suspicious when I told her that Barbara and I were married, especially since I looked about sixteen). I calmed Barbara's sobbing, wrung out her tear-drenched clothes, and spent the next month speaking French and getting to know the local citizenry as I marched from one end of town to another seeking odd jobs (the only sort appropriate to an odd person).

Meanwhile, another obstacle reared its ugly head and sneered in our direction. Barbara's mother (who is anything but ugly; in fact, she's quite delightful) announced that, to help take a load off Barbara's mind, she'd drop everything and spend the year in Paris taking care of Barbara's daughter, Nanette. Why, you may ask, was this a problem? After all, good baby-sitters are hard to find. Especially in France. Well, you see, Barbara's mother comes from good Daughters of the American Revolution stock, and DAR women of her generation have a certain problem with sex. Within the confines of marriage, they seem perfectly capable of enjoying it. But they are utterly unable to talk about it, think about it, or imagine that their daughters might be having it under conditions defined in those days as "sin." So the impending presence of Mama Steele meant that the whole purpose of my trip to France was in serious jeopardy. How could I possibly slip into Barbara's bed—or into Barbara—on a regular basis if her mother sat up in a rocking chair all night watching Barbara's bedroom door?

Then, one evening, a female friend to whom I was confessing my woes came up with a solution. For six months, Barbara had insisted that I make an honest woman of her. I had steadfastly refused. Not that I had anything against honesty, mind you. I didn't think I could stand even the tiniest fib. Though some of the white lies chronicled in this book might indicate just how little I knew myself. Nonetheless, cleaning up Barbara's morals seemed to involve marriage. And marriage, I'd learned from my grandmother, my mother, and my aunts in New Jersey, was a state of warfare between the sexes which I regarded with the same enthusiasm I reserved for pleasures like being sautéed in hot sauce.

Nonetheless, there was an irresistible appeal to my female counselor's logic. How *do* you sleep with a girl when her mother is in the same apartment? How do you do it over and over again, pretty much whenever you want (or whenever she doesn't tell you to keep your distance because your breath smells like dead pollywogs), without the mother having you arrested by the vice squad. Or without the girl's father, in Barbara's case a father the size of a steam shovel, using you as raw material in his latest recipe for squirrel ragout? You get married.

So pushing aside my memories of my parents, aunts, and uncles dusting each other daily with mustard gas, I dashed to the phone, called Barbara at Middlebury, and told her we were getting hitched. I didn't bother to ask her consent. There was no time. We had only three weeks left before we were due to head for Orly Airport, and Barbara was still legally married to a 6'3" poet.

So I jumped off the line, leaving Barbara to terrified visions of being tied for the rest of her life to someone who looked like a mutated Muppet. I hastily counted the money I'd made by writing works of enduring literature for the Scouting movement, made an appointment with the cheapest divorce lawyer I could find, discovered that we'd have to get Barbara on a plane for Mexico the minute she finished her sentence at Middlebury in order to give the law ten days to validate the quickie amputation of her previous spouse and still allow ourselves twenty-four hours in which to get married and pack for France, and that the whole thing would cost me approximately twice as much money as I had. So I called Barbara's mom.

Barbara's parents, as you remember, had been horrified by her first husband. Anything that could walk, talk, breathe, and was approximately male would, in their opinion, be a vast improvement. I fit all the above criteria, more or less. So they ignored my peculiar tendencies, and gave me the rest of the money to pay for the divorce. Then they even volunteered to plan and pay for the wedding. Nice people.

They didn't bother to ask Barbara if she still wanted to go through with it. She didn't. But the wheels of fortune had begun to grind, and those wheels had something in common with the fifty-dollar car Barbara had shared with her boyfriend—they had no brakes.

◆

I'LL SKIP THE PART about how, on the plane back from the divorce mill in Juarez, the jazz musician Art Blakey sat next to Barbara and convinced her to ditch me and come live with him and how—following the recommendations of a book on North Korean brainwashing techniques (yes, for real)—I stood Barbara under a naked light bulb (this is the truth) for twelve hours, badgering her into forgetting Blakey and going through with the ceremony that would chain her to me. She finally gave up when dawn arrived and it became obvious that I wasn't going to let her sleep unless she said yes.

Then, a week before the marriage (a nice, atheistic affair) was due to occur, another thought hit me. I was about to become the father of a five-year-old. In fourteen days, my newly-acquired child would enter first grade in the Parisian school I had found for her. And first grade is a vital time. It's when you learn to read and write. But Nanette, despite her Francophonic name, wouldn't know how to speak the language. Not a word of it. Not a single *s'il vous plait*. And with that obstacle in her path, she would never learn to read. Her only contact with literature would be the pictures in *The Adventures of Tintin* comic books. She'd never get a job, and would end up on welfare, drinking Sterno, unable even to sell drugs because she'd never mastered arithmetic. My sense of duty as an about-to-be-minted parent blared out one simple message: we had to cancel our trip to France. So Barbara and I never made it to the Sorbonne after all.

Meanwhile, Barbara's mother had organized a splashy yet unpretentious celebration at Kingston's famed Governor Clinton Hotel, complete with live musicians. She'd attempted to hire several dead ones, but they'd been unable to attend.

And my parents took care of our honeymoon. More specifically, they drove us back the 110 miles from Kingston to New York City after the ceremony and the party. On the way, my mom and dad demonstrated proper marital procedure by shrieking maniacal insults at each other for the entire three and a half hours. By the time Barbara and I arrived back in our own territory, prepared to enter married bliss, we were in a cold sweat.

To top it all off, Nanette, now *my* charming daughter, staged a riot when I denied her the right to destroy our new $80 bargain-store stereo system, a wedding gift from my brother and my best friend in high school, both of whom were impoverished students. Suddenly, our landlady, the spitting image of a Salem witch, banged on the door to see what all the commotion was about. To secure the apartment a week earlier, I'd told this highly moral woman that Barbara and I were already married. Nanette, my resourceful stepchild, hauled the bride and groom that had adorned the top of the wedding cake out of the garbage and revealed with an evil leer that we'd just been hitched that morning. In those days, that was shocking.

Realizing that she was now doomed to several thousand years in purgatory for harboring a couple gift-wrapped in evil, the building's proprietress turned a disturbing shade of blue and collapsed. Nanette crossed her arms and beamed in triumph.

MOTHER OF FIVE RUNS OFF TO EUROPE WITH TWENTY-THREE-YEAR-OLD JAZZ MUSICIAN, LEAVES CHILDREN WITH...ME?

Most books conclude with the couple clasping each other in their arms, declaring their undying devotion, and disappearing into a blank swatch of paper at the end of page 248, presumably to live blissfully forever after. This is an act of literary fraud. In the vast majority of boy-meets-girl, boy-gets-girl, boy-loses-girl, boy-gets-girl-again tales, the part after the ending is where the love story really fumbles or goes over the goal line. Alas, authors, pounding away at the typewriter with a bottle of Old Mushrat Rye on their right, a couple of cigarettes in each side of their mouth, and a pile of alimony checks waiting to be paid, can only shudder when they think of what occurs after the words "I do." These poor souls, alas, are missing out on the best part. Because it's *after* the courtship that the love affair begins.

But first, a digression. It was now 1965. The seeds and stems of the new decade that I had helped sow three years earlier were spreading like crabgrass. California was luring young women into a wonderland of fringed leather jackets, flower power, light shows, and sex with any passing object that bore an upright protuberance of the correct dimensions. Sugar cubes were sliding down gullets from coast to coast. People everywhere from Kansas to Carnaby Street were attempting to start their own Haight-Ashburys. And the mutant remains of my own legacy were about to pounce on me in Brooklyn.

Brooklyn? How in the world did my new family and I land in a borough of New York whose name was so peculiar that it was used as the punchline a dozen times per episode in the Colgate Comedy Hour, one of the biggest laugh shows of the early 1950s?

After I married Barbara, I realized that my new spouse had thrown the total responsibility for her daughter into my hands. Being Jewish and all, I probably would have grabbed the responsibility and run with it even if it hadn't been fired at me like a shell from Saddam Hussein's only-half-mythical giant cannon.

You'll recall that Barbara and I had started living together in one of New York's more colorful slums—the Lower East Side. As a previous chapter vividly recounts, I had suspended our Parisian migration when I realized that if my newly-acquired child entered first grade in a country gauche enough to speak French, she was highly unlikely to learn the three R's, and would probably become a washerwoman. This didn't seem a suitable fate for the offspring of a Semitic father, even if she wasn't my offspring in the strict biological sense, and even if her profoundest wish was that I'd disappear by spontaneous combustion at the nearest possible instant, thus leaving her to tyrannize her mother in peace.

Don't ask me why, but I had the feeling that the school down the block from our inner-city apartment in the land of high-speed lead projectiles would do Nanette even less good than a year of pedagogical headbanging in the Republic of *Parlez-vous*. So I marched off to the Dean of NYU's graduate education department and asked her if there were any good schools in neighborhoods that Barbara and I could afford. After all, I was a mere freshman in college, and without an income, private school is somewhat difficult to pay for. The lady dean was kind enough to provide the necessary information, and I hunted for apartments in the neighborhoods that might allow us to sneak Nanette into an institution for the potentially sane. There were only two of them: Riverdale and Brooklyn.

I subwayed out to Riverdale. Much too snooty.

This is how we were Brooklynized. We moved to Cobble Hill, a territory that had only been gentrifying for about five years, which means that you could still rent an entire floor in a run-down slum brownstone for $125 a month, but that most of the other parents in the neighborhood were on their way into the Mercedes set and had pressured their school into acting like an actual hall of learning.

But there is more to raising a child properly than merely getting her into a decent grammar school. Not to mention getting her into her clothes in the morning. As an avid student of psychology, I had read one of legendary psychologist Harry Harlow's more obscure studies on infant rhesus monkeys. In the researches that gained him his fame, old Harry had proved that infants need mother love more than they need mere food and chicken wire. But in the lesser-known experiment I'm referring to, Harlow had demonstrated something far more intriguing—that even if they are deprived of their mothers, baby monkeys turn out socially hale and hearty provided they have an opportunity to bond, cavort, and make mischief with a group of other youngsters their own age. So, wanting Nanette to grow up like a healthy rhesus monkey, I diligently hunted down every kid her age in our new neighborhood, set up dates for my struggling stepchild with each of them, then forced her to go off—much against her will—and play with utter strangers.

The scheme worked. Within six months, Nanette had bonded to the group and become the leader of the pack, much to the chagrin of the pack's parents, since Nanette was still a five-year-old from hell.

Acting as Nanette's social secretary, I rapidly became acquainted with most of the parents in the neighborhood, all of whom were far older and wealthier than I. Of particular note among this mixed klatch of single mothers, flagrant bohemians, writers for *The New York Times*, and what would be known in the 1980s as Yuppies, were the folks up at the corner. First of all, they had a girl Nanette's age who made my daughter look like a saint. I mean, anyone who spent more than ten seconds within arm's length of this little terror rapidly ended up crippled for life. Naturally, the monster in question became one of Nanette's best friends. And the demon's parents rapidly took a shine to us.

This parental twosome who occupied the entire brownstone on the corner was something utterly alien to my sensibilities—the epitome of upscale Connecticut suburbia. In fact, a Connecticut suburb was precisely where they had lived until they'd moved to Brooklyn, seeking street-crime and adventure. The husband was the comptroller for the Itek Corporation. Though I had no idea of what the company did, it sounded impressive. The wife was a clothing designer who pulled in a hefty $450 a week (approximately $172,799.61 a year in today's dollars).

In his spare time, hubby was active on the show-dog circuit, where he judged pedigreed bulldogs, or something of the sort. He was perfectly suited for the job. Because of a certain squared-off and determined Anglo-Saxon facial structure, he simply compared the dog's physiognomy to his own, and the canine that resembled him the most walked away with a blue ribbon, painfully afraid that wearing such a frill might make him look like a sissy. Just to top off the station-wagon image, the couple had five, yes, I kid you not, *five* kids!

At first I couldn't figure out why these people continually invited us to dinner. Anyone with his eyeglasses on could have told you that we came from radically different cultures. Barbara, Nanette and I lived at our crumbling end of the block eating a diet of lentils and chicken hearts, then lounged about on furniture that we had hauled in off the street (actually, there was very little lounging in the Bloom household, since I worked like a maniac from 9:00 a.m. until 10:00 p.m. trying to maintain my 4.0 grade point average, and Barbara was taking a double dose of graduate courses in education so she could become a teacher and support us). The Wentworths (the family of *haute bourgeoisie* with the quintet of kids from a horror comic) dined on whatever was most elegant at the moment, spent more on a single meal that we invested in groceries in a month, then burped off the results on the kind of couches you see in pictures in *Architectural Digest*, pieces of furniture each of which cost the equivalent of sixty years income for an average family from Kenya.

But gradually, the truth began to emerge. Mr. Wentworth was not entirely on the straight and narrow. His weekends at dog shows all over the East Coast provided him with the opportunity to do more than merely sniff the schnauzers. A good many very wealthy and attractive women showed up as either the owners of prize-winning pooches or as fellow gavel-bangers passing judgement on the innocent hounds. *Monsieur* Wentworth was apparently slipping between the sheets with as many of these canine loverettes as he could get his hands on.

What's worse, the man had a few bolts loose in his cast-iron cranium (you know how Anglo-Saxon workmanship has been going downhill ever since the unions got a hammer lock on the aristocracy in jolly old England). Mr. Wentworth (Cyril to his friends) liked to drink, a well-respected Anglo custom (on my first trip to Britain, I was astonished to discover that the entire population of the office in which I was working took a multi-hour alcohol break promptly at two o'clock every day and repaired to the pub downstairs; I later found out that it is illegal to sport a British accent unless you can certify that your blood cells have ceased the nasty habit of swimming in normal hematological fluids and are afloat in an undiluted stream of brewed or distilled beverages). In addition, Wentworth Sr. had a temper not unlike those found in the psychiatric wards at Bellevue.

One day when the cat displeased him, he threw it out the third-story window. Said cat managed to land on its feet, but carried on bravely from that point with a distinct and ineradicable limp. Yes, even the family feline kept a stiff upper lip. And during one of Wentworth's frequent disciplinary sessions with his mob of children, who, like my one daughter, seemed to have come from the mail order catalog sent out by the devil's subterranean retail operation, good old Cyril had broken one of his youngsters' arms.

Then there was Heather, the mom. Suburban life utterly bored her. I mean, she'd come from some Novocained state like Nebraska and had not headed east just to learn how to daintily cover her mouth when she yawned. She wanted life, lust, and adventure. It was The Sixties. She wanted to be a Hippie!

There were numerous candidates in our neighborhood who could have helped her in her quest. For example, there was the mother of another of Nanette's close friends. This child's mama—Orange—had originally been married to the man to whom Allen Ginsberg dedicated his seminal poem "Howl." Orange sat around making necklaces from individual beads so fascinating in their intricacy that you could get utterly lost just wallowing in the aesthetic tricks contained in a single one. She complemented her bead stringing by ingesting a variety of illicit substances—LSD, methedrine, and God-knows-what-all else. And she augmented her income by importing marijuana. Thirty or forty one-kilo bricks of the stuff often covered her bed from one end to the other, waiting to be broken up, sifted for unsuitable plant parts, and divided into thousands of portions which she could put into tiny polyethylene bags and sell for $20 per. What's more, Orange was charming, reasonably attractive, and—I much later discovered—certifiably insane.

Then there was the gentleman who lived downstairs from this queen of psychedelia. He had been a member of the Chad Mitchell trio until he fell into a vat of lysergic acid and saw whole new aspects of the universe—like the spiritual innards of Alpha Centauri. He had then dropped out of his fabulously successful singing career and been replaced by some hopeless nerd named John Denver (whom I would work with twenty years later). Then the newly illuminated former singer had begun to study religion. Today, the Chad Mitchell renegade is a successful Unitarian minister. A psychedelic steward of human souls.

With competition like this, how Barbara and I became Heather Wentworth's hippies of choice is utterly beyond me. I mean, we didn't take drugs, and I was a God-damned workaholic! Maybe Heather heard my stories and realized something that had not quite dawned on me: that I had accidentally helped the Hippie Movement get its start.

Nonetheless, Heather and her corporate husband seized on us as their passport to the netherworld of bohemian bliss. They had us over for dinner all the time, thus contributing most of the calories that kept our monthly diet above the starvation level. Meanwhile, Nanette (my daughter) and Paulette (the toughest of their daughters) formed a crime syndicate for six-year-olds and stole $20 or $30 in cash at a crack from the Wentworths, from Barbara, from me, and from any other neighborhood parents naive enough to allow the duo into their homes and to leave a couple of dollars on the bedroom dresser for emergencies. Then the partners in larceny would skip school for the day and go off to Coney Island to spend their loot (which is some feat for a first-grader, when you think about it, since even *I* couldn't figure out how to get from our apartment to Coney Island).

Eventually Barbara's and my company was not enough to satisfy Heather Wentworth's cravings for hippiedom. Nor was possessing a husband who slept with other women while highly competitive bulldogs watched. So, at the age of thirty-five, Heather found herself a twenty-three-year-old jazz musician and decided to run off to Europe with the lad. A good, solid, hippie thing to do. What's more, the saxophone master was only four years past his sexual peak, and the odds seemed pretty good that he'd be able to keep up with the demands of Heather's locomotive-like libido.

But Heather was not the kind of mother who simply abandons her children, then forgets them. No, she sought out good homes, *then* abandoned them. In short, she deposited her brood with her friends.

Since we were high on the friends list, we were chosen to operate *in loco parentis* for the oldest female, Beryl. Beryl was roughly fifteen, and had come out about the way you'd expect from a thoroughly dysfunctional family. She was the next best thing to a limp parsnip, and had totally withdrawn from humanity. In the entire year she lived with us, I don't think she had a conversation with us once. She went to school, came home, and spent the rest of the day and early evening indulging her worship of Bob Marley.

In case you're not up on Caribbean arcana, Bob Marley is the patron saint of Jamaica. In Rastafarianism, the home-grown Jamaican religion, God is Haile Selassie, former Emperor of Ethiopia. One day God (that's Haile) will descend to Jamaica, apparently piloting a large passenger ship, something along the lines of the Queen Mary. He will load up his faithful followers and take them from their imprisonment in Babylon (that's Jamaica) to the New Jerusalem (Ethiopia), which will flourish as a paradise on earth and rise high above all the other kingdoms (not to mention dictatorships and democracies) on the planet.

Marley, a singer and composer of reggae, the Rastafarian musical form, not only became capable during his lifetime of drawing crowds of 120,000 to soccer stadiums everywhere from Ireland and Italy to Zimbabwe, but Rastafarians felt that Marley was to Haile Selassie (who, you will recall, is God) what St. Paul was to Jesus. I know. Sixteen years later, I would become Bob Marley's publicist.

Meanwhile, Beryl Wentworth, the lumpily lassitudinous teenager, returned from her classes every day, shut herself in her room, and spent the rest of the afternoon and evening drawing pictures of her hero's face.

Beryl's arrival was the beginning of a Wentworth tradition. No matter what Heather (the wandering mother) was up to, she could always fall back on us as surrogate parents for her kids. A year after she departed from the States, she returned. She'd discovered that while her twenty-three-year-old lover's pelvic appurtenances were, indeed, able to function much as she had hoped, he had certain other drawbacks. Most notably, he was a heroin addict. As they schlepped from Venice to Vienna to the Place Vendome, she tried to cure him of his habit. But she didn't have much luck. Hence, she reentered the US without the self-puncturing musical whiz, collected the kids she had deposited hither and yon, unloaded them on a commune in Massachusetts, then went off to Woodstock, a haven of hippiedom, to gallivant some more.

This led to one of Nanette's more daring escapades. By now the year was 1970. My daughter was eleven, and had become the Moriarty of Mischief. She told us she'd be staying overnight at a friend's house, then trooped off in what seemed to be the right direction. At 2:00 a.m. I got a furious phone call from someone I'd never heard of asking if I knew where my daughter was. Of course, I knew. She was staying with a friend. The man on the other end of the phone snorted in a mixture of anger and contempt, clearly meaning to question my competence as a parent. Then he explained that Nanette had run away to the commune in Massachusetts to be with her friends, the Wentworth gang (and in their case, they qualified for this term as thoroughly as any social group ever put together by Jesse James or the Dalton boys). How did he know? He was the commune's head. I was rather disturbed, to say the least. But under the irritation was an absolute awe at Nanette's navigational skills.

The commune leader sent Nanette back. And the rest of the Wentworths arrived soon thereafter. Their mother had decided to reassemble them as a family unit (minus father Cyril), rent the apartment immediately beneath us, and rely on our friendship and support while she dedicated herself to one old hobby and one new one—sex (the one she'd been perfecting for quite some time), and the large-scale consumption of alcohol (a skill which came with some difficulty, but to whose mastery she applied herself with a heroic determination).

So her kids were in and out of our shabby apartment all the time, knowing that we were about the only stable—not to mention sober—people in their lives.

There were other episodes—like the year that Paulette, the Wentworth hellion who at the tender age of five had been capable of turning her peers into chopped meat through the dexterous application of her teeth and fists—came to live with us. Now sixteen years old, she struck up an affair with the boy across the street, an exceedingly good-natured lad with a constant smile on his face and a girth similar to Shamu the Whale's. He came from a nice, Dominican family. And when I say came, I mean came to stay. He ended up sleeping with Paulette every night and emerging from her bedroom every morning with his usual marvelous grin. How the two of them (Paulette was also rather large-boned) managed to fit into a single bed designed for an underfed monk is beyond me.

It wasn't until Paulette later married the blimp-like lad and had his child that we all discovered he'd gone into the family business—smuggling cocaine. Eventually, after enjoying a good deal of her husband's merchandise, Paulette divorced him. She is a successful sales executive in the garment industry today, her child is an adult, she and Nanette have remained good friends, but we never hear from her anymore.

Meanwhile Paulette's mother, Heather, showed that though she may have been as pickled as a gherkin, she still retained her sexual prowess. The government was conducting its decennial census, and had hired whatever flotsam and jetsam it could find to canvas neighborhoods inquiring about how many inhabitants were squirreled away in each abode. A young man arrived at Heather's door sporting a beard, an official clipboard, a smile, and a sense of humor. Heather flung open the door to reveal herself in her full glory—blurred only mildly by a black, see-through negligee. The census taker, who turned out to be a struggling commercial designer, put down his clipboard and didn't leave for six years.

Heather stuck around downstairs until her children were all grown and the former urchins didn't need to drop in on us—or move in, as the case may be—all the time. Then she went out into the world to seek more escapades...and more men. When she hit roughly fifty, she found a male in a personals column who advertised that he had money, a large home, and owned a boat. She married him and retired to the comfort of alcoholism. Eventually, it would kill her.

Beryl, the Marley fanatic, wedded a Rastafarian who turned out to be an enthusiastic participant in four popular Jamaican sports: sex, smoking cannabis, playing soccer, and killing rival Rastas. After fathering a son—who today is uncommonly handsome and delightful, but probably a psychiatric time bomb—Beryl's husband was killed in one of those raucous little gang battles believers in Haile Selassie have such fun with. Today, I believe Beryl is living on welfare. She never talked to us while she was holed up here, and she's maintained the practice ever since, so it's kind of hard to track her movements. However, one thing is certain: she's a second-generation casualty of the spiritual quest with which I'd helped kick off The Sixties, a quest that apparently soured as it aged.

THE SUMMER OF
THE GREAT POLYGAMY EXPERIMENT

Barbara's discontent came to a head in 1967. Her discontent with what? With me, of course. You'll recall that in September of 1965, when she'd married me, Barbara was none too happy about finally being knotted to the man she'd attempted to corner for the previous ten months. Guess what? Things went downhill from there. Within the first weeks after I moved in with her on the Lower East Side, the smile that lit my spirit had disappeared. She was glum, grumpy and resentful. If she acted civil more than once in six months, it was a major break in the clouds.

To motivate myself, I'd visualize Barbara's smile day after day for periods as long as twelve months at a time, twelve months when there was no Barbara smile in sight. In fact, when I came home and walked into the kitchen, Barbara would often pull back to the farthest diagonal corner of the room, shrinking from me as if I was spitting, leaking, and sneezing the Ebola virus. "Don't get near me," she'd say in a line you've read before, "your breath smells like dead pollywogs."

By that time, I'd shucked my Prussian psychotherapist and had found a male shrink named Murray Stern. He was the opposite of the brain untangler who had turned her back on me. He was tall and warm. And he let me see his face. I'd walk into Murray's office, sit across from him, and explain that I was in a state of unaccountable and almost indescribable emotional pain. "It feels like I'm in the middle of a whirlwind," I'd say, "the wind is whipping around shards of glass and tin. And every one of those shards is cutting me." Then Murray would ask one of the wisest questions ever tossed at an emotional sufferer. "What happened last night?" What happened the night before the agony began? I'd think. Recalling emotionally scarring moments is not easy. At least not for me. "Ummm, Barbara told me to stay on the other side of the room. She said my breath smelled like rotting pollywogs. Then, when we went to bed, she turned her back on me." Voila. The unaccountable whirlwind of blades was no longer unaccountable. The slashing vortex went straight back to a moment of rejection.

Nonetheless, from the time she'd seized on me in the NYU library, I'd been faithful, loyal and true. That continued during our marriage. I was not a perfect husband...I'm sure there was lots of room for legitimate complaint. My dishwashing was appalling. The food I made contained bargain basement ingredients even cats wouldn't touch—the aforementioned chicken hearts and a brand of cut-priced canned mackerel with an unpleasant silver slime on its surface, the last remains of its flashy, pimped-up skin. After all, I had to feed us protein on a bread-and-water budget. But I was faithful to a T. And it wasn't for lack of temptation.

Back before I'd started living with Barbara, temptations had been few and far between. Yes, there was my period of sexual good fortune on the West Coast. But New York was different. When you're alone and feeling it sharply, you give off a perfume of desperation. Women avoid you like the plague. Then I'd started living with Barbara. That lifted the odor of isolation in a radical manner. Suddenly, half the females in the city seemed to want me.

Well, maybe only four.

The week I moved my things over to Barbara's, I was squeezing through the door of a poetry writing class along with an exiting mob of fellow wannabe Gerard Manley Hopkins's when this red-headed girl who wrote things that I considered absolutely grotesque (multiple-choice poetry with postage-stamp-sized pictures inserted in the text) slipped next to me and slid a small piece of paper into my hand. I unfolded it after she disappeared around a corner and discovered it was a strange little poem about someone with lizard lips. Lizard lips? What did that have to do with me? Sorry, but I'm a little dense. Suddenly it hit me. It was a love poem. What's worse, it was directed at yours truly, the man whose misshapen smile every bug-eyed chameleon on the planet recognizes as akin to his very own.

Suddenly, the girl's poetry seemed far less contemptible. I deigned to talk to the creature, who turned out to be a graphic artist and the aforementioned member of the Warhol crowd. A few days later, she asked me to move in with her. I turned her down, gently, I hope. I was being faithful to Barbara.

Then there was the woman in one of my literature courses. She was intelligent, attractive, a bit older than I was—but then, who wasn't? Barbara was, too—had a five-year-old daughter like Barbara, and had been married to some member of the Van Doren family who'd gotten cancer at the age of twenty-seven and had left her an uncommonly young widow. She made it clear that I would be an admirable replacement. I said no, I hope without hurting her feelings. I was still being faithful to Barbara.

In my 17th century poetry class was the most interesting temptation of all, a gorgeous, extraordinarily brilliant girl who did not seem hobbled by the slightest bit of ignorance or naiveté. She was dressed in black leather—complete with leather skirt, leather boots, leather blouse, and leather jacket. She'd been a stripper for a while, had indulged in a few lesbian relationships, had married a filmmaker, and had gone back to school. While her husband was off in Afghanistan making movies, she'd decided that the man she *really* wanted was, you guessed it, the Woody Allen/Kermit the Frog look-alike. *Me*. And she was passionate about it. My handwriting was enough, she said, to drive her to orgasm. Now, I admit I was tempted. I enjoyed this woman's effervescent intellect to the nth degree. And her body was mind-boggling. But, in the end, I couldn't do it. Still being faithful to Barbara.

The fact is, I stuck to the one I was with, and that was that.

Well, along came 1967, the end of my junior year. Barbara had put in two years as a teacher while I studied my ass off at NYU. Not that teaching wasn't fun for Barbara, mind you. The school board had sent her to a junior high in Bedford Stuyvesant where the kids stabbed their principals for sport. It was rated the most dangerous educational institution west of Beirut. And Barbara's students were so inspired by the notion of learning French that they spent the entire class on their feet playing basketball with wads of paper torn from their textbooks. To score extra points, they attempted to throw each other out the windows.

To lighten her burden, the school administrators had suggested that Barbara double as an art teacher. Aside from one required undergraduate course in art history, this was a subject she knew nothing about. So every night

Barbara would come home, literally cry for an hour or two, then try to learn enough about drawing stick figures to prepare lesson plans for the next day.

Meanwhile, I took care of the shopping, the cooking, the carpentry, and Nanette.

I also tried to be helpful with Barbara's vocational dilemma. I sought more advice from the head of NYU's graduate school of education. The one who had pointed me to Brooklyn. Unfortunately, this backfired. The dean recommended a book written by a *New York Times* reporter who had gone underground as a teacher in the most dangerous school in the city, a junior high on a par with a war zone in Syria. After the principal was shot by a student, the intrepid reporter fled in fear for his life. Alas, it turned out that the whole saga had occurred in Barbara's school. Not a good book to show Barbara if I wanted to cheer her up.

To soften her sorrows, I wrote some of Barbara's papers (remember, she was attempting to get a graduate degree in education), and ultimately helped engineer an escape from pedagogy by inserting her into the New York Library system. Nonetheless, Barbara's resentment was building. Then the dam broke. One evening in the spring of 1967, she sat me down in a cheap Algerian restaurant a five-minute walk away from our apartment in Cobble Hill, Brooklyn, and told me point-blank that she wanted me to go out and have an affair. Why? She wanted to have an affair and she didn't want to feel guilty.

At the time, I happened to be editing the NYU literary magazine. More about how this happened in a minute. It was a sordid task that I had been dragged into much against my will. But it did have its perks: I was surrounded by intriguing young women. And one of them, in particular, was more intriguing than the rest. She wasn't the best-dressed person in the world. In fact, her very dishevelment put her on my wavelength. I can't manage to shevel properly either. What's more, she had a mischievous smile, a wonderful verve, a quick mind, a mouth-watering shape, and she seemed to find me fascinating. We'd taken to three-hour phone conversations every night, utterly wrapped up in each other. I was reasonably certain this couldn't interfere with my marriage. After all, for three years I'd proven remarkably adept at being faithful to Barbara. But now Barbara was telling me to ditch fidelity.

So I called up the girl with whom I'd had the Platonic exchanges of telephonic passion—Betty Sue Cross—and asked if I could meet her at her place. The next night, the Platonism gave way to aphrodisia. It turned out that under Betty Sue's walking laundry hamper of carelessly tossed-on skirt and blouse was a tiny waist, a slender torso, small, firm breasts, and hips like a perfect pear. A body that stunned me. But there was a problem. In the throes of passion, instead of climaxing, she broke out crying. Somehow our love making hit the spot where the loss of her mother when she was still a child had lacerated her heart. It didn't matter. I thought she was wonderful.

A few days later, when I was waiting alone in Betty Sue's apartment for her arrival, Betty Sue's roommate, Page, marched in and told me she'd been deeply hurt. I was sleeping with her roomie and wasn't sleeping with her. How could I be so cruel! Apparently, the Sexual Revolution had finally reached the East Coast.

A few nights later, I met Page at a sparely furnished but neatly kept Manhattan apartment she'd borrowed, in a huge thicket of 1940s middle-income brick buildings called Stuyvesant Town. We spent the night together, and it was an amazement. By 10:00 p.m. we had our clothes off, and by 10:02 my hands made one of the most astonishing discoveries of their lives—not to mention mine. My fingers and palms saw her body with a clarity and amazement that mere eyes can only wish for. She was a wonderland of curves, smoothness, and bits of fuzz in unexpected places, textures, and shapes that your hands can see in ways far more wondrous than your sight. Though the sight of her was beyond belief, too. For example, her breasts were small and high, and between them was a down you could not see, but that delighted your touch. My hands were so entranced that I was still on a voyage of discovery, gently touching and stroking her at 6:00 a.m., when the sun rose.

Suddenly I had not just the one woman I had intended to be faithful to for life, but three. Two more than I'd bargained for. And there was a twist. Remember how my Aunt Rose had introduced me to music by immersing me in *Peter and the Wolf?* Then, when I was roughly eleven, the Buffalo Philharmonic Orchestra had announced that it was going to perform *Peter and the Wolf* live. My mom knew I loved the piece and took me to see it. The conductor whose name appeared on the concert program was Willis Page. He was Page's dad.

Thus started the summer of the Great Polygamy Experiment. I was now sleeping with three women. You couldn't tell it at the time, but in the grand sweep of history—the sweep for which Mother History uses her push broom—this made sense. The coming months of 1967 were about to get a name, one very relevant to Barbara's demand that I cast a wider sexual net: The Summer of Love. And the Summer of Love would become a Sixties landmark. A landmark that, like so much of The Sixties, echoed the Sexual Revolution I'd been a part of in 1962.

◆

AT FIRST, THE AFFAIR with Betty Sue was a lark. Not Lark Clark, the girl I'd put together with Tom Reichmann for a deep dive into subway-tunnel romance. It was a slide, a glide, a delight. I figured, as everyone did that summer, that sex was a casual entertainment. You'd enjoy it immensely, and no one would get hurt. And that, in the beginning, was the way it seemed. Page, the roommate, would come out to Brooklyn and stay with Barbara while I spent the night with Betty Sue on Tenth Street, near First Avenue, in Manhattan. Page and Mrs. Bloom would indulge in a royal rollick, killing a half gallon of Almaden Chablis, gobbling a giant cake straight from the bakery box, and digging out the filling between the layers with their fingers.

Betty Sue and I would dive into the perplexities of passion. Everyone was good friends. One Sunday in June, Barbara, Betty Sue, and I even subwayed to Manhattan and walked hand in hand in hand north through Central Park to the Guggenheim Museum, like poster children for the Summer of Love. Sure, there were occasional difficulties, like the time the sister of my best friend from high school showed up to visit and was shocked into speechlessness. She trudged up our Brooklyn hallway just as I was running back and forth between opposite ends of the apartment trying to calm down two weeping women. And she happened to ring the doorbell while I was frantic and didn't have a stitch of clothing on. Being greeted by a breathless nudist who asks that you just take a walk around the block and give him a chance to get the rapidly separating pieces of his cosmos strapped back together can throw a twist into your system. I never saw her again.

Then something dark heaved beneath the surface of this sexual Disneyland. The power of attachment. I began to need Betty Sue like a drug. I fell in love with her. I wanted to be a permanent part of her life. The candy-coated fantasy of the polygamous playground was being melted by some primal pull toward involuntary monogamy. That pull was overwhelming, an obsession, an undertow of emotion that sucked in all of consciousness.

Betty Sue seemed to be going through very much the same thing. And, what's worse, the summer was about to end, and someone was planning to return to the city whose existence Betty Sue had neglected to mention to me...her live-in boyfriend. Betty Sue and I had embarked on what even she'd thought would be a temporary entertainment. And we'd found that the frills and flounces were merely a disguise with which the primal pull of permanent coupling entices us into its trap.

There was something more. I was often impotent with Betty Sue. That's not something I was used to. But you become hideously ashamed of yourself when the organ you need to consummate an act of love refuses to inflate. Why this inability to stiffen, something even the dumbest garden hose can accomplish without a hint of performance anxiety? I suspect it was the image of my New Jersey aunts, the towers of power who screamed at their husbands non-stop. In the back of my mind, in some dusty closet, towering over dust bunnies the size of dinosaurs, those aunts had made being in love with a woman a cause of terror. Ahhh, the joys of intimacy panic. Something I had apparently not conquered, despite shackling myself to Barbara.

It was all downhill from there. Betty Sue tried to end it and go back to her boyfriend. After all, he was down to earth, sensible, and was about to get an engineering degree. No, he didn't understand her emotions. Not a bit. But he was solid. And tall. I was not. I understood her emotional core powerfully. But that's because within me was an emotional whirlwind, the kind that even seagulls find challenging. And worse, I was married. But getting rid of me was hard. We'd see each other to say goodbye and end up rumpling her sheets and our emotions again, even though consciously that wasn't what we'd planned.

Many months later, in the deep freeze of December, when the first issue of the literary magazine that had flung us together in the first place finally came out, I threw a party at my apartment for the staff. I lay in a gargantuan supply of cheap muscatel—an alcoholic beverage highly recommended long ago by the kindly Californian fruit picker we met in a box car in 1962. The price of this connoisseur grape extract was perfect for an impecunious college student. It was on par with chicken hearts and silver-slimed mackerel. Apparently I swigged down nearly a case of the stuff. Then I told Betty Sue's boyfriend about our affair. In fact, I offered to trade Betty Sue to him for another glass of fermented grape juice. Then I blacked out, and can't remember the incident to this day. Since I don't drink, this'll give you some idea of how desperate things had gotten.

That weekend, something else strange occurred. Barbara hadn't wanted to be around for the party. She was as discontented with me as ever. So she had fled upstate to visit her parents. When Betty Sue called Kingston to tell her that I'd ingested four gallons of muscatel and was still unconscious twenty hours later, Barbara had a sudden revelation. Up to that point, she'd figured she was saddled with me. She'd married me to have a father for her child—actually, more like a baby-sitter. The further into the relationship we'd gotten, the more she'd felt burdened, trapped, strapped to a marriage she really didn't want. Now, when Betty Sue phoned Barbara, something snapped. Barbara realized that I was about to slip from her grasp. The relationship that had seemed like imprisonment suddenly struck her as something she didn't want to lose. She came back to New York...fast. And she returned with a whole new attitude.

Among other things, she didn't want me to have an affair anymore. That's when we both started to enjoy the relationship. And the result has probably been the greatest pleasure in my life.

SATORI AT LAST

Eventually, I graduated from college and got a Phi Beta Kappa key. But I still haven't found a single lock it fits.

Barbara became tired of supporting student husbands and subtly discouraged me from accepting the four graduate fellowships I'd won in physiological psychology—a field that would later get sneaky and change its name to neuropsychology. She was tired of having student husbands. The implication was simple. If I went to grad school, she would leave. But since she never said it in so many words, she could deny that she'd ever issued an ultimatum. Sort of like drinking a bottle of Jim Beam when she was a teenager, then heading into the back seat of her fifty-dollar car with her boyfriend for the evening. Why the liquor? So the next morning she could blame anything that she had deeply wished would happen on the alcohol. It's called "deniability."

There was another problem. One of the things that fascinated me was mass human emotion. Ecstatic emotion. The gods inside of you and me and their role as power sources in the forces of history. Adolf Hitler had exhilarated the people of Germany by staging torch light parades. Six hour, night-time marches of 25,000 SA and SS men, nine abreast, carrying torches and goose-stepping down the Unter den Linden boulevard through Berlin's massive triumphal arch, the Brandenburg Gate, to the Presidential Palace and the Reich Chancellery. And those parades had accomplished something extraordinary. They had exhilarated and exalted their audience, the people crowding the sidewalk so thickly that if you pulled up your feet, the press of bodies surrounding you would still hold you upright. Torch light parades gave their viewers something spookily close to an out of body experience. The sort of experience I'd had when dancing on a stage at the Park School of Buffalo.

We all need to feel that we are a part of something bigger than our selves. And the folks on the sidewalks of Berlin got a sense of rising to a level of the sublime by merging into not just one, but three things higher than their individual identities. Hitler called it *"ein volk, ein reich, ein führer"*—one people, one state, one leader.

Volk was not just a trivial word. It was a peoplehood, a supposedly distinct master race, allegedly gifted by three thousand years of evolution with its own collective soul. A collective unconscious superior to the deep self of any other group on earth. And if you were in the audience of a torch light parade, you rose out of your self and became one with that overarching collective soul. You became one with the empyreal. You became a molecule in the tidal wave of an over-race destined to take over the world.

Hitler had tapped the gods inside. He had roused one of the varieties of the religious experience. And the mass passions that this little man with the mustache had stoked were the forces of history. Alas, Hitler had used these forces for evil.

Now the job was to find those gods and figure out how to use them for good.

My task since I'd held onto the doors of a blue Frazier when I was thirteen while my parents tore at my socks and tried to wrestle me to Temple Beth El had been to find the gods inside. And through those gods, to find the mass passions that made Hitler's torch light parades the thrill of a lifetime. My task had been to track down the mass passions that shift and tweezle history. And to see how they fit into the evolution of the cosmos.

Was I going to find those mass passions by going to Columbia University for courses in psychology and to Columbia's med school for courses in physiology? Not on your life. I'd be condemned to a career giving college students pencil and paper tests in exchange for a psychology credit. In classrooms of students filling out tests, I'd be far, far away from passion. And even farther from the sort of mass passion that froths, foams, and forms history's sucking currents. Not to mention even farther from the gods inside. In other words, grad school loomed as an Auschwitz for the mind. And I had a shot at something I knew nothing about. Something so soaked in mass passion that it was ridiculous. I had a shot at another adventure. Going into the terra incognita called popular culture.

◆

How DID THIS STRANGE exit strategy show up? Or was it a strange entry strategy? An entry into the dark underbelly where new mass moods and new myths are brewed? Just possibly the land of the gods? The land of the gods inside? Let's flash back a minute to the literary magazine that helped launch the summer of the Great Polygamy Experiment. How in the world did I get involved with a literary magazine?

I'd taken poetry seriously ever since A. E. Housman had grabbed me by my rhyming couplets. In fact, poetry seemed a perfect way to wince with agony without making noises out loud. Poems were an iambic pentameter ouch. A necessity for someone with non-stop clinical depression. NYU had a specialist to aid students terminally addicted to verse—its poet in residence, Robert Hazel. Apparently named after one of my grandmother's favorite and most aromatic health aids, witch hazel. Though he never had a discernable aroma.

I didn't know it, but Hazel had mentored semi-famous writers like Wendell Berry, Bobbie Ann Mason, Ed McClanahan, and Rita Mae Brown. All people I'd never read and never heard of. Seven years later, Hazel would go on to be the poetry editor for the magazine *The Nation*. And I took one semester of poetry writing after another from this poor man, who was thus forced to read the contorted stuff I was pouring forth. It's hard to believe, but the poor man was not driven into madness by my tortured doggerel. Or maybe he was. One day, when poetry class was over and I was about to exit the classroom, Hazel ordered me to stay. In fact, he commanded that I wait until everyone left, then close the door, grab a chair, and put it in the you-are-about-to-be-balled-out position across from his desk.

When we were alone, Hazel locked his eyes on my face and said, "Look, you. Last year I asked you to be on the staff of the literary magazine. You never showed up. This year, I'm telling you—you are the editor of the literary magazine. You don't have a single way out. You don't even have a faculty advisor. The minute you go out the door, you ARE the literary magazine. Now go."

This was a problem. I hated college literary magazines. Stage a rip-roaring party, invite sixty Irish soccer hooligans, offer them thirty bottles of one hundred proof Drunken Leprechaun Mash, wait until 2:00 a.m., when the Celtic uproar would deafen the deck flagman on an aircraft carrier, put a literary magazine in the room, and the partiers would freeze like statues, turning their let's-burn-a-police-car fun into silence. Silence complete with a premature hangover.

Why? Just look at the cover. It's a shade of blue designed to put even sloths to sleep. If a bird's egg were colored this ghastly hue, the mother bird would give up and sit on some other female's nest. Or on some other female. What's worse, the appalling typeface threatens to scratch out your eyeballs and inject Nembutal into your exposed optic nerves. The font and its positioning are so awkward that they should immediately excuse themselves, gather up the magazine behind them, and hide in the nearest bathroom, offering themselves up as toilet paper.

So when I exited Hazel's classroom, I was in a state of shock. In fact, I was stopped dead in my tracks in the corridor outside of Hazel's door. I was stunned. From the inside, my face felt like a frog run over by one of those mining trucks in Arizona with tires five feet taller than you are.

But a funny thing happens when you possess an uncontrollable blabber-mouth and a delight in sailing half-baked insights at the professor like meringue pies, then catching as he throws a raspberry pie back. In other words, when you're one of those obnoxious students who, in an amphitheater with 150 other pupils madly taking notes, ends up in a dialog with the PhD on the stage. Kids know you who you don't know. Stewart, the barker at the Crazy Horse, the transvestite nightclub, had been one of those fellow students. Now, two years later, in a moment of need, another amphitheater Samaritan came down the hall, saw me standing stock still, and stopped. "You look troubled about something," he said, "can I help you?" The very same words a kindly passerby had said in front of San Francisco's City Lights Bookstore when I couldn't find the beatniks. There is a secret kindness in the hearts of even the worst of us.

"Yyyyyesssss," I stuttered, "I've just been made the editor of the literary magazine…" And my face, still as distorted as a Denver omelet scrambled with a spiked football shoe, must have said the rest. "Why don't you come downstairs with me for a cup of coffee," my anonymous benefactor said, "and we'll talk about it." Despite all the coffee invitations in odd places like the streets of San Pedro and Salt Lake City's airport, and despite my one-time-only amateur attempt at coffee with Barbara, I'd never actually taken a potential host up on this sort of invitation. But I was as limp as chloroformed cat. So I meekly followed to the stairs at the end of the hall, down the flights from the third floor to the first, out the door to Waverly Place, and twenty feet east to a coffee shop. He ordered coffee. I ordered water.

Then this nameless instant caregiver asked me one of the most important questions I'd ever been tossed in my life. "If you could do anything with this magazine that you wanted," he said, "anything at all, what would it be?" It was the hideous visual nightmare of literary magazines that bothered me. Graphics so bad that if you asked for my advice on how to commit suicide, I'd tell you to take two college literary magazines and call me in the morning. So I said, "I'd turn it into a picture book."

And that it is what I did. I went to Barbara number two, the visual artist with the red hair who hung out with the Warhol crowd, and asked where I could find artists. She pointed me to one. And I rapidly acquired others. Many of those others were not NYU students. But it didn't matter. I wanted a magazine so delicious that even one glimpse of its cover would suck you in. A magazine so glorious that every two-page spread would wrap itself around you and entrance you like the light shows at a concert hall that impresario Bill Graham had opened just a few blocks away from NYU on Second Avenue in the East Village, the Fillmore East. In the Fillmore's light shows, images of shifting color blobs metamorphosed on the ceiling, the walls, and the floor below your shoes. But I wanted the images in the magazine to be far crisper and more compelling than anything that the Fillmore's Josh White Light Show had ever produced.

One of the most brilliant of my artist recruits was a scrawny person even shorter than I am, which is not easy—some dachshunds are taller than I am—slender, with a Snidely Whiplash mustache, and a charisma that outbulked the Hulk. His name was Peter Bramley. It was an era of underground comics, and Peter was a cartoon master, able to fill a single astonishing 11x14 inch page with an overall composition that grabbed you by your eye sockets, screwed in two light bulbs, then turned on the switch. Why? Hidden in the big picture were hundreds of little pictures, like Hieronymus Bosch on cannabis.

Peter had a pretty wife and a baby, but they will change my life in just a few minutes. So hang tight.

The first issue of the radically re-conceived literary magazine—The Washington Square Review—was a smash. Among other things, it was twelve inches by twelve inches, oversized and square, printed on a quality of paper more delicious to the touch than the skin of a new lover—Page, for example—and bursting with color. The NYU Art School, which had never paid attention to the Liberal Arts School and its stupid literary magazine before, bought forty copies for its archives. Robert Hazel, the poet in residence who had strapped me into editorial slavery, was ecstatic. I had no idea of where the money that I was spending on paper with extraordinary heft and texture, and on a fine-art printing firm capable of making masterpieces came from, but I rapidly found out. It was something called the Student Activities Committee. Who even knew that that there was such a thing? But the committee commanded that I appear at one of its meetings. I showed up to take my punishment like a man…and they doubled my budget.

So, in December and January, a few days after I offered to sell Betty Sue Cross to the engineering student she was living with for a glass of muscatel, I began to plan *Washington Square Review* issue number two. And Peter Bramley of the weasel mustache was one of my prime co-conspirators. With the new budget, I was planning even more extraordinary paper than issue number one. And not just the full four-color printing of the first issue, but five color printing. In addition to the standard blue, red, yellow and black, we were going to have silver. But there was going to be a theme. And as that theme emerged, half of my staff quit. Why?

This was going to be the sex and death issue. A delicately colored dragonfly on the cover was superimposed on the cross-shaped ground plan of a cathedral. The pastel colors of the insect were set in a deep frame of black and silver. The two-page spread behind the cover was a photo of a massive cemetery in black and silver. The names of the staff members were printed on the pathway to a crypt. We had high gloss, thick paper, as irresistible to the touch as a lover's earlobes to your lips. And we featured a terrific short story on, what else is there to write stories about? Sex. A story in white knockout type on black, a tale richly illustrated with Peter Bramley's pictures.

But the second issue got no response from the Student Activities Committee. In fact, no response from a single soul at NYU. And none from Robert Hazel. Then one day I ran into Hazel turning a corner at Waverly and University Place across the street from Washington Square Park. He was not happy to see me. I asked what he thought of the new issue. "Did you have to put in that poem by your friend Jason Schneider that starts with masturbation?" he said, and walked away from me as quickly as he could. He was disturbed by the very subject that the Boy Scouts had ordered me to write about. The very topic that Anton van Leeuwenhoek had shared with the Royal Society in 1688. I was a pariah in the halls of ivy. Or in the NYU buildings that pigeons used as public toilets. I mean, this was Manhattan, not Harvard Square.

But that wasn't the end of issue number two. Not by a long shot. It was sold in bookstores up and down Eighth Street, the main drag of Greenwich Village. The art director of *Look* magazine, *Life Magazine*'s competitor as the leading big-format picture magazine in the country, called and asked if I could trek up to midtown Manhattan to meet with him. The art director of *Evergreen Review*, the leading Bohemian magazine in North America, called and made the same request. Then came a call from the very organization that kept coughing me up the way a cocker spaniel regurgitates a cigar it has mistaken for a sausage, the Boy Scouts of America. The art director of the Boy Scouts' official, big-format, glossy, gorgeous monthly magazine, *Boy's Life*, wanted a meeting, too. Idiotic how it had never occurred to me that New York had more than just NYU. It was the art-directorial capital of the Western hemisphere.

Oh, and long into the future, Jason Schneider, who had written the masturbation poem that blasted Robert Hazel's bile, would become the editor of *Modern Photography* and *Popular Photography*. Plus the literary offerings in *The Washington Square Review* issue number one would win two National Academy of Poets' prizes. Or so I was told. By the poet who was awarded the prizes.

A month later, school ended. I graduated magna cum laude and Phi Beta Kappa thanks to the lesson of the egos, a lesson derived in part from my misadventure with *Ten Steps to Organize a Boy Scout Troop*. The idea of dressing up for graduation was no more appealing than wearing a suit to go to High Holiday services had been when I was thirteen. So I skipped my graduation ceremony. Instead, I accepted an invitation from Orange, the highly-bohemian mother of one of Nanette's best friends, to go see a Country Joe and the Fish concert with her and a circle of friends. Country Joe and the Fish was the quintessential Sixties band. It was San Franciscan, psychedelic, sang songs of protest, and was famous for this cheerful chorus:

And it's one, two, three, what're we fighting for?
Don't ask me, I don't give a damn
Next stop is Vietnam
And it's five, six, seven, open up the pearly gates
Well there ain't no time to wonder why
Whoopee! We're all gonna die

That was the night I realized that I had lost my Sisyphean rock. For four years, I had awakened every day with a mission—get A's and graduate. Now that goal was gone. All I had when I woke up in the morning was the prospect of grad school at Columbia in September. And that was not a goal that could provide a structure for the day.

At the Country Joe and the Fish concert in a seatless, standing-area-only auditorium somewhere in the Morningside Heights neighborhood of northern Manhattan, on the fringe of the Columbia University campus, Orange passed out little black pills to all of those in her party. I took what I was given. Always be gracious to your hostess. It was some sort of speed. And you remember what happens with speed. Twelve hours of heaven, ninety six hours of hell. During that hell, in the dawn of the next day, I sat with a huge bottle of Valium in front of me seriously contemplating suicide. I don't even remember where I was. But when your sense of purpose goes, your emotional agonies arise like post-industrial dragons lifting their heads from the poisonous slime around an oil refinery. Orange saw what was on my mind, grabbed the valium bottle, and insisted that I spend the night at her place. When she took me to her bed, we got naked between the sheets, and she let me slip between her welcoming thighs. It was one of the most comfortable and obligation-free acts of intercourse in which I've ever engaged. I owe her thanks.

Meanwhile, Orange called Barbara about my contemplation of self-annihilation. Barbara called my uncle Fred, my mother's brother who had been the focus of my grandparent's minimal money for college and had become a medical doctor. And Uncle Fred recommended a consummation that once upon a time I had devoutly wished—incarceration in a mental institution.

Actually, my time in the prison for those with discombobulated brains—the nut house—was a learning experience. But that's a subject for another book.

After two weeks, the authorities let me out of the institution early. For good behavior. And that's when my life was changed.

◆

I WENT TO VISIT Peter Bramley, my brilliant artist, at his apartment on Second Avenue and Tenth Street. I climbed the two flights of stairs, entered, and found a room devoid of furniture. Seated on the wall-to-wall carpet were three figures—Peter, his wife Florrie, and their three-year-old, Gareth. All of them were crying. I wanted to know what was wrong. Peter and Florrie explained that they were broke. Their furniture had been dispossessed. Their electricity and phone were about to be cut off. And they were being evicted.

Now, look, Peter's work was a friggin' astonishment. And I hadn't yet found a summer job. I'd been too busy analyzing the behavior of a bunch of folks who were as crazy as I was from deep within the locked building that housed them—and that housed me—the loony bin. So I asked Peter to give me the portfolio of his art. I figured I'd show Peter's artwork to a dozen people. They would see his brilliance. They'd give him work. He would be able to pay his rent and get his furniture back. And I could return to looking for a summer job. The whole rescue, I estimated, would take two weeks.

But Peter had a dream—founding an art studio with two other artists. So we put together a portfolio that included all three of them. Peter dubbed us Cloud Studio. And I began to schlepp the studio's portfolio to magazines, book publishers, record companies, advertising agencies, and anyone else I could find in the yellow pages who might need art work. Including the art directors who had called me after the second issue, the sex and death issue, of the *Washington Square Review*. By the end of the summer, I had gotten *New York* magazine interested in doing a feature on our studio. But I hadn't sold a thing. And Barbara was making it clear that if I went back to school in September, I could kiss her good bye. Although I'd be forbidden to actually get close enough to give her a kiss.

So in September I called Columbia and asked for a year off. But instead of putting a year into Cloud Studio, I put in three. And that's how I escaped the Auschwitz of the mind of grad school and entered a field I knew nothing about—popular culture. The culture of the kids who used to beat me up. But hidden deep inside that culture was the myth making machinery of modern society. And that machinery might, just might, if I was lucky, lead to the gods inside. Not to mention to their product—the forces of history.

◆

THE FIRST YEAR, WE Cloud Studioniks earned $75 a week per person. Pathetic, right? But it allowed Bramley to pay his bills. Two years into the process, we were creating book covers for companies like Harper & Row and Bantam Books, we were providing illustrations for the Institutional Investor Magazine, and, most important, we were doing all the artwork for ABC's seven FM radio stations, radio stations that were using our art in seven major cities to help establish a whole new kind of radio—progressive radio, album rock. What's more, I'd invented a new animation technique for NBC-TV, and ABC had asked me to found an ad agency to handle their account. I declined. I didn't want to learn how to buy time on radio and TV. Not my cup of borscht. And, to show you how low some publications will sink, I'd been featured on the cover of *Art Direction Magazine*—in a cartoon drawn by Peter Bramley

But the really-big deal came when Matty Simmons, the man who had helped invent the credit card for American Express, started to treat me as if I were his son. Something that Maurice Girodias, the legendary pornographer who had been the first to publish *Lady Chatterley's Lover, Lolita*, and Henry Miller, had also begun to do. Matty Simmons had taken the plunge into publishing. And he'd had an idea. Once a year, a bunch of kids at Harvard turned out a magazine that hit newsstands all over the USA and sold out instantly. Matty wanted that crew to do a magazine once a month. The Harvard kids went for it. The magazine they'd done in Boston was called the *Harvard Lampoon*. Matty's monthly variation was called the *National Lampoon*. And Matty chose us—Cloud Studio—to art direct the magazine. This meant we got a monthly check. A big one.

Peter and another of the artists didn't like the fact that I'd get a share of this bonanza. So they voted me out of the studio. An act of cruelty and greed that would pay off big time for me.

What saved me? Attention Deficit Disorder. Which means you actually DO pay attention, but to more things than most adults approve of. On the side, I'd been buying wildly unconventional, custom-made outfits from a designer located a mere five blocks away from Cloud Studio on the Lower East Side's velvet strand of hippie businesses, Second Avenue. In fact, I'd been co-designing some of these clothes myself. And I'd been hankering to write for magazines. Why? The Albert Einstein imperative—to be a scientific thinker, you have to be a writer. One day I'd walked into a brand new underground fashion magazine financed by one of the founders of *Rolling Stone*. The new magazine was called *Rags*. I figured an eager new magazine might need artwork. But instead of leafing with popping eyes through Cloud Studio's portfolio, they gawked at my outfit: purple bellbottoms with a purple tunic and a huge, handmade leather belt holding up a handmade leather pouch for bills, change, a handkerchief, and a few pets. Do you have more of these clothes, they asked. Yes, I have a whole closet full of them, I replied. Do you think you could write about them, asked the editor, a quick-thinking blond with serious acne scars but a wonderful personality. You bet, I said, leaping at the big chance to do an Einstein.

So I went home, wrote an article about business suits as the ultimate self-imprisonment devices and about the sort of liberating outfits my designer and I were putting together. I modeled four of these eye-busting outfits for Rags' photographer. And guess what? They asked if I could write more.

So I got up every morning at six, went directly to the typewriter, slugged a cup of coffee, and typed. Then I went into Cloud Studio and hauled its portfolio uptown, thus threatening to snap my vertebrae. Carrying an artists' portfolio is a bit like carting an anesthetized baby hippo with a handle in its back. At seven pm, I'd get home, make dinner for Barbara, Nanette, and myself. Then I would sit at a solid-metal, 1940s Remington -non-electric typewriter and smash away at the keys until 11:00 p.m. Something you must understand about the sturdy pre-electric Remington. To move just one key, you have to hit it with the force of four Arnold Schwarzeneggers pounding the nose of a single villain. Then, on weekends, I'd write from dawn to dusk.

When I was up to roughly a hundred articles for *Rags* and had been named a contributing editor, another contributing editor walked in, this one a slender, woodsy blond who liked to spend her time in leafy locations like upstate New York dressed in a manner the deer would have found acceptable—medium sloppy. Said my fellow contributing editor, she, too, was starting an underground magazine, *Natural Lifestyles*. Would I agree to be a contributing editor? So my deadlines increased, but my spare time did not. This was a problem. Then Cloud Studio was kind enough to vote me out, thus giving me the time I needed to out-type Tom Wolfe.

One afternoon I was covering a national parapsychology convention for *Natural Lifestyles*, whose editor loved to toss me into the lunatic fringe and see what my science-obsessed mind would make of it. I was scribbling notes like a Babylonian scribe taking dictation from the king when a twenty-year-old male wearing a suit jacket walked up to me and asked if I'd like to edit a magazine. Hmmmm, edit a magazine. That sounded like something that would allow me to write by day and end my 6:00 a.m. and 10:00 p.m. battles with my cast-iron Remington. Having written on stalking, tracking, and organizing troops for the Boy Scouts, I didn't ask what the magazine was about. I figured I could write about anything. See what a real Boy Scout training will do for you?

In those days there was no Google in which to look things up. So I went to a meeting with the magazine's publisher not having a clue. The magazine was called *Circus*. But it didn't cover the sexual improprieties of clowns and the scandals among elephants. It was about something I'd just begun to pay attention to during my frequent visits to ABC's seven FM station headquarters on Sixth Avenue. Yes, at ABC the promotion manager for the stations had taught me that you could tell Carol King from James Taylor by the sexual cues in their names. A hint: James was the male. Ahhhhh.

Gerald Rothberg, the publisher of *Circus*, explained to me that his magazine was about rock and roll. Umm, what? Say that again? And Gerry was desperate. He'd had two editors. They'd both quit. The next issue of the magazine was due at the printers in two weeks. Could I do the work of two editors and put together a finished copy of a magazine on a subject I knew nothing about in fourteen days? All by myself? Sure. Why not? Anything to get up at 7:00 a.m. like a normal human being. And that is how I came to be credited with founding a new magazine genre: the heavy metal magazine.

The man who gave that credit was Chet Flippo, one of the founding editors of *Rolling Stone* in San Francisco, the man who had put together *Rolling Stone*'s East Coast office in New York. Chet felt he was lacking in academic cred and tried to make up for this deficiency by writing a master's thesis on the history of rock journalism, thus giving himself a dollop of respectability. One day Chet sent me six pages of his thesis by messenger. I had no clue to why. Messengers were very expensive. But I opened the big manila envelope from Chet, fetched out half a dozen sheets of typewritten paper, and read them. They told the tale of a person who worked in a converted broom closet on yet another manual typewriter (yes, Gerry Rothberg generously allowed me to work in a windowless converted storage closet across the hall from his six-window corner office overlooking the East River). This prisoner of a room designed for brooms, wrote Chet, was turning straw into gold. Yes, the miracle man in the mop cubicle was increasing the circulation of a forlorn monthly rock magazine that hadn't stood a chance by 211 percent in two years and utterly reinventing the field of rock monthlies.

What Chet didn't get into his thesis was the real secret. When you land in a field you know nothing about like an alien from Alpha Centauri, you are able to evaluate the way things are traditionally done with antennae and bug-eyes, thus giving yourself a fresh perspective, a perspective those mired in the field do not have. And you can apply the techniques of Martin Gardner's *Scientific American* Mathematical Games section to see what works and what does not. Then you can listen to your publisher and steal tricks from European magazines whose astronomical sales figures he envies. What's more, you can pickpocket the secrets of a magazine your publisher keeps on a pedestal, secrets of a weekly that has been guiding your bohemian eccentricities for nearly two decades—Henry Luce's *Time* magazine.

And, above all you can love the kids you're writing for. You can be grateful to them for letting you into a secret world your own peers once shut you out of, adolescence. Yes, you can make up for a major deprivation—the lack of a teenagehood. All that can motivate you to excite, thrill, and entrance your audience. And to invent new ways to get a daily feel for what they like and what they loathe.

That, ladies and gentlemen, is how I stumbled from art into a career in another branch of popular culture I knew nothing about—rock and roll. Thanks to *Circus* magazine, I ended up five years later as what Delta Airlines' in-flight magazine called "one of the most prestigious pop publicists in the world." Yes, I founded my own public relations company, cleverly named The Howard Bloom Organization, Ltd., and passed my working hours with fellow eccentrics like Michael Jackson, Billy Joel, Prince, Paul Simon, Bob Marley, Diana Ross, John Cougar Mellencamp, Lionel Richie, Kiss, Queen, Aerosmith, AC/DC, Billy Idol, Joan Jett, David Byrne, Peter Gabriel, ZZ Top, Grandmaster Flash and the Furious Five, Kool and the Gang, Run DMC, and Bette Midler. Not to mention Michael Lang, who was still buying designer toys to furnish his posh apartment on New York's unaffordable Central Park South with the proceeds from Woodstock number one, but couldn't pass up the chance to burst the seams of his Swiss bank account by launching Woodstock number two (the twenty-fifth anniversary edition). What's worse, he is apparently plotting a fiftieth birthday of the bacchanal in the mud of Max Yasgur's farm. I don't know how he'll guarantee the presence of the mud.

One day in 1971, just after I'd been named editor of *Circus*, I was required to attend my first rock concert. The band was one of a flush of British blues groups that had been big in the late Sixties, but were now on their last legs. The two most important of these bands had been Chicken Shack and Fleetwood Mac. This concert was Fleetwood Mac at Carnegie Hall.

The performance began normally enough. There were three thousand of us in the audience. While the lights were up and there was no band onstage, we were all insanely self-conscious, aware of how the people behind us and on either side of us viewed us. We were trying to look intelligent and under control. In other words, we were trying to look cool. Then the lights went down, the band took to the stage, the music began, and I got my first glimpse of that mystical thing that happens at concerts. We lose our sense of performing for the audience of folks near us and are sucked into the performance onstage. We lose the self-consciousness of the interior makeup department I'd seen at work when I was on peyote. We are lifted out of our selves. We become a part of something bigger.

Then, half an hour into the show, something strange happened. The power went out onstage and the house lights, the lights over our heads in the audience, went on. The magic that had sucked us out of our selves was in danger of disappearing.

The stage had no lighting at all. But Mick Fleetwood, a tall, gangly string bean of a man, came to the very lip of the proscenium, getting as close to us as he could get without jumping down and breaking a leg. He raised his fist in the air, and said something to the effect of, "Fuck this. We're going to rock and roll." The audience was galvanized. Yes, including me. We were all together in this, riding over the forces of calamity and telling them to go intercourse themselves. We were a part of something higher than ourselves. We were exhilarated and exalted. We were what Hitler's torch light parade audiences had been, a group with a collective soul, a soul uplifted by challenge and fired by ecstasies. But we were elevated and galvanized without a hint of scapegoats, violence, and war. By total accident, I had found my way into the land of the gods.

A land in which I'd learn to "empath" people like Michael Jackson and Prince by remembering the out of body experience I'd had when dancing on a stage in high school. A land in which the marginal insanities that sometimes bring truth—and deity—the madnesses admired by William James in his *Varieties of the Religious Experience* come alive. A land on the outer margins of the forces of history.

◆

TEN YEARS LATER CAME the best thing that ever happened: Barbara delivered an ultimatum. By then, she'd escaped from the Bedford-Stuyvesant knife fights that punctuate a teacher's life, gotten a degree in library science, and had worked her way up to second in command in the New York Public

Library's second-largest reference section—at a library in a neighborhood nicknamed Fort Apache—the South Bronx. Barbara announced that she was planning to leave the New York Public Library to embark on something new. What unexpected field did she want to go into? Working at my company, The Howard Bloom Organization, Ltd, the biggest PR firm in the music industry. I absolutely forbade it. I put my foot down. I issued strict orders. I got out my stone tablets and chiseled "thou shalt nots." I even skulked around pretending to be a burning bush.

Not that I was being arbitrary, mind you. Barbara was my joy and my refuge. The music biz was a sizzling wok of stress. My clients frequently employed oriental torture techniques to stir-fry my nerve endings. My staff was a Freudian kindergarten. Since I couldn't afford to pay high wages, many of my not-entirely-faithful team members were neurotic drug enthusiasts whom I had scraped from the underside of the earth and pushed, shoved, and dragged into productivity. But keeping them from going over their perpetually enlarging deep-ends was a moment-to-moment task.

Then there was the normal instability of the music industry, which made the earth beneath my feet ripple like a perpetual Pakistani earthquake. Every few months the inevitable would happen and I'd lose a client. Since I'd inserted my whole soul into each client, a chunk of me was macheted away. The emotional effect was like a monthly amputation. So I needed Barbara as an escape. Or so I thought.

Apparently, the Mouse (as Barbara was known) was not impressed by my imitations of the voice from the whirlwind. The day after I absolutely vetoed her planned career move, she appeared in my office, took over a desk, and stayed for the next five years. Which shows you who wears the pants in this family.

The result was miraculous. Instead of sitting at my desk twelve hours straight using gigawatts of energy to retain my composure while all hell broke loose, I could now punctuate my torments with hug-breaks. I'd grab Barbara as she walked by, plonk her down on my lap, smoosh my lips all over her face (especially her tiny nose), and nibble her ears (her lobes are the most wonderful tactile devices the creator ever concocted—better than the texture of freshly-baked pita). If I didn't nab her on the stairwell (we had a two-story office on Manhattan's 53rd Street near Lexington Avenue) and flatten her against the wall, thus intolerably embarrassing every member of the Howard Bloom Organization, Ltd, with public displays of unadulterated mush, Barbara would sneak up behind me as I ascended to the second floor and give my bottom a good, hard pinch.

The staff loved it. It was like having a slightly randy mommy and daddy on the payroll.

What's even better, ever since the summer of the Great Polygamy Experiment, Barbara's angelic smile had returned.

It all goes back to the wisdom of the murderers. You remember, the ones who tried to straighten out my life in a Hudson on the way to the San Francisco Bay.

First on the homicide-experts' list of rules for reforming a lost soul was, and I quote, "Ya gotta have a goal in life." It really doesn't matter what it is. My first was to find satori, which somehow eluded me. My next was to get through college with decent marks. Straight A's. And the one that followed was to raise Barbara's kid and make Barbara smile again—all of which involved entering a variety of rather strange occupations.

Now that my stepdaughter has a kid of her own and Barbara's grin is semi-permanent, I'm back to the goal I started with when Einstein became my hero—to figure out the nature of the universe. And to pinpoint where your inner gods and mine fit into the cosmos' big picture. However, unlike Albert, I'd prefer to do it with my daytime clothes on.

The murderer's second lesson was, "Ya gotta have a woman." That's where Barbara comes in. True, I'm the demonstrative one in the family. I initiate most of the kissing and the expressions of affection. As for Barbara, if she has a slight cold, she wipes her nose on my shoulder, which, for some strange reason, I find endearing.

◆

OK, SO I ADMIT we're not sentimental. What do you expect from a couple who never went through the paroxysms of romance? For example, there was our twenty-fifth anniversary. Normally, we forget this yearly occasion until after it's occurred, then we suddenly realize that the fifth of September whiffled by a few days ago, poke each other in the ribs, and say, "My God, we missed it again." We reminisce, and are delighted that we've been together ten, twenty, or whatever number of years. I babble a lot about what a good time I've had and how it's been the best years of my life. Barbara tosses in some similar musing and is generally tickled that I count my existence as having started to include fun on a regular basis for the first time after I began living with her.

But our twenty-fifth anniversary was marginally different. First of all, we didn't forget the date. How could we? My cousin—the one who put me up at his home after I had the momentary mental breakdown in Israel and who set me up as a researcher at Rutgers—called and made a fuss.

Later in the day, I bought Barbara a batch of roses, a gourmet Danish with cherries on top, and a Nestle's Crunch. Barbara came home from her day of high-powered political meetings in Manhattan bearing a tiny wind-up frog with a giant smile on its face that hopped with mechanical glee across my dinner tray. And two days after the big event, we headed for the local 440-acre park, designed by Frederick Law Olmsted, who'd created the sylvan wonderland across the street from my bedroom in Buffalo. We passed the creek where we'd spotted chipmunks last year (the first chipmunks we'd ever seen in the Big Apple), through the glade where we'd spied wild rabbits, and over the rutted puddle where we'd once encountered an elegantly slender, luminously green snake. We circled the lake, where a male white swan was trying to court a female. She was skillfully avoiding him, and he was half-flying to chase her, sticking his long neck out straight, opening his six-foot wingspan, and flapping so low that his feet dragged in the water, then settling down to paddle after her, tucking his chin into his chest as if to cut down on aerodynamic drag. Ahhh, the lengths to which a male will go to woo a female.

We came out of the far side of this nature patch and entered neighborhoods the likes of which we'd never imagined existed in Brooklyn during our first twenty-five years here—houses like the ones in my hometown, built around the turn of the twentieth century, big, sprawling domiciles with balconies in odd places, whimsical turrets, Ionic columns holding up massive porticoes like those of ante-bellum plantation mansions, strange Dutch curving roofs, Victorian greenhouse-like second floor solariums with arched glass tops and sides, a riot of early 1900s imagination poured into the shape of gables, stained glass windows, and sharply peaked roofs. And we had our anniversary talk about how good it has been, and how much fun we've had, and how my life has been different, very different, because of it, and how I've had pleasures I never imagined could exist. I still didn't believe it had been twenty-five years. Five was more believable.

A friend recently commented that Barbara plays an essential part in my life. But the statement was just a bit off. Barbara *is* my life. Which, I guess, means the quest of The Sixties is over. Satori has been found.

◆

I WROTE THAT ENDING in 1995. It's now 2016, and it turns out that there is one more form of satori that emerged as a result of accidentally contributing to the start of The Sixties. Edna St. Vincent Millay, T. S. Eliot, William Blake, Albert Einstein, Friedrich Nietzsche, and Phil Fish had laid out a mission: come to understand as much of everything as you can. Yes, everything. Be bold. Use adventure as a tool of understanding. Then gather every science you can comprehend, all the history you can gather, a bit of the arts, and your personal expeditions into the wilds where science has not yet been applied—from riding the rails with fruit pickers to helping establish Amnesty International in North America, going into the trenches with the NAACP, and working with rock stars. Meld all of that together to forge new perceptual lenses, new lenses with which you can see everything inside of you and everything outside of you from a radically new point of view.

Don't be the mole digging a hole so deep that you can't see the world around you. Be the eagle who flies over the landscape. Be a synthesizer who puts the puzzle pieces unearthed by specialists into a big picture. Into a sweeping, awesome narrative that covers the history and future of this universe. A universe in which the greatest amazements are in the minds, the unnamed emotions, and the creations of human beings. In the minds, emotions, and creations of you and me. That's the goal that you glimpsed with the help of the Roswell Park Cancer Institute, LSD, peyote, and methedrine. That's the aim you learned to strive for without drugs. That's the target you're still aimed at today. With all of your heart, your soul, and your brain.

Strive to see the infinite in the tiniest of things. How? By going off the beaten track. By stepping outside the normal perceptual frame. By moving beyond the tools of grad school and the lab. By surfing the seas of passion, religion, and politics. By scholarship plus adventure. Remember the lesson of Sisyphus: the joy is not in the endpoint, it's in the pursuit. And that grand chase, that push for new insight every hour and every day, is the most exhilarating satori of them all.

EPILOGUE

Remember what happened when you were sixteen? You were working at the world's biggest cancer research lab—The Roswell Park Cancer Institute. You did not want to be like the mentor who had been assigned to you, biochemist Phil Fish, a wonderful man who spent five years trying to synthesize just one molecule. You did not want to be a mole digging a hole so deep that all you could see was the darkness, the dirt ahead of you, and the dark soil on either side. You wanted to be the eagle who soars over the landscape and sees how all of the narrow results of the specialists converge in a big picture. A soaring, stunning big picture. The sort of big picture that Edna St. Vincent Millay and William Blake would have cheered for. The sort of big picture that the Spirit of The Sixties would have thanked you for. But there was no name for what you wanted to do. And names count. Words change realities.

The closest thing to a name came from a forgotten nineteenth-century philosopher, Herbert Spencer, a man who was once regarded as the most important philosopher of his century, then fell into disrepute. Spencer lived on the Strand in London, in the building, the "establishment," of a new magazine, *The Economist*, where he was an editorial assistant. But his real goal was yours: to sew all the narrow scraps of the scientific specializations—from physiology and embryology to sociology and psychology, two fields he helped establish—into a massive tapestry, a grand panorama. An evolutionary panorama. Yes, it was Spencer who coined the phrase "survival of the fittest" and who popularized the term "evolution," not Charles Darwin. Spencer had a word for what he was doing: "synthesis." And what he was after, he said, was a "synthetic philosophy."

In fact, Spencer was so wedded to the construction of his synthetic philosophy that when one of the most brilliant women of his age, Mary Ann Evans, fell in love with him and wanted to marry him, he said no.

Mary Ann Evans lived in a building across the street on the Strand—the establishment of the radical publisher John Chapman. Like Spencer, she edited a magazine—the *Westminster Review*. And that magazine, like *The Economist*, was turning people's heads. Spencer found Mary Ann fascinating. He loved her company. He used the free tickets he was given to take her to concerts and plays. He walked with her on their way back from the theater singing their favorite songs. He even took her to the biggest event of the century, the Great Exhibition of 1851, an exposition of new technologies from all over the world mounted by Queen Victoria's techno-lusting husband, Prince Albert, in a breath-taking, breakthrough, all-plate-glass building supported by slender cast-iron beams built specifically for the purpose—the Crystal Palace.

Spencer, like many of Mary Ann's friends, felt she should do more than editing. She should write her own books. The push from friends helped. Mary Ann wrote her first book of fiction, *The Sad Fortunes of the Reverend Amos Barton*. But she didn't want to be regarded as a writer of fluff. She didn't want to be pigeon-holed by her femaleness. So she adopted a *nom de plume*, a male name, George Eliot. And she became a superstar.

Mary Ann Evans was in love with Herbert Spencer. As you know, she wanted to marry him. But Spencer was already married. To his work. To putting all of the sciences together in one big picture.

Nonetheless, one hundred years later there was still no name for what Spencer had tried to do. And there was no word for what you wanted to do. Words matter. Remember the word "dropout." And the difference between a "cleaning woman" and a "babysitter."

See if this word helps. See if it captures what you wanted to achieve.

Omnology—an academic base for the promiscuously curious, a discipline that concentrates on seeing the patterns that emerge when one views all the sciences and the arts at once.

The Omnologist Manifesto

We are blessed with a richness of specializations, but cursed with a paucity of panoptic disciplines—categories of knowledge that concentrate on seeing the pattern that emerges when one views all the sciences at once. Hence, we need a field dedicated to the panoramic, an academic base for the promiscuously curious, a discipline whose mandate is best summed up in a paraphrase of the poet Andrew Marvel: "Let us roll all our strength and all Our knowledge up into one ball, And tear our visions with rough strife Thorough the iron gates of life.

Omnology is a science, but one dedicated to the biggest picture conceivable by the minds of its practitioners. Omnology will use every conceptual tool available—and some not yet invented but inventible—to leapfrog over disciplinary barriers, stitching together the patchwork quilt of science and all the rest that humans can yet know. If one omnologist is able to perceive the relationship between pop songs, ancient Egyptian graffiti, mysticism, neurobiology, and the origins of the cosmos, so be it. If another uses mathematics to probe traffic patterns, the behavior of insect colonies, and the manner in which galaxies cluster in swarms, wonderful. And if another uses introspection to uncover hidden passions and relate them to research in chemistry, anthropology, psychology, history, and the arts, she, too, has a treasured place on the wild frontiers of scientific truth—the terra incognita in the heartland of omnology.

Let me close with the words of yet another poet, William Blake, on the ultimate goal of omnology:

To see a World in a Grain of Sand
And a Heaven in a Wild Flower,
Hold Infinity in the palm of your hand
And Eternity in an hour.

That, ladies and gentlemen, is the spirit of The Sixties. And that's The Sixties' gift to you and me.

ABOUT THE AUTHOR

"I know a lot of people. A lot. And I ask a lot of prying questions. But I've never run into a more intriguing biography than Howard Bloom's in all my born days."

—**Paul Solman**, Business and Economics Correspondent, PBS NewsHour

T. S. ELIOT, EDNA St. Vincent Millay, William James, Albert Einstein, and the beatniks drove Howard Bloom to adventure in the terra incognita of human extremes, then to attempt to write about his discoveries so clearly and deliciously that anyone with a high school education could understand them. That was the imperative behind his explorations in the Sixties. And that remains the imperative behind his life today. The variety of experiences it's led to has been mind-boggling.

Bloom has been called "next in a lineage of seminal thinkers that includes Newton, Darwin, Einstein, [and] Freud," by Britain's Channel4 TV, "the next Stephen Hawking" by Gear Magazine, and "The Buckminster Fuller and Arthur C. Clarke of the new millennium" by Buckminster Fuller's archivist, Bonnie DeVarco. Bloom is the author of *The Lucifer Principle: A Scientific Expedition Into the Forces of History*, *Global Brain: The Evolution of Mass Mind from the Big Bang to the 21st Century*, *The Genius of the Beast: A Radical Re-Vision of Capitalism*, *The God Problem: How A Godless Cosmos Creates*, and *The Mohammed Code: How a Desert Prophet Gave You ISIS, al Qaeda, and Boko Haram—or How Mohammed Invented Jihad*.

Bloom's second book *Global Brain* was the subject of an Office of the Secretary of Defense symposium in 2010, with participants from the State Department, the Energy Department, DARPA, IBM, and MIT. Bloom is founder and head of the Space Development Steering Committee, a group that has included astronauts Buzz Aldrin, Edgar Mitchell (the sixth man on the moon), and members from the National Science Foundation, the Department of Defense, and NASA. He has debated one-one-one with senior officials from Egypt's Muslim Brotherhood and Gaza's Hamas on Iran's global Arab-language Alalam TV News Network. He has also dissected headline issues dozens of times on Saudi Arabia's KSA2-TV and on Iran's global English language Press-TV. He has probed the untold story of the Syrian Civil War with Nancy Kissinger. And he is co-conceiving the core module of an energy infrastructure for the solar system at Caltech funded by the Keck Institute for Space Studies, GE, and the Air Force Research Lab.

Bloom's scientific work has been published in: arxiv.org, the leading pre-print site in advanced theoretical physics and math; *PhysicaPlus*; *Across Species Comparisons and Psychopathology*; *New Ideas in Psychology*; *The Journal of Space Philosophy*; and in the book series: *Research in Biopolitics*. He was invited to lecture an international conference of quantum physicists in Moscow—Quantum Informatics 2006—and the concepts Bloom introduced were later used in a book proposing a new approach to quantum physics, *Constructive Physics*, by Moscow University's Yuri Ozhigov.

In addition, Bloom's work has appeared in *The Washington Post*, *The Wall Street Journal*, *Wired*, Knight-Ridder Financial News Service, the *Village Voice*, *The Huffington Post*, *Cosmopolitan Magazine* and the blog sites of Psychology Today and the *Scientific American*.

Bloom has founded three international scientific groups: the Group Selection Squad (1995), which gained acceptance for the concept of group selection in evolutionary biology; The International Paleopsychology Project (1997), which created a new multi-disciplinary synthesis between cosmology, paleontology, evolutionary biology, and history; and The Space Development Steering Committee (2007).

Bloom explains that his focus is "mass behavior, from the mass behavior of quarks to the mass behavior of human beings." One of his key topics? The forces of history. And he has lived those forces.

To plumb the depths of mass emotion, Bloom dove in 1971 into a field he knew nothing about—pop culture. He was credited by *Rolling Stone* founding editor Chet Flippo with "creating a new magazine genre—the heavy metal magazine." Then he founded the biggest PR firm in the music industry—The Howard Bloom Organization, Ltd.—and helped build or sustain the careers of figures like Michael Jackson, Prince, Bob Marley, Bette Midler, Billy Joel, Paul Simon, Billy Idol, Peter Gabriel, David Byrne, John Mellencamp, Queen, Kiss, Aerosmith, AC/DC, Grandmaster Flash and The Furious Five, Kool and the Gang, Run DMC, and roughly a hundred others. He contributed to the success of films like *The Great Gatsby, Down and Out in Beverly Hills, Outrageous Fortune,* and *Purple Rain.* And he did it by focusing not on profits but on soul.

Bloom did more than explore the forces of history, he helped make them. He helped launch Farm Aid and he helped establish Amnesty International's American presence. He worked with the United Negro College Fund, the National Black United Fund, and the NAACP, and he put together the first public service radio campaign for solar power (1981).

Bloom returned to science full-time in 1988. Since then, Bloom has done stints as a visiting scholar in the Graduate School of Psychology at NYU and as a core faculty member at the Graduate Institute in Meriden, Connecticut. He's been flown to Moscow, Amsterdam, Paris, Vienna, Seoul, Kuala Lumpur, and Chengdu, China to lecture. He's also lectured at American locations from Nellis Air Force Base and the Eisenhower Center for Space and Defense Studies to Yale University. He is currently on the board of governors of the National Space Society.

Topping it all off, Bloom's computer houses a not-so-secret and not-at-all humble project, his 8,100-chapter-long Grand Unified Theory of Everything in the Universe Including the Human Soul. Pavel Kurakin of the Keldysh Institute of Applied Mathematics of the Russian Academy of Sciences says that,

> *"Bloom has created a new Scientific Paradigm. He explains in vast and compelling terms why we should forget all we know in complicated modern math and should start from the very beginning. Bloom's Grand Unified Theory opens a window into entire systems we don't yet know and/or see, new collectivities that live, love, battle, win and lose each day of our gray lives. I never imagined that a new system of thought could produce so much light."*

Concludes Joseph Chilton Pearce, author of *Evolution's End* and *The Crack in the Cosmic Egg*, "I have finished Howard Bloom's [first two] books, *The Lucifer Principle* and *Global Brain*, in that order, and am seriously awed, near overwhelmed by the magnitude of what he has done. I never expected to see, in any form, from any sector, such an accomplishment. I doubt there is a stronger intellect than Bloom's on the planet."